THE HEART OF ALL NATIONS

PIERBATTISTA CARDINAL PIZZABALLA

The Heart of All Nations

Faith and Hope in the Holy Land

TRANSLATED BY
MICHAEL J. MILLER

IGNATIUS PRESS   SAN FRANCISCO

Original Italian edition:
Il potere del cuore. Venticinque anni a Gerusalemme
Second expanded edition © 2017, Fondazione Terra Santa—Milan
Edizioni Terra Santa—Milan

Cover photo © 2020 Reuters/Ammar Awad
Cover design by Enrique J. Aguilar and Thomas Jacobi

ISBN 978-1-62164-886-4 (PB)
ISBN 978-1-64229-401-9 (eBook)
Library of Congress Control Number 2026931491
Printed in the United States of America ♾

Contents

A NEW MINISTRY, AT THE SERVICE OF ALL

Apostolic Administrator of Jerusalem, 2016–2020

APPENDIX: WE MUST NOT BE AFRAID

Latin Patriarch of Jerusalem, 2020–2025

Foreword

by J. D. Flynn

Just one week after the world was shocked by the attacks of October 7, 2023, Pierbattista Cardinal Pizzaballa attracted global attention with an offer of extraordinary sacrifice.

As he discussed the 251 hostages taken from Israel—children among them—the cardinal was direct: "I am ready for an exchange, anything, if this can lead to freedom, to bring the children home. No problem. There is total willingness on my part," he told reporters.[1]

Hamas did not take up the cardinal's offer.

But the world heard him. Pizzaballa captured hearts in that moment; the idea of handing himself over was a powerful model of what it means to be a disciple of Jesus Christ.

As the cardinal continued to find a way for peace, visiting a parish in Gaza and talking solutions with anyone who would listen, he became respected among Catholics as a moral authority whose words were backstopped by moral witness.

He remains an object of fascination and admiration, and a source of hope for Catholics inspired by his integrity, devotion, and obvious faith.

And *The Heart of All Nations* points to the faith behind the man, the long history and intellectual work that backstops

---

J. D. Flynn is cofounder and editor in chief of *The Pillar*.

[1] Justin McLellan, Catholic News Service, "Jerusalem Catholic Patriarch Offers in Exchange for Israeli Hostages", *United States Conference of Catholic Bishops*, October 16, 2023, https://www.usccb.org/news/2023/jerusalem-cardinal-offers-himself-exchange-israeli-hostages.

the cardinal's powerful gesture, and which accounts for it, from his own mind and heart.

Long before he was a cardinal known around the world, Pizzaballa was an eleven-year-old Catholic from Italy's Bergamo region, entering a Franciscan minor seminary and beginning a journey of formation in the heart, mind, and faith of Saint Francis of Assisi himself, and in the 800-year-old tradition of Franciscan life and spirituality.

Each stage of his life, in vows, in priesthood, in Holy Land ministry, and in episcopacy, has been, in many ways, a deeper immersion in discipleship of Christ along the specific path of the Poverello, the poor man from Assisi, whom Pizzaballa has lived to emulate.

In fact, if there is one thing to know about Cardinal Pierbattista Pizzaballa—one thing which stands in the diverse texts of *The Heart of All Nations*—it's that Pizzaballa can only be understood if he is seen as a Franciscan friar, with the attributes, and values, and methods of the Seraphic Father Francis himself.

His Franciscan character—that unique and joyful following Christ discovered and prescribed by Francis—is evident in the addresses, homilies, and reflections of this book. And at the heart of that spirituality is a love for Jesus Christ, discovered in the poor, revealed in Scripture, and intimately present in the Cross.

In his singular text meditating directly on Saint Francis, Pizzaballa captures the heart of the Franciscan spirituality.

"Francis' point of departure is a faith that becomes concrete experience and will manifest itself also through his spiritual journey: from the encounter, then, all the rest is generated," the cardinal writes. "First of all, then, the encounter with Christ, this transforms his existence by activating mechanisms of preaching that are in the first place the proclamation of a lived experience."[2]

This Franciscan notion—that evangelization is the "proclamation of a lived experience"—is consistently manifest in the texts of *The Heart of All Nations.*

Preeminent is the palpable closeness between the cardinal and the crucified Christ, which is expressed no matter how he speaks, because it seems such an animating aspect of his own life.

"Sometimes, we have a vague, abstract idea of salvation, and speak of it as something that will happen someday. . . . This is not Christian salvation," he insists.

Instead, "the pages of the Gospel about Capernaum speak of a very concrete salvation, and of a God who comes to dwell in the space of everyday activities."[3]

In fact, the basis of the cardinal's theology of the Church, as he explains, is rooted in the experience of Christ, because he maintains that "knowledge always comes by way of experience."

"Saint Francis", he writes, "is a very concrete man, and the place to encounter Christ is the Church: there is no other way for him, because the Church, through the sacraments, gives us the opportunity to have an experience of Christ, especially in the Eucharist."[4]

Evident in the writing of Pizzaballa is the deep Franciscan immersion in Sacred Scripture. Pizzaballa's work is biblical theology, in the truest sense; Scripture is alive in the cardinal's writing and preaching because Christ is alive for him,

[2] "Francis of Assisi Between Contemplative Spirituality and Apostolic Life".

[3] "With the Eyes of the Apostles: A Presence That Upends One's Life".

[4] "Saint Francis of Assisi Between Contemplative Spirituality and Apostolic Life".

and Christ is found in the story of God's love for his people that unfolds in Sacred Scripture.

Connected is the Franciscan sense of concreteness, sacredness of place itself, which is common to his confreres since they first gathered at hermitages, caves, and tiny chapels in Umbria's woods and valleys.

"How do I encounter Jesus today?" he asks. "I am not always ready for the encounter, but I know what my points of reference are: the Word and prayer, the Holy place and the persons, together. The relation with the Holy Place continually recalls the event spoken of by the Scriptures, making it a close memory."[5]

In other words, Jesus is real because he can be really encountered not only in Scripture, but in the Holy Land spaces where the Lord walked—vividly imagined and revered by Saint Francis, and experienced in daily life by the cardinal.

"Today in Capernaum we still see the streets that Jesus walked along, the doorstep of Peter's house, and we can imagine what the life of the inhabitants was like at that time. There are kitchens with ovens, flooring, and stairs, and we can conjecture what the thatched roofs were like. Among those houses is the one also belonging to Jesus: only a privileged few can still touch it."[6]

Also clear is the Franciscan preference for peacemaking—in and through Christ— a Franciscan pursuit since Francis' own foray to Egypt, where we met with Sultan al-Kamil.

In his essays on Jerusalem, for example, the cardinal is clear that he aims to hear and understand the people among whom he lives, that he is seeking the human fraternity with which Francis began evangelization. But the cardinal is clear

[5] "With the Eyes of the Apostles".

[6] Ibid.

that peacemaking is not the fruit of affective collegiality or natural understanding.

Instead, he is clear that making and finding peace can be accomplished only through witness to the Gospel itself.

"Living out the Gospel in the Holy Land," Pizzaballa writes, "where meeting one another often proves to be complicated and where past and present violence mark the life of entire communities, both social and religious, to the point of becoming the sole criterion for interpreting relations—means, for a Franciscan, trying to break that vicious circle of violence and fear by witnessing to salvation."

Later in the text, he is more direct: "True peace is born when the person and the relations are integral, complete, and full."[7] And what is the source—the only source—of that fullness and integration?

For Pizzaballa, the answer is clear: Jesus of Nazareth, who transforms those who encounter him.

Some years ago, another prominent Franciscan prelate—the Capuchin Archbishop Charles Chaput—commented on the strange dual vocations of bishops.

"When I was ordained a bishop, a wise old friend told me that every bishop must be part radical and part museum curator—a radical in preaching and living the Gospel, but a protector of the Christian memory, faith, heritage and story that weave us into one believing people over the centuries."[8]

For Pizzaballa, living in a place that becomes so easily a

[7] "Francis of Assisi Between Contemplative Spirituality and Apostolic Life".

[8] Archbishop Charles Chaput, "Address at the University of Notre Dame 2016 Bishops' Symposium", Archdiocese of Philadelphia, October 19, 2016, https://archphila.org/archbishop-chaputs-address-at-the-university-of-notre-dame-2016-bishops-symposium-reclaiming-the-church-for-the-catholic-imagination/.

kind of living museum for all salvation history, this is likely more true than it is for others.

And the cardinal's work reflects a desire for both preservation and radical witness. He urges his flock to experience Christ in Word, sacrament, and place. But he urges them on, too, to the power of speaking in bold signs, to creativity in vibrant proclamation of the faith.

The Christians of the Holy Land, he says, should "safeguard", "keep visible", and "defend . . . the 'also-Christian' character" of their land, while at the same time recognizing that their call to "a vibrant testimony of faith and belonging," to be open to "new forms of creativity" in the proclamation of the Kingdom.[9]

In that sense, Pizzaballa is useful for Catholics no matter where they live; the Church today is embroiled in questions he's addressing: the balance between preserving the traditions of our patrimony and finding "new forms of creativity" for effectively proclaiming the Gospel to a world in which Christian faith cannot be presupposed, in which believers are a minority in a swath of once-Christian places.

In short, Pizzaballa is living out and reflecting on the tensions of looking deeply into Christian history and presenting it anew in the commission of the New Evangelization. These are universal challenges.

In a Franciscan key, they might be seen in the call to Francis from Christ Crucified: "Francis, rebuild my Church."

In his own way, Saint Francis understood this first in terms of concrete work, with stone and mortar, and then the path of providence became clear—the way in which Francis would usher in a new era of holiness, renewing the Church and pointing to her reform, by inviting Christians to deeper discipleship of Christ on the Cross itself, to radical

[9] "The Universal Vocation of the Churches in the Holy Land".

identification with His crucifix, and joyful participation in the Resurrection.

The Church today is in need of its own reform and renewal. And whatever other models are needed, there is a need in our time for those who take up the radical call to personal holiness and evangelical witness at the heart of the Franciscan charism, and for the resonance of that call to inspire penitential reform and joyous renewal.

Pizzaballa has perhaps risen in global prominence by providence, as an example of that life—in *The Heart of All Nations*, the call to "rebuild my Church" is expressed by His Beatitude as a call to personal conversion and holiness, and to fruitful, tangible witness to a life in Jesus Christ.

"We believe that the Paschal Mystery is God's final, definitive intervention in history, for all," he writes. "The most unexpected and surprising one. We believe that after having saved us from nothingness, from slavery, from exile, God had to save us again from one last enemy, which is death, in other words, sin. We believe, and today we announce, that death is every place in life where God is absent, where man is unrelated to Him."

"And today," he adds, "we believe in and announce that God the Father has made room for Himself in the life of each one of us, forever. The Resurrection is His life breaking into ours."[10]

The words and wisdom of Cardinal Pizzaballa have brought the Resurrection more tangibly into my own life. That is the Franciscan charism in every generation, and indeed, the witness to which every disciple of Jesus Christ is called. May the insights of *The Heart of All Nations* be a source of inspiration, encouragement, and exhortation to those who wish to follow Jesus Christ.

[10] "Do We Believe?"

The Power of the Heart

2004–2016

On May 5, 2004, Father Pierbattista Pizzaballa, O.F.M., was appointed Custos, the custodian of the Holy Land, a function traditionally entrusted to members of the Order of Friars Minor since 1342. The Custos' duty is not only to protect sacred Christian sites, but to serve as a chief delegate for the Church in the region, in its charitable works and in its dialogue with other religions. Father Pizzaballa filled this office until 2016, when Pope Francis named him apostolic administrator (archbishop) of the Latin Patriarchate of Jerusalem. Collected in this section are some of his most illuminating addresses and reflections during his many years as Custos.

The Ten Commandments, Revelation, and the Covenant

Speech at the Pontifical Lateran University

January 17, 2006

The Ten Commandments—the Decalogue—are at the basis of our action and constitute "the pole star of the faith and morality of the people of God" and "the great code of the ethical civilization of all humanity".[1] I will present several reflections on the biblical passage in which they are recorded.

The Covenant

In the first place, the excerpt in which the Decalogue is found must be situated in its context. The event narrated in chapters 19 to 24 and 34 of Exodus constitutes the nucleus from which the law of Israel developed. The Decalogue, after chapter 34, is considered to be among the most ancient documents of this pericope, and its "marvelous characteristic in comparison with what preceded is that of a more general and universal code for Israel which is valid always and everywhere. . . . All the other legislative documents are

---

Speech given on January 17, 2006, at the Pontifical Lateran University in Rome, on the occasion of the Seventeenth Conference for Jewish-Christian Dialogue. The theme was "Hear, O Israel! The First of the Ten Commandments: 'I am the Lord, your God'".

[1] From the commentary by Bishop Vincenzo Paglia, president of the Episcopal Commission for Ecumenism and Dialogue of the Italian Bishops' Conference, and Rabbi Giuseppe Laras for the 2006 Giornata per l'Approfondimento e lo Sviluppo del Dialogo Ebraico-Cristiano.

said to have originated in some way from Sinai. This is true not only for the cultic legislation but also for the Decalogue; this code, [though] promulgated in the land of Moab, comes from the Covenant on Sinai (Deut 5:2) and is dictated to Moses on Mount Horeb."[2]

The Sinai event, in which the Decalogue was given, is *par excellence* the foundational act of Israel. This event is subdivided into three parts: the theophany (Ex 19), the terms of the Covenant (Ex 20), and the code of the Covenant (Ex 20, 22–24), which is a set of more precise and detailed laws. The whole Book of Exodus speaks about the revelation of God and puts God before all else, starting with His apparition to Moses and the revelation of His name. The encounter of Israel with God at Mount Sinai, in summary, is a fundamental point of all salvation history. It is a reflection "on the long adventure of the people of God, who are called to discover God in a different and deeper way than the rest of humanity: What does this special tie of Israel with God mean? What is entailed in this new way of knowing God that started on Sinai?"[3]

Israel's reactions are different, depending on the occasion: their fear of discovering God (Ex 20:19 and Deut 5:23–33), their rejection of him (the golden calf, Ex 32), their enthusiastic acceptance of him (Ex 24:3–4). Israel certainly experiences an intense bond with God, and the perception of His transcendence is heeded profoundly by the people that has come closer to Him.

The Decalogue is not called "law" but rather "Words", or the revelation of God and His communication with those who already know Him. Its purpose is to perpetuate the re-

[2] Enzo Cortese, *Le tradizioni storiche di Israele. Da Mosé a Esdra* (Bologna: EDB, 2001), 128.

[3] Ibid., 125.

lation created from the beginning: deliverance from slavery. The prologue to the Decalogue explains what kind of relation this is, namely, the relation between the savior and those who are saved. Although we know that the Decalogue is a rather ancient document, the account is constructed in such a way as to make it seem that the episode is prior to the Decalogue, and the latter is the seal of the whole revelation: God is the one who addresses His Word to those who are saved and marks out for them a path to travel. Therefore, in my opinion, it is not possible to separate the Decalogue from the context of the revelation and the Covenant between God and the people; the Decalogue cannot be merely a great moral code for humanity, a freestanding criterion for establishing good and evil, right and wrong, and so on. The Hebrews and the Christians, believers in the one God and in His one revelation, must not separate this foundation of their life as believers from its context and from its roots: the one, exclusive revelation of God to His people and the Covenant that He contracts with them.

The First Word

The Decalogue contains two kinds of precepts: those that define the right attitude toward God and those that regulate our conduct with our neighbor. This is, however, an artificial distinction: the two kinds form an indivisible unity; one cannot be observed unless the other, too, is observed at the same time. In the New Testament also there is a passage that takes up this theme again and clearly emphasizes it:

> One of the scribes came up and heard them disputing with one another, and seeing that he answered them well, asked him, "Which commandment is the first of all?" Jesus answered, "The first is, 'Hear, O Israel: The Lord our God,

> the Lord is one; and you shall love the Lord your God with all your heart, and with all your soul, and with all your mind, and with all your strength.' The second is this: 'You shall love your neighbor as yourself.' There is no other commandment greater than these." And the scribe said to him, "You are right, Teacher; you have truly said that he is one, and there is no other but he; and to love him with all the heart, and with all the understanding, and with all the strength, and to love one's neighbor as oneself, is much more than all whole burnt offerings and sacrifices." And when Jesus saw that he answered wisely, he said to him, "You are not far from the kingdom of God." And after that no one dared to ask him any question. (Mk 12:28–34)

The first commandment requires that God be acknowledged as the one savior, and it rules out the deification of false absolutes and created representations of the transcendent God:

> I am the Lord your God, who brought you out of the land of Egypt, out of the house of bondage.
>
> You shall have no other gods before me.
>
> You shall not make for yourself a graven image, or any likeness of anything that is in heaven above, or that is in the earth beneath, or that is in the water under the earth; you shall not bow down to them or serve them; for I the Lord your God am a jealous God, visiting the iniquity of the fathers upon the children to the third and the fourth generation of those who hate me, but showing mercy to thousands of those who love me and keep my commandments.
>
> You shall not take the name of the Lord your God in vain; for the Lord will not hold him guiltless who takes his name in vain. (Ex 20:2–7)

Another passage from Deuteronomy helps us to understand this text better:

> Take good heed to yourselves. Since you saw no form on the day that the LORD spoke to you at Horeb out of the midst of the fire, beware lest you act corruptly by making a graven image for yourselves. . . . But the LORD has taken you, and brought you forth out of the iron furnace, out of Egypt, to be a people of his own possession, as at this day. (Deut 4:15–20)

The text explains that the people did not see God, but heard Him. Between God and Israel, moreover, there is a privileged relationship: "So that you might be a people of his own possession, as you are today"; the Decalogue is the concrete, tangible sign of this relationship. The people, therefore, must be on guard against clinging to other experiences and must choose life (Deut 30), remaining faithful to their Lord. God allotted the idols to all the other peoples (Deut 4:19).

The deep bond between God and the people, symbolized by the event on Sinai and made still more profound over the course of Israel's history, requires a great moral and religious commitment, both within the nation and in its relations with the outside world. This first commandment in reality declares a mutual belonging: the people belong to God, and in a certain sense God belongs to His people; the Decalogue is the concrete sign of this bond.

The Prohibition Against Making Images

Much has been written about this prohibition, and in its early years Christianity, too, was divided and torn. Remaining in the biblical context, however, there is nothing abstract about the prohibition against making images and the invitation, on the contrary, to refer continually to the experience of salvation and of deliverance from slavery.

In the first Testament, in which this prohibition is absolute, the expression "face of the Lord" is used very often—at least four hundred times. To see, to seek the face of the Lord means to encounter Him, to have an experience of Him, to carry on a relationship: the relation with the Lord is understood as something concrete.

Reading some of the Psalms, in particular Psalms 17 and 24, helps us to understand how to seek the face of the Lord means to live in a certain way, according to God's law, concretely pursuing justice. One verse of Psalm 17 is particularly significant: "As for me, I shall behold your face in righteousness; when I awake, I shall be satisfied with beholding your form" (Ps 17:15). This verse communicates a fascinating truth: in doing justice, that is, in observing His commandments, in remaining faithful to the one Covenant, we will contemplate the image of God. Therefore there is no need to make other images.

In short: "The Law and the Sinai Covenant are closely connected with the experience of God. Paradoxically, unfaithfulness to the law, the related punishments, the partial failures of the divine plan, the anguish and the disappointments of the leaders and responsible parties are tragically involved in all this, yet they, too, bring us to God. Moses reached the heights of mysticism precisely through these trials and not in the tranquility of a convent. He did not arrive in the Promised Land, but he arrived at the peak of divine contemplation at Sinai and on Mount Nebo, at his death."[4]

The believing Christian, meditating on these passages, cannot help thinking about the many New Testament references and about the figure of Jesus: the concepts of covenant,

[4] Ibid., 131.

commandment, faithfulness, justice, seeking and contemplating the face of the Lord are all brought into relation to the person of Jesus.

In theological reflection, we should in any case avoid what is called "expropriation": if the old Covenant remains, then the Israelites are still the privileged people to whom it is addressed, as Paul acknowledges (Rom 9:4): "Our Christian interpretation of the law is sometimes different, but we have it in common, and it keeps us united."[5] To do justice, that is, to keep the commandments, binds us all in the same way, because we all eagerly desire the face of God.

[5] Ibid.

Jerusalem According to the Christian Vision

Speech at the Lassalle-Haus, Switzerland

September 14–15, 2009

When speaking of Jerusalem, the political element, linked to the Israeli-Palestinian conflict, certainly predominates. The international community pays a lot of attention to this city, and there are countless initiatives related to it throughout the world. Furthermore, references to religious themes are obviously inevitable. Very often, however, these religious references to Jerusalem, especially from a Christian perspective, remain vague and are placed in a context that is liturgical and devotional, or sentimental-religious. We hear people speak of Jerusalem as the Mother Church, but without ever clarifying what this expression really means: that Jerusalem takes us back to our origins and our past. It is more difficult to hear and discuss what Christians today think of the current meaning of Jerusalem.

In discussions about the political and religious future of the city, its Christian character often disappears. The small number of Christians and the differences between local Churches leave the Christian voice almost completely devoid of influence; perhaps only the Holy See still has a moral voice in this context, but I doubt that this voice is really perceived as decisive.

Speech given at the Lassalle-Haus, a center run by the Swiss Jesuits near Zurich (September 14–15, 2009).

The Religious and Theological Significance of Jerusalem

> The name of the city henceforth shall be: "The LORD is there."
>
> Ezekiel 48:35

> Jesus said to her: "Woman, believe me, the hour is coming when neither on this mountain nor in Jerusalem will you worship the Father."
>
> John 4:21

With the arrival of Christianity, it could be argued that the Holy Land, and Jerusalem with it, lost its centrality in the faith life of Christians. In Judaism, in fact, reference to Jerusalem is fundamental, and it is an integral part of the prayer life and religious identity of the Jews. In Islam, the pilgrimage to the Holy Places is an indispensable moment, marking the journey of faith of the faithful Muslim. The Christian, on the other hand, simply worships God "in spirit and truth" (Jn 4:24) and can do so anywhere in the world. Most Christians will never travel to the Holy Land or see Jerusalem in person. Today, a significant effort is underway, with some noteworthy results, to promote pilgrimages to the Holy Land, but the number of pilgrims remains modest compared to the number of Christians in the world.

We speak also about the heavenly Jerusalem, citing various passages from the Old and New Testament; Jerusalem appears there as the place to which we all aspire, while touching on the theme of the earthly Jerusalem seems less relevant.

On the other hand, we are scandalized by the religious divisions among Christians, divisions to which Jerusalem bears witness; in this city, which is seen as a sort of reflection of the heavenly Jerusalem, there is an almost messianic expectation of peace and common life, as if the inhabitants of the Holy City were supposed to be different from the inhabitants of the rest of the world.

In conclusion, we often remain tied to an emotional and religious position. Therefore, we must ask ourselves: What is the meaning of Jerusalem today, and what is its importance as the Holy City par excellence in the life of a Christian?

Christianity Is Incarnation

Christianity is an incarnation. This might seem like an obvious statement: God who becomes man is the essence of the Christian faith. His incarnation is the culmination of salvation history; God revealed himself in history.

Now, if there is a history of revelation, there is also a geography of revelation: if there is an incarnation and it is embedded in history, there must also be a place in which this incarnation manifested itself. History and geography are therefore mutually necessary elements. If we were to ignore one of these two aspects, the event itself would be denied. For this reason, it has always been essential for the Church not only to look at Jerusalem as a spiritual summons, but at the same time to maintain a physical presence in the city. It is part of the Church's life to affirm: "I know that you seek Jesus who was crucified. He is not here; for he has risen, as he said. Come, see the place where he lay" (Mt 28:6).

From the beginning, the Christian community has gathered in the Holy Places to celebrate a memory, which is not a simple recollection of a past event. Today that event nourishes the life of the Christian: the Resurrection of Christ is the actual fundamental event of our faith life; it is a present reality. Even today we need to run to see the empty tomb of Christ. This is why it is important for us to be in the Holy Places, to be custodians of the actuality of that event; Jerusalem is the heart, the symbol, of this principle.

What has happened in Jerusalem throughout the entire history of revelation, and in particular the events of the redemption accomplished by Christ, speaks to us about the desire for reconciliation between God and man and for unity among all men; just think of the moment of Pentecost. This is why, for Christians, Jerusalem is the place symbolizing their aspiration for reconciliation and unity and, at the same time, the conflict and divisions present in this city generate turmoil and anxiety more than anywhere else in the world.

Jerusalem, the Mother Church

We cannot think of Jerusalem only as a great museum or a set of Holy Places in which we celebrate a memory. It is also a crossroads of peoples and nations, made up of "living stones", that is, human beings. Everyone calls the community of believers who live there, specifically the Church, "Mother Church". What does this expression mean?

Jerusalem is the Mother Church because, being the first among the Churches, she is the one that gave birth to all the others, and she is not an apostolic Church, that is, founded by an apostle: Christ Himself is the one who founded her. The Church of Jerusalem was not founded by saints or apostles, but is the place from which saints and apostles set out to start other Churches.

She is furthermore the Mother Church because she was born as a Church that is local and at the same time universal. The Pentecost event is particularly significant: "They were amazed and wondered, saying: 'Are not all these who are speaking Galileans? And how is it that we hear, each of us in his own native language? Parthians and Medes and Elamites and residents of Mesopotamia, Judea and Cappadocia, Pontus and Asia, Phrygia and Pamphylia, Egypt and the parts of Libya belonging to Cyrene, and visitors from Rome, both Jews and proselytes, Cretans and Arabians, we hear them telling in our own tongues the mighty works of God'" (Acts 2:7–11).

The Church of Jerusalem, therefore, arose from the beginning with a universal vocation. All the nations were there, all of them heard the apostles speaking in their native languages. Jerusalem is the reminder of the harmony and unity of the beginnings.

Even today, this city is the only place where the Churches live together, in a situation of wounded sensibilities, but at the same time on a vital journey in search of unity and sharing. Each Church has her own cultural center and seat of the hierarchy in another part of the world, but all, without exception, have their heart in Jerusalem. In this sense, Jerusalem is a mother, because it is not the expression of one of the Churches, but of them all, which are forced to share space and time here. It is an imperfect but still valid way of preserving unity.

Jerusalem, finally, is the Mother Church because its bond with the Holy Land also connects it in a unique way to the history of which this Land is the custodian. The Revelation of the Old and New Testament here becomes the history of the local peoples and cultures. The life of the Mother Church is inextricably linked to these cultures, and in particular to its relationship with Judaism and Islam. This relationship is often a source of conflict, yet it is constitutive of the very life of the Church: without a relationship with the other two monotheistic faiths, the Church could never continue to live and grow in this Land. We are a minority; without a relationship with the other two peoples who constitute the majority, we will have no future, not even with regard to the simplest and most insignificant aspects.

Jerusalem is, in conclusion, the place and the treasure that encompasses a series of meanings that are still relevant for the faith life of the Churches and of Christians: the link between history and geography, between event and place, memory and the present day; it is the origin and the source for all the other Churches; it is the representation of the call to universality and unity, which today are certainly wounded but still vital. It also represents the inescapable link with Judaism and Islam, as well as with the origins of Christianity.

> Gathered beneath the walls of this city, sacred to the followers of three great religions, how can we not turn our thoughts to Jerusalem's universal vocation? Heralded by the prophets, this vocation also emerges as an indisputable fact, a reality irrevocably grounded in the complex history of this city and its people. Jews, Muslims, and Christians alike call this city their spiritual home. . . . Jerusalem, in fact, has always been a city whose streets echo with different languages, whose stones are trod by people of every race and tongue, whose walls are a symbol of God's provident care for the whole human family. As a microcosm of our globalized world, this City, if it is to live up to its universal vocation, must be a place which teaches universality, respect for others, dialogue, and mutual understanding.[1]

Jerusalem is therefore a complete model of the Church. In it, all the constitutive elements of the original Church—localism and universality, place and memory, unity—persist, although in a wounded condition, touched by human sin.

[1] Benedict XVI, Homily in the Josafat Valley, Jerusalem, May 12, 2009.

Jerusalem for the Local Church—and for Other Churches Around the World

Local Christians

Jerusalem's local Christians are few, currently no more than ten thousand, and belong to various denominations. There is a strong international presence, especially among religious. The local Church, however, is Arab: the local Christians are Arabs; most members of the hierarchy are Arabs; Arabic is the language used by the majority of Churches.

The local Arabic Churches, however, also have a strongly universal structure. They all have strong ties with the various Churches around the world, and for this reason they are considered somewhat distinct from all the other inhabitants of the city. Many social activities conducted by Christians still take place in buildings that recall one of the various Western cultures, with strong language ties: Christians study in Arabic, but also in English, French, German, Italian, Spanish, etc.

It is also clear that a local Christian's view of Jerusalem coincides with that of the people to whom he feels he belongs: a Palestinian Christian will want to defend the city's Christian character at all costs, but, at the same time, he will identify with the desires of his people and the vision of those who govern that people. The Palestinian view of Jerusalem is rooted in deep historical, political, cultural, social, religious, and economic ties with the city, ties that span centuries. East Jerusalem, as defined by its pre-1967 borders, should be the capital of Palestine, and West Jerusalem the capital of Israel, with each state enjoying full sovereignty over its respective part of the city. East Jerusalem should be connected and integrated as part of the Palestinian state.

Churches Around the World

There are enormous differences in approach and culture among the Churches with respect to Jerusalem. The Orthodox Churches have a different approach from that of the Protestant communities, and the latter in turn distance themselves from the Catholic Church. They all refer to this city for the reasons described, but as far as practical aspects are concerned, in the social and political sphere, there are plainly many differences between them.

In general, communities around the world support the Church of Jerusalem. Specifically, most of the initiatives of the local communities are funded by Churches abroad: schools, hospitals, and various activities could not exist without this support.

Pilgrimages are increasingly widespread: almost all Churches—not just the Catholic Church—organize visits and pilgrimages to the Holy Places. In this sense, Jerusalem truly seems to have returned to being a "house of prayer" for all believers. Pilgrimages are increasingly becoming moments of encounter not only with the Holy Places, but also with the communities. Such encounters are a valuable source of mutual enrichment and help people to become aware of the political and social problems that afflict the city and affect the Christian community in a particular way.

On this last aspect, the positions of the various Churches vary and often translate into political choices. There are Christian denominations—particularly evangelicals—that, for religious reasons, support the Israeli position, and there are Churches that, instead, demonstrate greater solidarity with the local Arab Churches, assuming the role of ambassadors in their respective countries of the voice of the local Christians.

The Holy See

Regarding Jerusalem, the distinction often made between the "question of the Holy Places" and the "question of Jerusalem" is unacceptable for the Holy See. It is, in fact, obvious that the Holy Places derive their meaning and use in worship from their intimate connection with the surrounding environment, a connection that must be understood not merely geographically, but also and especially in its urban, architectural, and, above all, human and institutional community dimensions.

The papal documents on Jerusalem certainly contain emphases and subtle differences. Those drafted between 1887 and today can be divided into three periods: from 1887 to 1947 (the year of the first Arab-Israeli war), when the popes speak about the Holy Land in general and about Jerusalem, they insist primarily on the need to protect the physical integrity of the Holy Places and on the needs of local Catholics; from 1947 to 1964 (the year of the pilgrimage by Pope Paul VI), the emphasis is placed on protection of the Holy Places, on freedom of access for all believers of the three religions, and on the right of each to have control over its own sacred places; from 1964 to the present, the emphasis shifts to Jerusalem in a global context and to the preservation of its identity and vocation. Specifically, the documents refer to (1) the Holy Places and the surrounding areas; (2) the guarantee that everyone can keep his cultural and religious identity; (3) freedom of religion and conscience for residents and pilgrims, and (4) the cultural dimension.

Jerusalem is a treasure for all humanity. Given the obvious conflict and the rapid transformation of the Holy City, any solution that is unilateral or obtained by force is not, and can by no means be, a solution. According to the Holy

See, any exclusive claim, whether religious or political, is contrary to the very logic of the city itself. Every citizen of Jerusalem and everyone who visits this city should be able to breathe in the message of dialogue, coexistence, and respect that it evokes. Exclusive claims cannot be made based on numerical or historical grounds. That said, there is nothing that can prevent Jerusalem, in its unity and uniqueness, from becoming the symbol and national center of both peoples who claim it as their own capital.

But although on one hand Jerusalem is sacred to Jews, Christians, and Muslims, on the other hand it is also sacred to many, many people from all over the world, who regard it as their spiritual capital or travel there on pilgrimage, to pray and to meet their brothers and sisters in faith. It is therefore a cultural heritage for all, including those who simply visit as tourists.

The Holy See maintains, therefore, that it is imperative to find a concrete solution to all the problems of this city, while respecting its particular characteristics. In the Apostolic Letter *Redemptionis Anno* (1984), Pope John Paul II wrote: "I am convinced that failure to seek an adequate solution to the Jerusalem question, as well as resigning oneself to a postponement of the problem, only further jeopardizes the desired peaceful and just harmony of the crisis in the entire Middle East."

What does the Holy See mean by "adequate solution"? It means recognizing that the current situation is one of conflict and that Israelis and Palestinians, with the collaboration of all those who can help them, must reach an agreement that corresponds to their specific, legitimate, reasonable aspirations and respects the principles of justice. From the perspective of the Holy See, in any case, the resolution of a territorial dispute alone is not sufficient for Jerusalem, precisely because it is a unique reality, the heritage of the entire world. And the entire world has shown itself to be fully aware of this when, for example, it has sought to defend this heritage through certain United Nations resolutions.

The Holy See therefore continues to call for Jerusalem to be protected by a special status guaranteed at the international level. This implies that the city's historical and material characteristics, both religious and cultural, should be protected and that there should be equal rights and treatment for those who belong to the communities of the three religions that are present, in a context of freedom in terms of spiritual, cultural, civic, and economic activities. The Holy Places must also be protected, along with the rights of freedom of religion, worship, and access for residents and pilgrims, whether they come from the Holy Land or from other parts of the world.

Political and Social Aspects

Overall, Palestinians, except for the most extreme elements, have a decidedly unified vision of Jerusalem: their idea is of a shared city that is the capital of two states and home to the three great monotheistic religions. The Palestinians' principle is that Israel must withdraw from all the occupied Palestinian territories, including East Jerusalem.

On the other hand, Israelis also consider this city their unique and indivisible capital. If Palestinians cannot conceive of a future Palestinian state without Jerusalem, the same is true for Israelis: there is no Judaism without Jerusalem. Within the Israeli ruling class, there are then different positions regarding the future of the city, particularly with regard to the possibility of sharing it with the Palestinian side. In any case, it is clear that, sooner or later, the two sides will have to meet to define its status, which remains the most important issue for both. It is also clear that, in order to find an agreement, they will have to identify common criteria of reference, and it is especially on this point that we, as Christians, believe we have the right to make our voice heard.

We want to insist on the need to preserve the Christian character of the city as one of the constituent elements of its universal configuration. By "universal configuration" we mean the reality in which Jews, Muslims, and Christians, for centuries, have inhabited and shared the same spaces and, at times, the same traditions: Jerusalem would lose its universality if it did not maintain its public and visible character, including, of course, its Christian character. "Universal" means, then, open to the world but also with the lives of the world within the city itself.

By "Christian character", we refer, in the first place, to the possibility of praying publicly in the city; here, in fact, the European custom of dedicating a more private sphere to prayer is not relevant. Muslims pray publicly, Jews observe the *Shabbat* publicly: Christians must be able to do the same, according to their different traditions. We also mean supporting—or at least not hindering—the various Christian institutions (schools, hospitals, and so on), and maintaining the Christian presence and its natural demographic growth, along with the natural bonds between the Christians of Jerusalem and their brethren in the Holy Land. Without the daily relationships that exist with Christians in various parts of the country, and particularly in Bethlehem, it would become very difficult to keep the various Christian institutions of the Holy City active.

Jerusalem's identity includes a sacred character that does not belong only to individual sites or monuments, as if these could be separated from one another or isolated from their respective communities: the sacred character involves Jerusalem in its entirety, its Holy Places and its communities, with their hospitals, schools, cultural, social, and economic activities.

Israelis and Palestinians, in seeking (1) a political agreement that will end their conflict over Jerusalem and (2) a definitive and lasting political and territorial solution, cannot ignore the fact that the city encompasses aspects that go far beyond their legitimate national interests. Likewise, Israelis and Palestinians cannot avoid taking into account the efforts and requests of all the legitimate parties involved; in this, they should not feel limited in any way but, on the contrary, respected and reassured. Finally, the two sides should ensure that the city's current universal character is preserved and work to ensure that it remains the place where Jews, Muslims, and Christians continue to meet along the streets of the Old City, each group with its own mentality and traditions, which are so uniquely linked to one another.

> This is the hope, this the vision, which inspires all who love this earthly Jerusalem to see her as a prophecy and promise of that universal reconciliation and peace which God desires for the whole human family. Sadly, beneath the walls of this same City, we are also led to consider how far our world is from the complete fulfillment of that prophecy and promise. In this Holy City where life conquered death, where the Spirit was poured out as the first-fruits of the new creation, hope continues to battle despair, frustration, and cynicism, while the peace which is God's gift and call continues to be threatened by selfishness, conflict, division, and the burden of past wrongs. For this reason, the Christian community in this City which beheld the resurrection of Christ and the outpouring of the Spirit must hold fast all the more to the hope bestowed by the

Gospel, cherishing the pledge of Christ's definitive victory over sin and death, bearing witness to the power of forgiveness, and showing forth the Church's deepest nature as the sign and sacrament of a humanity reconciled, renewed, and made one in Christ, the new Adam.[2]

[2] Ibid.

The Universal Vocation of the Churches in the Holy Land

Address at the Special Assembly for the Middle East of the Synod of Bishops

October 12, 2010

In the Holy Land, we strongly feel the limitations of a perspective and a pastoral approach that too often start from problems and from the concrete situations rather than from the vocation of Christians and of the Churches in those special and blessed lands.[1] I think, instead, that today it is necessary to begin again from the specific vocation of the Churches in the Holy Land. Moreover, this seems to me to be the meaning of the invitation that the Holy Father addressed to us in the inaugural homily of the Special Assembly of the Synod of Bishops, when he asked us to adopt the perspective of God, who sees this Land from above.[2]

Address at the Special Assembly for the Middle East of the Synod of Bishops, held in Rome from October 10 to 24, 2010. The theme of the Assembly was "The Catholic Church in the Middle East: Communion and Witness. 'Now the company of those who believed were of one heart and soul' (Acts 4:32)."

[1] See *Instrumentum Laboris* for the Special Assembly for the Middle East of the Synod of Bishops, 2010, no. 6, https://www.vatican.va/roman_curia/synod/documents/rc_synod_doc_20100606_instrumentum-mo_en.pdf.

[2] "This 'land' is not of this world; the whole of the divine plan goes beyond history, but the Lord wants to build it with men, for men and in men, beginning with the coordinates of space and time in which they live and which He Himself gave them. With its own specificity, the land we call the 'Middle East' makes up part of those coordinates. God sees this region of the world, too, from a different perspective, one might say, 'from on high'. . . And we too, as believers, look at the Middle East with this view,

It is important, then, first of all to recall the first manifestation of the Church in Jerusalem on the day of Pentecost: "'[We are] Parthians and Medes and Elamites and residents of Mesopotamia, Judea and Cappadocia, Pontus and Asia, Phrygia and Pamphylia, Egypt and the parts of Libya belonging to Cyrene, and visitors from Rome, both Jews and proselytes, Cretans and Arabians, we hear them telling in our own tongues the mighty works of God!' And all were amazed and perplexed, saying to one another, 'What does this mean?'" (Acts 2:9–12). This universal gathering of all languages in Jerusalem and the fact that they met in God is not only a memory of a past but is still present and future. Today, as then, the Church of Jerusalem is born and develops with a universal vocation and openness. Every day, the Friars Minor of the Custody of the Holy Land are respected witnesses and often generous promoters of the physical and spiritual movement that brings millions of people to return and meet in this city in search of the center of faith and Christian life.

As a Christian community that lives in the Holy Land, we must therefore, first and foremost, rediscover the fact that we live in the places of our origins. However, it is not simply a question of places; we are the living memory of the Incarnation, which occurred not only in time, but also in a specific space: living with vitality in that space is a vocation and a service to the entire Church. We are therefore asked to recover this awareness; it is necessary for pastors and faithful of the Churches in this Land to deepen their own knowledge of the Holy Places, which are an important

from the perspective of the history of salvation." Benedict XVI, Homily for the Opening of the Special Assembly for the Middle East of the Synod of Bishops, October 10, 2010.

opportunity for evangelization and prayer, as well as a fundamental point of the Christian identity of the Holy Land. Jerusalem, in particular, cannot be seen merely as the site of a conflict between opposing factions: it remains the point of departure and arrival for anyone who shares the faith of Abraham.

The pilgrimages that arrive in the Holy Land from all over the world, as well as the presence of Jewish and Muslim faithful around the same sacred area of the Holy City, appear to the eyes of faith as a fulfillment, albeit partial, of the prophecy of the gathering of all peoples on Mount Zion to learn the ways of the Lord and walk in His paths (see Is 2:2–4; Mic 4:2–4).

Therefore, there is a need for renewed attention to formation and catechesis, both of those who are preparing to be pastors and of the faithful, so that everyone may be up to the challenges that evangelization and mission present in our time and in this Land of ours. A pastoral approach that focuses more on the Word of God, studied, meditated on, and proclaimed, appears indispensable.[3] The difficulties and even prohibitions that the explicit proclamation of the Gospel encounters in our lands must not cause us merely to preserve what already exists; they also require us, as individuals and as communities, to be creative, capable of eloquent and incisive testimony.

Pilgrimages, on the one hand, and the multilingual, multiracial and multi-ritual nature of the Church in the Holy Land, on the other, push us to be an increasingly "extroverted" Church, hospitable and open to others. The Church here has always been a minority: being a minority is part of our identity, and we must accept it. This condition re-

[3] See *Instrumentum Laboris*, nos. 8, 62–69.

minds us that we are not made and do not live for ourselves, but are to enter into relation with those who meet us, and it forces us to be proactive: this undoubtedly is happening. Indeed, despite being a little more than one percent of the population, the one Church, through her work, reaches more than five percent of the inhabitants. In this regard, I mention the Custody's service in the areas of education, assistance and university training, which is offered not only to Latin Christians but also to the faithful of other confessions and religions. In recent years, moreover, the Custody has opened its doors to collaboration in the pastoral care of groups of Hebrew-speaking Catholic faithful and immigrants.[4] The centers for study, research, reception, and social communication, founded and supported by the Custody—such as the Franciscan Center for Eastern Christian Studies in Cairo, the Memorial of Saint Paul in Damascus, the Magnificat Musical Institute in Jerusalem, the Franciscan Multimedia Center, and the Faculty of Biblical Studies and Archaeology in Jerusalem—are open to Christians of all denominations.

Being a minority must not prevent us from giving a vibrant testimony of faith and belonging, from developing thoughtful and strong cultural proposals, the only possible space for discussion in our Land. In conclusion, it must not close us off but, rather, open us to new forms of creativity, which are not only permitted but sometimes absolutely expected by our brothers and sisters of other religions.

For us who live in the Holy Land, ecumenical commitment is first and foremost a meeting of people, of brothers and sisters who, beyond their differences, share the common Christian journey and the commitment to peace, but

[4] Ibid., nos. 49–53.

it is also a daily expression of the labor handed down to us by the prejudices and history that become concrete and tangible in this Land.[5]

Regarding the delicate and painful political landscape, I would simply like to emphasize what is not always clear even to ourselves: that it is up to us Christians of the Holy Land—who do not claim territories or positions of privilege—to safeguard, to keep visible, and to defend jealously, in all possible forms and public venues, the also-Christian character of this Land and of Jerusalem, which is neither taken for granted nor, perhaps, always accepted.

[5] See *Instrumentum Laboris*, 82.

The Significance of the Holy Places for Christianity

Talk at the Second Annual Symposium on Interfaith Dialogue, Jerusalem

October 19, 2010

The theme of tolerance and respect among believers in different faiths who live in the Holy Land is important for all people of goodwill. Tolerance and respect for the other person require in the first place an experiential knowledge of the historical roots of the different religions that have coexisted in this Land for centuries.

With respect to the Holy Places, the Christian religion has much in common with the other monotheistic religions. Christians believe in one God, Creator of heaven and earth, and that God wants to participate personally in the history of humanity. The Christian view of creation and redemption is rooted in the history of salvation, which unfolded over several millennia in this part of the world: the entire region, therefore, is considered by Christians also as a sacred place, which speaks about God and, in a special way, about the historical reality of Jesus of Nazareth.

It would not be correct, though, to speak about the Holy Places within a spatial-temporal dimension without making some reference to the persons who live there. The space

A talk prepared on the occasion of the Second Annual Symposium on Interfaith Dialogue (Jerusalem, October 19, 2010), titled "Ethics and Tolerance in Religion". The text was read at the Symposium by Franciscan friar Noel Muscat, since then-Archbishop Pizzaballa was at the Vatican as a participant in the Synod of Bishops' Special Assembly for the Middle East.

reserved for the deity, and therefore made sacred, at least from the biblical perspective of the Jewish-Christian tradition, cannot be a mere empty space. Salvation history speaks about a God who "descends from heaven" in order to be with His people: the God in Israel is an itinerant, nomadic God, who accompanies His own people on their journey from slavery to freedom. He is furthermore a God who speaks to His people, through the mediation of the prophets and of the Sacred Scriptures. Thus the Land that we now call Holy is not an empty space reserved solely for God; rather, the persons who dwell in it are the ones who sanctify it, because they act as a sign of the presence of God in the world.

If we apply this idea of a tangible presence of God among His people to the Christian perspective, we see that Christianity believes in a historical manifestation of God in the person of Jesus Christ, who became man and lived among the people of this Land. So for Christians, too, every person who lives in the Holy Land becomes an expression of the sacredness of this region. Every human footprint on this Land is a symbol of the sacred footprints of God and, for Christians, of those of His beloved Son Jesus Christ, who, as the Gospel of John says, "became flesh and dwelt among us" (Jn 1:14). Consequently, all people of goodwill who live in the Holy Land and believe in the God of Abraham have a common denominator for dialogue, mutual respect, and religious tolerance.

On the other hand, it is true that, as everyone knows, the respective Holy Places often coincide here and are the cause of conflicts and tensions between believers. Similarly, though, in no other place on earth is there such a wealth of interreligious coexistence, marked also by sincere aspirations for peace and friendship. From this perspective, the

Holy Land is truly a miracle of human coexistence in the name of the one God, and, in the case of Christianity, it is also a miracle of ecumenical coexistence in the name of Jesus Christ. No doubt, the signs of division among believers are unfortunately highlighted somewhat more than the positive signs of fraternity and respect.

The historical sources indicate that, from the foundation of the Roman Province of Palestine in the year 6 until the battle of Yarmouk in 636, Christianity was born and became the predominant religion in this Land, particularly during the Byzantine period. The first Christian community to spring up was the Hebrew-Christian one in Jerusalem. This same initial nucleus was what subsequently guaranteed the persistence and the development of the Christian faith from the generation of the apostles of Jesus until the period in which the memoirs of the disciples were put into writing, eventually making up the Gospels and the other writings of the New Testament, which Christians consider sacred and inspired by God just like the other Sacred Scriptures of the Hebrew canon. These same Christians preserved the memory of the Holy Places associated with the life of Jesus Christ, in particular Nazareth, Capernaum, the Grotto of the Nativity in Bethlehem, and the Cenacle, Golgotha, and the Holy Sepulcher in Jerusalem. The period in which the Hebrew-Christian community flourished in the Holy Land is therefore fundamental for the connection with the person of Jesus of Nazareth Himself. Among these first Hebrew Christians there were relatives of Jesus and other disciples.

With the Edict of Milan by the Emperor Constantine the Great in the year 313, Christianity became the state religion of the Roman Empire. From Constantinople the influence of Byzantine art, spirituality, and culture spread to these regions; during the Byzantine era, furthermore, the

Hebrew-Christian community gradually faded away, yielding its place to the Christianity that was imported from Constantinople.

This second period was the high-water mark, the glory days of Christian hegemony in the Holy Land; it was and remains a unique period in the long history of dominions and power struggles, in reality the only period in which Christianity dominated in that Land, except for the brief time of the Crusades.

Leaving aside the political aspect of the Byzantine rule, we can in any case mention some elements that testify to the importance, for Christians, of this Land and of its Holy Places.

First of all, the Byzantine period was marked by a growing fervor for pilgrimages. We possess precious documents of pilgrims who came from the West, which provide useful information about the Christian life and presence in the Holy Land during that era. Among them, the diary of the pilgrim woman Egeria, which goes back to the late fourth century, is one of the most interesting: it describes the magnificence of the Holy Places, which then were resplendent with mosaics of gold and silver, in particular the three basilicas that Helena, the mother of the Emperor Constantine, had had built in 325, after the Council of Nicaea. Two of these splendid places of worship exist to this day, but have undergone profound and substantial changes, especially the Basilica of the Holy Sepulcher in Jerusalem and the Basilica of the Nativity in Bethlehem. The third basilica, known by the name of *Eleona*, on the Mount of Olives, was destroyed during the Persian invasion in 614 and was never rebuilt.

The second striking fact during the Byzantine rule was the flourishing of monasteries in the desert, particularly on the arid hills of Judea, in the region between Jerusalem,

Bethlehem, and the Dead Sea. None of these monasteries, or *lavra*, exists today; the most famous is the Monastery of Mar Saba. The ideal of a life in seclusion in the caves of the desert, together with the ideal of a coenobitic or monastic life in a community, became the model for Christians after the end of the persecutions. When—for instance, during the first centuries of the Christian presence in the Holy Land—death by martyrdom did not exist, the choice of a higher life took concrete form in the so-called *fuga mundi*, a flight or retreat from the world inhabited by sin. The desert of Judea was the most suitable refuge for men with such high ideals of life, and the spirituality of the desert continued to enrich this Land with a sense of the sacred that had unique features.

The locations just described are therefore the Holy Places that to this day are venerated and visited by Christians and non-Christians alike. Together with the sacred places of Judaism and Islam, they make this Land truly special, and as a Christian friar who lives in Jerusalem, I perceive that they exert an attraction that deeply touches people's hearts.

Three popes came to visit the Holy Land in recent years: Paul VI in 1964, John Paul II in 2000, Benedict XVI in 2009. During his visit, Pope Paul VI called this Land "the fifth Gospel" to indicate that physical contact with the Holy Places becomes, for us Christians, a vivid reminder of the Good News preached by Jesus and handed down to us by the four written versions of the Gospel. Every time the pope travels to the Holy Land, he always insists on the fact that he comes as a pilgrim. It is truly touching to see how a papal visit always turns into a manifestation of respect for and veneration of the Holy Places, not only the Christian ones, but also the places sacred to Judaism and to Islam. This is another proof of the sincere desire of Christians to build bridges and to highlight the elements common to all who believe in the God of Abraham and who love this Land as the part of the world that belongs most to God.

One might easily be confused by the many rites and Churches that officiate in the Holy Places, particularly in Jerusalem and Bethlehem. Aside from the historical divisions that sadly have characterized the Christians—as well as other faiths—there is nevertheless an important positive aspect in this sort of rivalry, and that is the unshakable faith and the strong tie that unites all Christians to the places that speak about Jesus and His message. The worn-down stones of the ancient basilicas, the sense of being in a place where time has stopped, the voices of the monks who chant at the same time in Greek, Latin, and Armenian, the fragrant clouds of incense that accompany the smoke of the countless candles in the semi-darkness, all bear witness to a very steadfast commitment and to the determination to stay and to be present in these places that Christians consider the holiest in the world.

This is why the Christian Holy Places are open first of all for worship, but also for visits by Christians and non-Christians. Standing, even for just a few minutes, in the Basilica of the Holy Sepulcher, we realize that many people travel there in search of meaning. It is true, certainly, that they may still be disoriented or downright scandalized by what they perceive as total confusion, but many seek all the same to grasp the deep, hidden value of the sacred spaces and rites. It is our duty, as religious Christians, to help those who approach these places to go beyond human curiosity about what is "exotic" and to seek to understand that something great really happened there. The Christian message of the Holy Places is not that of a mysterious experience that cannot be shared with someone from outside, but rather the message of an experience that touches the heart and the profound meaning of life: the experience of God who is truly present in human frailty and who accompanies every human being on his journey in life.

Love and care for the Holy Places have characterized the Franciscan presence in this Land since the thirteenth century. The Franciscans have given the witness of a peaceful presence, which adopted a style different from the one that characterized the period of the political influence of Byzantium or of the Crusades: perhaps this has been the secret of their survival and perseverance even during insuperable difficulties. Moreover, they have always been at the cutting edge of the archeological excavations in the Christian Holy Places, and the respect paid in academic circles to the Franciscan archeologists is one of the proofs of the competence and seriousness by which they have distinguished themselves. Their activity is also an obvious sign of the sense of belonging, felt by Christians in general, to this Land and to the ancient sites that speak about Jesus of Nazareth.

At this point it is necessary to mention the "living stones" of the Holy Land: as we said, another reason why it becomes a holy place for us Christians is that we can live and pray there. From the time of the Hebrew-Christian community in the early centuries, the Christian presence has therefore been of very great importance. This aspect became more urgent and obvious when the Christians ceased to be in the majority and to hold power and became a small minority, as they are today.

The presence of a Christian community in the Holy Land, albeit a small one, is important so that the Holy Places do not become museums and religious works of art to be admired by the tourists, but rather may be active centers of worship, in which the sense of religious belonging is very much alive. The sacredness of the Christian Holy Places therefore depends a lot on the Christian community that lives there around them and prays in them. Of course this Christian presence is enlarged thanks to the thousands of pilgrims who crowd these places each year and are a sign of their international character. The international aspect is relevant, as a proof that persons of different cultures, languages, and countries of origin can truly meet in order to pray, united by one faith, in a Land that is holy for them, too; moreover, this does not reduce the value of these same Holy Places for the local Christians, and vice versa.

The thousands of pilgrims are also interested in visiting the places of worship of the other major religions that are present: in no other place in the world is it therefore so concretely possible to educate people to cultivate a sense of respect and mutual tolerance for the other faiths, and to study real ways of building a deeper understanding of the beauty of diversity in harmony.

Finally, the significance of the Holy Places for the Christians is closely connected with their faith in a God who sanctified this Land in the person of Jesus Christ, whom Christians adore as the Son of God, born of a Virgin from Nazareth in the city of Bethlehem, who lived for three years in the region of the Sea of Galilee, where He preached and performed miracles, and who traveled throughout this Land, even traversing the hostile, mountainous region of Samaria, on His way to Jerusalem, where He was crucified, buried, and rose again from the dead, so that He was then proclaimed the Christ by His followers. This same land is also the fundamental point from which the Good News of the Gospel of Jesus Christ spread: first from Jerusalem, then toward Samaria and the coastal cities, and finally toward the pagan world of the Mediterranean basin, through the preaching of the Apostle Paul of Tarsus, only to arrive at the heart of the Roman Empire in the city of Rome, the center of the activity of the Apostle Peter, the fisherman from Capernaum on the Sea of Galilee.

In conclusion, all the elements of this Land's sacredness for Christians are linked also to the promises made by God to Abraham and to his descendants; it is quite true that many places sacred to the Jews are so for the Christians, too. The presence of the Christian community among the Jews and the Muslims has not always been easy, and yet it is very significant that the three religions venerate the sacredness of this Land as one of the fundamental elements of their faith in one God: may this faith generate greater tolerance and dialogue, on the path of true peace and fraternity among equals.

Jewish-Catholic Dialogue in Israel Today

Speech at the Collège des Bernardins, Paris

March 2011

The Catholics in Israel are not in the majority of the Christian population, which for the most part is made up of the Greek Orthodox Church. This is an important premise for dialogue, because the Jewish world in Israel is not always able to make the distinction between Catholics and non-Catholics. When someone refers to the Catholics, you are more likely to think of Rome than of Jerusalem; often, too, in the Holy Land many of the ecclesial initiatives are organized by all the Churches together and are not limited to the Catholics. Furthermore, the Catholic Church and the Greek Orthodox Church have different approaches to Judaism. In Israel, the dialogue between the Catholic Church and the Jewish world, therefore, is one of the channels of dialogue, but not the only one.

We should also specify that the Roman Catholic Church in the Holy Land has a jurisdiction that goes beyond the borders of Israel: indeed, besides Israel, it also includes the Palestinian Territories, Jordan, and Cyprus. The same is true of the Maronite Church and for the Syriac Catholic Church; only the Melkite Church has a jurisdiction that falls entirely within the borders of the State of Israel.

Speech given during the twenty-first session of the biennial meetings between the International Jewish Committee for Interreligious Consultation (IJCIC) and the Holy See's Commission for Religious Relations with the Jews (Paris, Collège des Bernardins, February 27–March 2, 2011).

It is necessary, then, to distinguish the ecclesiastical authorities from the common believers, who often remain rather distant from the initiatives and official events dedicated to interreligious dialogue. From my point of view, this aspect should be reexamined: we must ask ourselves whether the time has arrived to abandon the halls in which our official meetings are held so as to start initiatives that are more connected to the everyday life of the believers. Often, indeed, the only meetings that take place at the level of the common believers are not official events at all, but rather situations in which the persons, for various reasons, meet each other—for example, at the workplace or in dealing with sickness. In this case, the distinction between Israel and the Palestinian Territories is fundamental, because a Catholic Christian from Bethlehem does not have the same encounter with Judaism as one who lives in Jaffa or Nazareth does.

Finally, the different rites and jurisdictions that make up the Catholic Church in the Holy Land make no distinction between Israel and the Palestinian Territories. Therefore, together with other religious reasons, it is preferable to use the wording "Churches of the Holy Land".

Social Life in Israel

Positive Aspects

FREEDOM OF WORSHIP

In Israel there are no problems with regard to freedom of religion or to the practice of one's own faith. Cases are reported, however, of especially offensive behavior near Orthodox Jewish districts and some *yeshivot* [rabbinical schools], in particular in Jerusalem. In the past, some communities have suffered as a result of this, but recently the situation seems to have improved; in any case, it must be acknowledged that freedom of worship and of expression are guaranteed without problems.

INCREASE IN THE CHRISTIAN POPULATION

In Israel—unlike what is happening in the Palestinian Territories—the number of Christians is not diminishing, nor is it increasing decisively. Certainly we do not observe the worrying phenomenon of emigration: this is a sign of the calm and economic stability of the Christians.

SCHOOLS

The Christian schools in Israel play an important role in preserving the Christian identity. They are also a decisive factor in the social life of the country, especially within the Arab part. To a great extent they are widely financed by the State, but the public funding, although considerable, is decreasing; this economic support for the Christian schools is essential, and this right is still guaranteed, despite everything: this arrangement is not a given in the rest of the Middle East.

ISRAELI SCHOOL BOOKS

The presence of Christianity in Israeli textbooks, on the whole, has increased. Certainly much work still remains to be done in order to update the image of the Christians and of the Catholic Church, which to some extent goes back to the Inquisition, the persecution, and paganism, but the efforts made in recent years must be appreciated.

CULTURAL INITIATIVES

Increasing numbers of visits are made by Israelis (in groups with a guide or individually) to the Christian places, such as the Christian Holy Places, schools, and villages. There is a growing awareness of the Christian presence and of its contribution to the cultural life of the country, in the past and in the present; sometimes, however, this realization is no doubt just beginning and can be found only in some segments of Israeli society.

HEBREW LANGUAGE

Hebrew is gradually becoming one of the languages of the local Church. The Catholic Church is in fact made up not only of Arabs, foreigners, and pilgrims, but also of Hebrew-speaking Israelis.

Problems

IDENTITY

Within the Christian community in Israel there is an obvious problem of identity. The Christians are Israeli citizens, but they are not Jews; they are Arabs, but not Muslims. This problem presents itself more frequently among the young people who live in surroundings far from the Christian world: in some areas of the country, for example in Jaffa and Ramle, there are students who attend Israeli public schools and know more about the Jewish religion than about their own Christian faith and identity.

IMMIGRATION

In recent years, among the numerous immigrants from the former Soviet Union, there have been tens of thousands of Christian descent. Initially the Church seemed to have opened up a new pastoral "channel". In reality, it proved to be rather weak, for various reasons. On the one hand, for cultural reasons: for the Church it is difficult to operate in a Jewish Israeli context; indeed, it is not a question of ordinary pastoral work, but rather a "frontier" that requires acting in new settings. On the other hand, on the part of Israeli society internally there is fatigue in welcoming these immigrants, who are sometimes considered as foreigners.

FOREIGN WORKERS

In Israel there are tens of thousands of foreign workers; many, after a certain period of time, leave the country, while others remain. Some of them give birth to their own children here, and naturally they acquire the fundamental rights: above all the right to education, which, among the Jews, is for the most part in Hebrew. The topic of foreign workers therefore presents an altogether new challenge to the Church.

DISCRIMINATION

Despite the considerable progress in recent years, in the Arab world, in relation to the Jewish world, a strong sense of frustration and discrimination remains. The Christians are no exception, and these feelings have a negative effect on the building of a relationship with the Jewish world.

IGNORANCE

The Church and the Christians lament a profound ignorance in their regard on the part of Israeli Jewish society and, generally, with respect to Christianity. Various efforts have been made, no doubt, but too often the Christians are still identified with the pagans, the idol worshippers, and so on.

Reflections

In the first place, it is necessary to acknowledge that in Israel there are not many opportunities for dialogue and that, in most cases, these opportunities are of little importance for social life. Certainly the religious authorities meet, but for the most part on institutional or formal occasions, and rarely for events of a strictly religious character; almost always these meetings have no impact on everyday life.

There is then another problem on the cultural level: the Church finds it difficult to understand Israel and its religious institutions, and vice versa. Often Israel considers the Church as a foreign entity.

Also present, however, are many personal ties of friendship and moments of encounter between small religious communities, families, or movements. In other words, although at the institutional level the relationship between Christianity and Judaism is of a formal sort, at the local level we find instead many initiatives for dialogue, often among foreigners, but more and more often among the local inhabitants, too. New ecclesial movements, families that work together, in which sincere friendships have developed, associations and groups that defend human rights, and many other occasions for meeting are often the source of fraternal ties. These personal contacts, in my opinion, are no less important than the institutional ones.

On the institutional level, finally, there is another source of difficulties, unconnected with the personal level. As we mentioned, the Churches in the Holy Land do not make a distinction between Israel and the Palestinian Territories, and this has many effects on the dialogue between Catholics and Jews. A Catholic religious authority, when he speaks with an Israeli Jew or a religious, must indeed consider not only his faithful in Nazareth and Jaffa, or Haifa and Ramle, who therefore are in Israel, but also those who live in the Territories, in Bethlehem or Ramallah, and this will affect their relations.

Elements to Consider in Religious Life

I will mention now some aspects of the Jewish-Catholic dialogue that directly involve the religious life of the Catholics in Israel.

In the first place, the theme of the Old Testament: in the local Christian community love for the Old Testament must grow. Indeed, the Old Testament is perceived now as a mainly Jewish, distant text. This change will depend on the various Churches and traditions, in which the Old Testament is read today to a greater or lesser degree. All the Churches, of course, are well aware that it makes up an integral part of the Catholic Bible, but some prefer not to study it, or put it aside from their own studies. Concerning this aspect, too, however, some changes can be observed: movements, ecclesial groups, and associations are taking steps in this direction. This year, for example, the Catholic Churches are dedicating their pastoral activities specifically to the knowledge and the circulation of the Bible. It must be remembered, moreover, that the Bibles are printed in Arabic. Finally, it is necessary to emphasize that a prejudice still remains and needs to be overcome, sometimes starting with the clergy.

On the other hand, with regard to the relation between Judaism and the Church, the Catholic Church, starting with the promulgation of the conciliar Declaration *Nostra Aetate*, has undertaken a long journey—accomplished through documents, possibilities for dialogue, and gestures—of reconciliation and overcoming misunderstandings with the Jewish world. Until now, however, this journey has taken only timid steps in Israel and is therefore just beginning; it is not easy to explain or to understand how important the dialogue with Israel is for the life of the Church.

For the Church in the Holy Land, it is difficult, then, to distinguish between the religious and the political Israel. The conflicts in the past and at present necessarily influence and condition the religious relation between the Church and Judaism; documents and gestures of reconciliation are perceived as a political surrender to the government of Israel, and not as a step forward in a common journey.

Finally, we should take into consideration the theme of the land, the faith, and the nation. The Catholic Church, unlike Judaism, does not establish a tie between land, faith, and nation. From the Catholic perspective, religious faith and one's tie with the land and the state are two distinct elements; in contrast, this bond is deep in Judaism, and we will have to keep working together on this aspect.

The Synod of the Churches of the Middle East

The recent Special Assembly of the Synod of Bishops for the Middle East, which was held in Rome in October 2010, was decisive from many perspectives; on many questions, it advanced discussions and topics that are now on the agenda of the Arab world, for example, the concepts of full and equal rights of citizenship, freedom of conscience, and so on.

The topic of Judaism and relations with Israel was not central to the discussions, but neither was it excluded a priori, and taking into account the eminently Middle Eastern context of this assembly, some resolutions can be considered important innovations: a sort of signpost for the future of the Churches in the Middle East. Therefore we will elucidate several of them.

In the first place, in the two sessions focused on interreligious dialogue, an Orthodox rabbi was invited to speak for the first time: Rabbi David Rosen. This highlighted the importance of our dialogue with the Jewish people. On the next day, after him, the floor was given to a Sunni Muslim and to a Shiite. Rosen's emphasis on the importance of the Christian communities of the Middle East was very much appreciated.

In the second place, in formulating the final message of the Synod, the Synod Fathers showed sensitivity with regard to the tragedy of the current conflict and its effects. Indeed, in the final message we read: "We reflected on the suffering and insecurity in which the Israelis live."

In any case, the entire message distinguishes neatly between the painful political questions—which could be a reason for distance between Arabs and Israelis—and religious heritage, which in contrast is common to Jews and Christians.

The eighth paragraph of the final message then describes members of the Jewish people as "our fellow citizens". In unequivocal terms, the document recalls:

> The same Scriptures unite us: the Old Testament, the Word of God, is for both you and us. We believe all that God revealed there, since he called Abraham, our common father in the faith, Father of Jews, of Christians and of Muslims. We believe in the promises of God and his covenant given to Abraham and to you. We believe that the Word of God is eternal.

Clearly recalling the heritage of the Vatican Council II, the message continues:

> The Second Vatican Council published the document *Nostra Aetate* which treats interreligious dialogue with Judaism, Islam and the other religions. Other documents have subsequently clarified and developed the relationship with Ju-

> daism. On-going dialogue is taking place between the Church and the representatives of Judaism. We hope that this dialogue can bring us to work together to press those in authority to put an end to the political conflict which results in separating us and disrupting everyday life in our countries.

The document then calls on Jews and Christians to make a joint commitment to the way of peace:

> It is time for us to commit ourselves together to a sincere, just and permanent peace. Both Christians and Jews are called to this task by the Word of God. In his Word, we are invited to listen to the voice of God "who speaks of peace": "Let me hear what God the Lord will speak, for he will speak peace to his people, to his holy ones" (Ps 85:9). Recourse to theological and biblical positions which use the Word of God wrongly to justify injustices is not acceptable. On the contrary, recourse to religion must lead every person to see the face of God in others and to treat them according to their God-given prerogatives and God's commandments, namely, according to God's bountiful goodness, mercy, justice and love for us.

In the eleventh paragraph, which acknowledges the international authorities which have sought to resolve the conflict between Israelis and Palestinians, the Synod Fathers express as follows their desire for a "a peaceful, just and definitive solution" in harmony with the political leadership of Israel and the international community:

> The Palestinian people will thus have an independent and sovereign homeland where they can live with dignity and security. The State of Israel will be able to enjoy peace and security within their internationally recognized borders. The Holy City of Jerusalem will be able to acquire its proper status, which respects its particular character, its

> holiness and the religious patrimony of the three religions: Jewish, Christian and Muslim. We hope that the two-State-solution might become a reality and not a dream only.

Finally, the message addresses as follows all men of good-will, wherever they may be:

> We condemn violence and terrorism from wherever it may proceed as well as all religious extremism. We condemn all forms of racism, anti-Semitism, anti-Christianism and Islamophobia and we call upon the religions to assume their responsibility to promote dialogue between cultures and civilizations in our region and in the entire world.

The synodal process concluded with the formulation of forty-four propositions to the Holy Father. These propositions will guide the process by which the pope will formulate his [Post-Synodal] Exhortation to the Catholics in the Middle East and are the points to which the Synod Fathers dedicated the most time. Most of these points have a pastoral character, and their purpose is to strengthen and encourage the Catholic communities. The forty-first proposition, at any rate, expresses the clear desire that the dialogue between Jews and Christians of the Middle East may be intensified and fostered:

> Judaism has a central place in the Declaration of the Second Vatican Ecumenical Council, *Nostra Aetate*. Initiatives of dialogue and cooperation with Jews are to be encouraged so as to foster human and religious values, freedom, justice, peace and fraternity. Reading the Old Testament and getting to know Jewish traditions lead to a better understanding of the Jewish religion. We reject anti-Semitism and anti-Judaism, while distinguishing between religion and politics.

This important proposition furnishes the necessary basis for the development of a new and positive relationship, in the Middle East, between Jews and Christians, together with Muslims.

During the Synod, in reality, debates took place, some of them very heated, since they were connected with political and religious questions, but everyone knows how much the two spheres intersect in this region. Hasty conclusions presented by some journalists, problematic statements pronounced by some prelates of the synod, and collateral events of a sociopolitical nature created the impression that the meeting had an anti-Semitic and anti-Israeli character. It was not like that at all, but unfortunately this seems to have been the final perception. The impact and the reactions in the Israeli media were strong and negative. Especially the controversy concerning certain statements about the land and the Jewish character of the State struck the Israeli public consciousness deeply, in a negative way.

On the other hand, the Church received these arguments with concern and weariness, because, from her perspective, the final formulations were drafted hastily and showed partiality.

The reactions just described are significant, because they clearly show who we are and where we are currently situated in our relations. They also suggest, though, what we would like to share, for the purpose of continuing our vital relationship of coexistence, to which we are all called.

The Importance of *Nostra Aetate*

Speech at a Meeting with the Chief Rabbinate of Israel

March 31, 2011

From the perspective of the document's contents, the structure of the Declaration *Nostra Aetate* is divided into five numbered sections.[1] After the prologue, which constitutes the first section, section 2 considers the different non-Christian religions and specifically mentions Hinduism and Buddhism. Sections 3 and 4 are dedicated to the Muslims, because of their monotheism and their various relations to biblical revelation, and to the Jews, because of their singular position in the economy of salvation, while section 5 contains the exhortation to universal fraternity.

As for the context and the debates that led to the final version, the document was originally designed as an appendix to *De Oecumenismo*, the document on ecumenism, and was supposed to contain only the Church's thought about the Jewish people. The need to inquire about relations with the Jewish people was deeply felt by the majority of the Council Fathers and much awaited by outside observers; from it arose the demand to widen the horizon to the other non-Christian religions, without prejudice to the principal role of

---

Speech given on the occasion of a bilateral meeting between the Chief Rabbinate of Israel and the Pontifical Commission for Religious Relations with the Jews, held in Jerusalem from March 29 to 31, 2011.

[1] Vatican Council II, Declaration on the Relation of the Church to Non-Christian Religions *Nostra Aetate*, which was promulgated by Pope Paul VI on October 28, 1965, and inaugurated a new phase in the Church of openness to interreligious dialogue.

Judaism in relation to the Church. The debates were among the most heated, also because of the difficulty that the Arab Churches had in accepting a document on Judaism.

It is by no means out of place to think that the declared, mysterious coexistence of the Old Covenant with the New would provide the Council Fathers with the basis, beyond pastoral or political advantages, for rethinking analogically the Church's relation with the other non-Christian religions, which would come to be included also, positively, in the theological consideration of the council precisely by starting from the new consideration of the Jewish question. The Jew, therefore, becomes for the Church the paradigm for the other. In other words, the particular relationship with Judaism was the element and the criterion that led the Church to inquire systematically with regard to the "Other".

There were additional factors that reinforced this perspective and sensibility: the first among them was the journey that Paul VI made to the Holy Land in January 1964, which several times offered the pope the occasion to speak to non-Christians and about them. Later on he would often recall this intense experience, for example in his message for Easter Sunday, March 29, 1964: "Every religion has within it gleams of light, which must not be despised or extinguished. . . . Every religion announces the dawn of faith; and in these moments we look forward to a resurgence of the best of all dawns, together with the full splendor of Christian wisdom."[2]

[2] See Paul VI, encyclical letter *Ecclesiam Suam*, August 6, 1964, no. 107: "Then we see another circle around us. This too is vast in extent, yet not so far away from us. It comprises first of all those men who worship the one supreme God, whom we also worship. We would mention first the Jewish people, who still retain the religion of the Old Testament, and who are indeed worthy of our respect and love. Then we have those worshipers who adhere to other monotheistic systems of religion, especially the Moslem

The Church, while confirming her awareness of being the new creation in Christ, daughter of Abraham according to the faith, recognizes in the call of Israel the beginnings of her own faith and of her election; moreover, she sees the Chosen People included in the one love of Christ for Jews and Gentiles. She knows how much she owes to Israel according to the flesh from which come Christ, Mary, and the apostles, and she is not prepared to extend simplistically to the whole Jewish people, of all time, the responsibility for the killing of Christ: this point is rather important.

The document, then, even in the special attention that it devotes to Judaism, which will be the dominant note in the succession drafts, too, seems to contain ideas that, at the council, would be the seeds of a "theology" of non-Christian religions. Alongside the traditional idea that men of goodwill seek God and worship him and obey the natural moral law and the mystery of the universal salvific will, we should not overlook the "Christological" motive of the one love with which Christ embraces the nations with a view to reconciling all the nations of the world with Christ.

What, then, is the new contribution of the document? It is, first of all, the first time that a council paid attention to those people—and we are talking about millions of them—who still do not know or do not acknowledge Christ and His redemption.

It springs, secondly, from an idea of Church-in-relation (*Lumen gentium*) and from the renewed concept of her identity. The clarification of the Church's identity that occurred with the Dogmatic Constitution *Lumen gentium* and was understood in terms of the long journey of salvation history, of

---

religion. We do well to admire these people for all that is good and true in their worship of God."

which Old Testament history is an integral part, required a renewed attitude toward those who now proved to be companions along this journey, and no longer competitors or enemies. The Church's profound awareness of her nature and essential mystery produced the need to elaborate this Declaration, for this reason judging it to be the mature and necessary fruit of the new understanding of the mystery of the Church that was being outlined precisely in the chapters of the Dogmatic Constitution on the Church and the liturgy.

The fundamental unity of the plan of salvation history from its one origin to its one end, which is recalled in the prologue of the Declaration, now required a new view of the relations with those who lived out, although in their own way, the relation with the one God, with a view to the one Salvation. The Declaration, as it was presented to the Council Fathers, started from the consideration of the new condition of the world, which was ever more unified, and therefore from the relations between people of different cultures and religions, which are ever more numerous; nevertheless, besides a practical necessity, the true theological foundation of the reflection was the *divinum consilium* [divine plan] of God, who created the entire human race and leads it to its end.

The document, however—and we must identify this as another novel aspect—has a pastoral character: it springs from a pastoral concern and does not intend to resolve problems of a dogmatic sort. *Nostra Aetate* is, in summary, the pastoral translation of the renewed theological self-awareness of the Church.

From the new Declaration, therefore, we must not demand a dogmatic definition about the validity of the non-Christian religions with respect to salvation or with regard to their place in God's salvific plan, but only pastoral guidelines, which can orient Christians in their daily encounter with people who do not share their faith. This does not mean that it is a document of lesser importance: pastoral work puts into practice what is believed. Faced with an increasingly pluralistic perspective and the multiplication of her interlocutors, the Church chooses to enter into relation.

Here instead are a few reflections with reference to the pastoral consequences. In the Declaration we read:

> Although the Church is the new people of God, the Jews should not be presented as rejected or accursed by God, as if this followed from the Holy Scriptures. All should see to it, then, that in catechetical work or in the preaching of the word of God they do not teach anything that does not conform to the truth of the Gospel and the spirit of Christ.
>
> Furthermore, in her rejection of every persecution against any man, the Church, mindful of the patrimony she shares with the Jews and moved not by political reasons but by the Gospel's spiritual love, decries hatred, persecutions, displays of anti-Semitism, directed against Jews at any time and by anyone.[3]

This passage is important, because it recalls clear pastoral approaches that are binding for the whole Church, which from now on are her ordinary life. In the first place, revise catechesis and rethink it in terms that are no longer anti-Jewish: we must no longer speak about the people who committed "deicide" but, on the contrary, show the Church's deep connection with her Jewish roots.

In the second instance, there is preaching: this, too, along with catechesis, will have to be rethought, in order to avoid

[3] *Nostra Aetate*, no. 4.

not only any form of accusation or disdain, but also, indirectly, superficial interpretations of Scripture, which are rather widespread, in which the Old Testament is presented as fraught with violence and the New Testament as rich in mercy and love.

Finally, an intervention will be needed in seminary formation programs and in centers of theological study: the theology of substitution must be replaced by a theology of relation.

From the postwar period on, thanks to *Nostra Aetate*, the journey of the Jewish-Christian dialogue has been rather significant. On the part of the hierarchy, it was expressed with the cancellation of the prayer on Good Friday *pro perfidis iudaeis* [for the faithless Jews] commanded by Pope John XXIII in 1959, the historic embrace between Karol Wojtyła and Rabbi Elio Toaff in 1986 in the Great Synagogue in Rome, the promotion of countless meetings of the International Committee for Catholic-Jewish Relations,[4] and the long-awaited opening of diplomatic relations between the State of Israel and the Holy See, which occurred in 1993, but also through a long series of documents by national episcopates and local communities.

In conclusion, as far as the expectations of the Christian community are concerned, although much still remains to be done, it must nevertheless be acknowledged that the Catholic community has come a long way in rethinking its own identity in reference to the people of Israel; its relation with this people is now considered indispensable. Moreover, the relation with many Jewish communities in the world is

[4] An organization made up of the International Jewish Committee for Interreligious Consultations and, representing the Catholic Church, the Holy See's Commission for Religions Relations with the Jews.

natural today; not always easy, but an integral part of the life of the Catholic and Jewish community.

We cannot say the same about the situation in Israel: Israeli Jewish society has a very superficial knowledge of Christianity in general and an almost total ignorance of Christianity in the Holy Land. Except for a few groups of specialists, almost all Israeli Jews know Christianity through stereotypes and prejudices. The contents of the textbooks in Israeli schools has improved in comparison to the earlier editions, but Christianity and relations with it remain objects of very little interest and are not regarded as important elements in cultural life.

It is therefore necessary to work more seriously, and not only in times of emergency, to make the dialogue between Catholics and Jews important in Israel, too: political and religious leaders must become stakeholders in the dialogue with the Christian community of the Holy Land, and this must likewise be a common commitment for Catholics throughout the world.

I think that it is necessary to admit, however, that we are still at the beginning of the dialogue and to acknowledge honestly the fact that, together with the chronic unresolved problems, for some time now the Christian-Jewish dialogue has been becoming particularly difficult, and the local communities are less aware of the annual International Day for Dialogue. Among the reasons for this we can point out weariness, repetitiveness, the illusion of having already rapidly reached the goal that was set, but also, perhaps, an excessively timid investment in the ordinary pastoral program of parishes, in the praxis of the lay movements, and in the curricula of theological studies. To this we must add also the influence of the news media and of the political situation in the Middle East, with the Israeli-Palestinian conflict at its center. More and more often, political opinions end up influencing and dividing the respective communities.

Perhaps the best way to return to that radical commitment is to follow the path of encounter, even more than of dialogue. Besides, as Massimo Giuliani wrote in a valuable article: "A dialogue is mature when it takes into account the historical imbalances, the psychological asymmetries and the theological conflicts without being upset by them; but it is mature also when it constantly watches over its own language and is careful not to transgress the limits of the other person's dignity."[5]

[5] Massimo Giuliani, "Ebrei e cristiani, un dialogo che rispetti le differenze", *Vita e pensiero* 2 (2005): 101.

With the Eyes of the Apostles

A Presence That Upends One's Life

Talk at the Rimini Meeting for Friendship Among Peoples

August 24, 2011

To live life and one's faith "with the eyes of the apostles", the *apostolica vivendi forma* of Franciscan memory, means having—even before and besides fidelity to a stable, unchangeable deposit—the deep conviction that here and now, in this fragment of our biographies and geographies, we can find "an immense assurance", because this certainty already dwelt "in this time" and "in this region". What, then, is our experience of Christ? What does Capernaum, a set of ruins, say about this experience? How does this Land still nourish, even today, the habit of experiencing Christ in everyday life? These questions are simple, but also compelling.

Before mentioning Capernaum, though, I would like to start from another, more distant place, the first one in which God dwelt on earth: the Garden of Eden. I will then address several passages from the Bible, the first chapters of Genesis and the first chapters of the Gospel of Mark, which seem to be very distant from each other, yet have something in common: being a beginning.

The Book of Genesis speaks about the "beginning", *bere-*

Talk given on August 24, 2011, at the Rimini Meeting for Friendship among Peoples, sponsored by Communion and Liberation. The title of that year's Meeting was "And Existence Becomes an Immense Certainty".

shit, not only to indicate what comes before everything, but also to announce the profound intention that motivates God's heart when He creates the world and man. He wants to be—freely and not out of necessity—a God with the world and for the world, with man and for man: a world and a man that were imagined, designed, willed, created, and loved. It can be said that if man is *capax Dei*, capable of God, this is possible because God willed to be *capax hominis*, capable of man, and therefore *capax mundi*, capable of the world.[1] The first truth about man is that he was made for this real relation, in which life is born and grows. Sin is imagining here that life is situated not within the relation between God and man, but outside of it or against it, in the flight into an imaginary world of power and self-affirmation: with Adam and Eve, man personally accepted this doubt. What was simply real—in other words, God, man, and their relation—is now marked by doubt; what remains is only a life that we must invent anew every day by ourselves, because man no longer knows God and does not know that everything has already been given. Salvation is the fact that there was a new encounter that gives life again to this world and to wounded man, whom God did not abandon.

The first chapter of the Gospel of Mark relates that, after John the Baptist was arrested, Jesus started His preaching and came into Capernaum; Mark the Evangelist explains that Jesus went to Capernaum to settle and live there. Jesus therefore comes to live within a wounded, fragmentary world that has become inhospitable to God and to man, and He does so simply, by sharing concretely in the life of His people.

Today in Capernaum we still see the streets that Jesus

[1] See Adolphe Gesché, "Dieu est-il *capax hominis*?", *Revue théologique de Louvain* 24 (1993): 32ff.

walked along, the doorstep of Peter's house, and we can imagine what the life of the inhabitants was like at that time. There are kitchens with ovens, flooring, stairs, and we can conjecture what the thatched roofs were like. Among those houses is also the one belonging to Jesus: only a privileged few can still touch it.

Those inhabitants, therefore, had not had an emotional or theoretical experience: Jesus was there, in the midst of them, even in their houses; the signs and wonders that upend their life occurred precisely within their ordinary context.

Turning to the text of Mark: the first day that Jesus spent in Capernaum was a special day: it was the Sabbath, the feast day that celebrates God's love for man, the deep bond between us and God. On that first day, four important events occurred.

The first (Mk 1:21–28) shows Jesus as He enters into the synagogue and speaks. His speaking can only be a teaching, a retelling to man of the truth about God. And then, suddenly, alongside the voice of Jesus, the demon's voice is lifted up, as in Eden. The demon shouts, and his voice seeks to be louder than the voice of Jesus, the Word. He wants man to listen to him again, and not to God's voice. He shouts across the distance between us and him: "What have you to do with us?" (Mk 1:24). The demon shouts his truth, his victory; by asking him why he is there, he tells God that he is a distant God and that his being there ruins man: "Have you come to destroy us?" (Mk 1:24). But on that day, in Capernaum, the voice of Jesus succeeds in silencing that ancient voice. It takes away man's doubt that now God can only be a distant God. Jesus replies to the man with the unclean spirit: "Be silent, and come out of him!" (Mk 1:25). When the Word speaks, evil must be silent. Finally, when the cries of the evil one cease, the real question reoccurs to man: Who is this man who speaks and silences in us the voice of the evil one, of doubt? Who saves us in this way? Has God become our neighbor again?

In the second event, Jesus, after leaving the synagogue (Mk 1:29–31), enters Peter's house and heals his mother-in-law, who was in bed with a fever. Then the mother-in-law, healed, starts to serve Him. Here Jesus goes to dwell within another fracture, not the one that separates man from God, but the one that divides man from his own brother, blockading him in his own solitude and making him incapable of serving. Jesus does nothing except make His way there: once again, He simply enters.

Then there is another very interesting passage (Mk 1:32–34), a third miracle. Toward evening, after sunset, the whole city had gathered in front of the door, and they brought to Jesus all the sick and the possessed. So Jesus went to the synagogue and there healed man in his relation with God; He entered the house and healed man in his closer, familial ties. The third miracle, which takes place when these first two relations are healed, is that an entire village is gathered in a new solidarity in sorrow and begs salvation of the one man who can give it.

Finally, in the fourth and last passage (Mk 1:35–39), Jesus goes away. Secretly, at night, He goes to pray. When the others notice this, they are astonished that He is no longer there; they seek Him and find Him. Jesus, however, replies that Capernaum is not the only town; there are towns elsewhere waiting for Him and calling Him: Capernaum is not a closed, isolated place, but rather a door that opens to the other. The salvation of Capernaum is an event by which man rediscovers his own solidarity with every other person: what happened in that town is what occurs now everywhere, to every human being, to every family, to every town. "Elsewhere", then, is all the other villages of Galilee, but above all it is the Father, and Jesus returns to a place of prayer to the Father, bringing with Him the man whom He encountered. He who dwelt with men can now lead man to his true dwelling place, to live in God.

Capernaum testifies that man's real life is the real Holy Land of the encounter with God: one encounters God by living His lifestyle, which is the style of relation, of encounter that is open to Him. In other words, once again there is a meeting place between God and us: namely, reality as it is. A life lived with and for others is the only meeting place with the Lord. By "life" we do not mean something abstract, but real life, and even someone who is not that well acquainted with his own heart knows that it is marked by ambiguity and sin. There is no experience of God that does not pass by way of the painful and very beautiful drama of each person's life. Salvation takes place among our households: the eyes of the apostles saw and contemplated this; living in the Holy Land, with the passage of time I have become convinced of this, and not by studying it in books, but because it was granted to me to experience it. In this respect, the Holy Land is an extraordinary place. Guarding the Holy Places is not merely a work of archaeology: to stay in the Holy Land as a Franciscan, and to preserve the memory of the Holy Places, obliges us above all to guard the testimony and the experience to which they refer. The Place of the encounter that goes so far as to obtain forgiveness must become a testimony to encounter and forgiveness. If Jesus dwelt in a land while giving the depth of truth and divinity to human concreteness, it is possible to dwell in this Land with Him and as He did; to paraphrase the theologian Karl Rahner: If the Word became man, every man can, potentially, be the Word.

This does not happen to us, however, unless each person's ideas have a depth and, furthermore, a grounding in life that is lived in openness to others as to The Other, because without this depth, ideas will be essentially excuses, and the other will become an enemy. On the other hand, if the ideas have experience as their basis, there will be no need to defend them, because life will be enough to express their truth value. The encounter with diversity compels us, moreover, to examine somehow the reality and the depth of our own experience.

For us, therefore, being in the Holy Land should be nothing but this: doing what Jesus Himself did—namely, dwelling in a lively way in this fractured world. We dwell in it in a very simple way, namely, by seeking above all to live out the Gospel. Mission, indeed, is living out the Gospel in the place and in the condition in which one is from time to time. To live out the Gospel is precisely this possibility of not fearing reality, life, but of standing within it, acknowledging in it a larger presence that can be encountered only by committing oneself to life as it is. The Gospel is the astonishment of being able to live through everything that happens, only because God is there, together with us. To live out the Gospel is to have this experience firsthand, that is, to stand concretely in one's own history, without seeking another path to be saved except the one that comes from the cross of Christ. To stand in one's own poverty and to let God save us continually.

Living out the Gospel in the Holy Land—where meeting one another often proves to be complicated and where past and present violence mark the life of entire communities, both social and religious, to the point of becoming the sole criterion for interpreting relations—means for a Franciscan, trying to break that vicious circle of violence and fear by witnessing to salvation.

Sometimes we have a vague, abstract idea of salvation

and speak of it as something that will happen someday, and therefore, while waiting, we try to do the best that we can. This is not Christian salvation: the pages of the Gospel about Capernaum speak of a very concrete salvation and of a God who comes to dwell in the space of everyday activities. On the other hand, if faith remains relegated to a certain practice or moment of the day, if it does not become attentive watching to recognize the passage of the Lord in history, if therefore it does not transform all of life, then reality will always be a threat against which we must defend ourselves. "Your faith has made you well" (Lk 17:19), the Lord says to those whom he encounters.

Jesus dwells in His Land with a set of concrete attitudes, such as peace, generosity, welcome, forgiveness; He could not dwell in our sinful world if His way of staying there was not forgiveness. When they present to Jesus in Capernaum a paralyzed man by lowering him through the roof (Mk 2:1–12), Jesus first of all forgives him. Only from there does the possibility arise of encountering the other, the one who is different, and of discovering how this encounter also reveals something that otherwise would never be discovered, about each one of us and about the relationship that we have with God.

One personal experience has strongly marked my stay in the Holy Land. Initially, in my first years in Jerusalem, my contact with non-Catholic and non-Christian realities was limited to crossing paths on the street with Jews, Muslims, and Christians of other denominations, and a simple awareness of the many traditions that, in various ways, influenced the life of the city. There were no personal encounters except for the common episodes that all inhabitants of Jerusalem have experienced: some bless you, others curse you, still others spit on you or stop you to talk to you. As a whole, therefore, my life was spent calmly within the convents; I had no particular occasions for dialogue; I lived inside the world that had always been mine: Christian, Catholic, religious. I had my questions, and I gave my answers to them.

Things changed when I was sent to study at Hebrew University in Jerusalem: it was my first real exposure to a reality that was totally foreign to me. I was studying the Bible and thus took courses offered by the Scripture department, in which all the students served in or aspired to religious ministry; at that time, however, I was the only Christian in the whole department. After the first inevitable difficulties, true friendships developed. In our relations and during the lengthy discussions that we carried on, I realized that we did not have a common language, in terms of a way of thinking, of concepts. In speaking about my faith, I managed to convey practically nothing, and not because I did not have the words, but because we belonged to two different worlds: we did not share the same way of understanding topics like the Trinity, the Eucharist, the Incarnation, forgiveness, the family, social life, and so on. The very concept of Messianic mission, which I thought was well known, is rather different, and the interpretation of history is completely different as well; the Old Testament, which is generally thought to be our common basis, in reality is not read and experienced in the same way.

Little by little I understood that my interlocutors were interested in my experience of Christ, but not so much in my reflections on it. My companions were for the most part settlers, that is, they came from the so-called settlements that had been occupied by Israel, or else they had ties to that world; their experience of faith and their reading of the Bible had led them to make forceful choices that were also debatable. What was my reading? There was no attitude of distrust or hostility with regard to me, but sincere curiosity; in confronting it, I was initially rather uncertain. I asked myself then what my experience of Christ was and how I could speak about it in a comprehensible and credible way.

Until then I had always moved in Christian and ecclesial circles, and my way of life reflected that world; I understood, though, that together with the effort to communicate I also had to seek to "purify" my motivations. I realized what the word "witness" means, the toil and the charm of it, and I noticed that one's witness becomes true when one makes a sincere effort to communicate it. There is no experience without witness, and no witness that remains enclosed in itself.

That period marked a sort of re-founding of my vocation. Contact with the Jewish world had driven me to reinterpret my experience, to compare it with that of others, to share it in a way that was new for me. I spoke about Christ to people who did not accept Him as Lord, although that did not divide us, but even strengthened our bond. I will never forget the continuous reading of the New Testament that we did together in the afternoons or evenings. Some even came from a distance so as not to miss those meetings, and I was not the one who insisted on holding them. Almost on every page I was asked what it meant, what it said to me and why; my interlocutors always identified a conceptual parallel in the rabbinic literature, and when I listened to their impressions, I was touched by their emotion. Sometimes, when in a friendly way I took the liberty to make a witty, slightly critical remark about matters concerning the Church—perhaps also unconsciously as a *captatio benevolentiae*, a rhetorical attempt to win them over—I shocked them.

They loved Israel; I was supposed to love the Church: I was not supposed to discuss internal matters with them. Witness was not only something I was commanded to do, but also a necessity; it was in a certain sense "imposed" on me by their friendship.

Therefore it was on the terrain of reality that I encountered my friends, and I also discovered that friendship is the experience that brings you back to reality, compelling you simply to be yourself. This experience of dialogue with persons who were radically different, followed then by encounters with connotations that were different but equally intense, transformed my relationship with Jesus; since then the things to do have not changed, but rather my way of relating to them. Those encounters prompted me to make, in an altogether new and more intimate way, a personal decision in relation to Jesus.

How do I encounter Jesus today? I am not always ready for the encounter, but I know what my points of reference are: the Word and prayer, the Holy Place and the persons, together. The relation with the Holy Place continually recalls the event spoken of by the Scriptures making it a close memory.

Relations in the Holy Land are marked by deep wounds, but precisely by experiencing them from within, it is possible to acknowledge the daily challenge to relate to Christ. Everything then becomes concrete, difficult, even necessary: forgiveness, generosity, freedom, charity, moderation, patience, and welcome become a necessity, and to resist these attitudes would be to resist Jesus.

In conclusion, the Franciscans in the Holy Land generally do what the other religious orders do; they pray, study, teach, welcome. But the meaning of what they accomplish is not in the works, but rather in the resulting opportunity to love human life, knowing precisely that every life is an opportunity for the presence of God, a sacrament of an encounter. The purpose therefore is relation: the Gospel of presence, the Gospel of remaining.

From our encounter with this Land, we Franciscans receive the grace of a real experience of Christ, because words are not enough here, or perhaps they are too much, and no one believes us anymore. What remains, instead, is an in-depth, concrete experience of our own humanity, beyond superficial appearances, on a journey of truth that is not easy. We have one assurance: the Lord continues to journey within human history, which remains a difficult story, but one that is inhabited and forgiven and, therefore, precious. We stay here with the gusto of someone who wants to bring to all that he does the unique newness of our faith, which is salvation, a salvation that affects everyone.

Therefore we keep the door open, as Peter's house was open to welcome the Lord Jesus. We open up to God the door of reality, and this means that we give Him what man frequently does not have the courage to offer Him: our own pain, our sin, our need to be saved. We do this with tenacity and the hope of those who want to assist the accomplishment of this salvation, to see the dawn of Capernaum even in a place where it might still seem to be night.

National Community, Religious Pluralism, Citizenship, and Peace

New Perspectives for the Holy Land

Talk at a Conference for the Community of Sant'Egidio, Rome

February 29, 2012

Today the issues of citizenship and participation must be framed within a comprehensive reflection that encompasses the concrete problems of increasingly complex socio-cultural contexts, but also enhances the available educational resources, which can lead to significant progress in the civil, spiritual, ethical, and political fields.

In contexts experiencing acute conflict or tension, such as the Middle East, one of the main educational challenges is to promote the transition from "belligerent citizenship" to "citizenship of peace" through educational action aimed at building a culture of shared peace and making progress in the area of democratic achievements, rights, freedom, and justice in public institutions. The education of new generations can make an essential contribution in this regard, a long-term investment in the future of democracy.

In this way, the prospect of peace and rights takes on a specific identity, countering the tendency to develop approaches that assume conflict as a normal element of social

---

Presentation given on February 29, 2012, in Rome, as part of the conference titled "Arab Spring: Toward a New National Agreement", organized by the Community of Sant'Egidio.

life. The culture of peace and rights then becomes a dimension endowed with positive characteristics, not a utopian ideal or a limited objective, responding only to urgent events, according to a narrow conception of peace as the resolution of conflicts and the reduction of violence. Contrary to this "minimalist" approach—which can nevertheless offer some useful tools—a shared culture of peace should be the result of a constructive approach that supports social conditions capable of generating positive peace. The latter refers to the existence of economic, cultural, intellectual, human, and political practices and relationships that contribute to the overall well-being of the citizens, integrating all dimensions of life, up to and including the ultimate goal of rebuilding interpersonal and social relationships as ethical and nonviolent relations.

Often, speaking about peace and dialogue in the Holy Land seems to be, on the one hand, a scenario far from any concrete possibility of being achieved and, on the other, a topic awaiting urgent and necessary solutions. This paradox is due to the fact that centuries-old tensions, political interests, and different cultures intertwine and clash in the Holy Land.

Yet this land is not only a site of conflicts; it is also the cradle of Western culture and, to a great extent, of Eastern culture as well. It gave birth to our faith and is an indispensable point of reference: what happens here has consequences for the rest of the world. If in some ways, then, this region seems to be hopeless, due to its millennia-long experience of conflict, paradoxically, it still remains today the place that gave rise to hope for many: Jews, Christians, and Muslims. "This one and that one were born in her" (Ps 87:5): we were all born there. This apparent contradiction still exists today: while hatred seems to erect insurmountable barriers, the Holy Land remains the place where the three monotheistic religions coexist as though in a beautiful mosaic, enriched by different traditions.

Hopes for a different future find their foundation in the past and in the history of this Land. From the perspective of the man of faith, who believes in the God of biblical revelation who remains faithful to His Covenant despite the infidelities of the people, the foundation of all hope is precisely faith: "Now faith is the assurance of things hoped for, the conviction of things not seen. For by it the men of old received divine approval" (Heb 11:1–2). Through faith, the prophets nourished hope for a different future, making it even a certainty: for the prophet, hoping is not only a leap toward the future, but also means believing that change is possible, indeed, that change has already happened.

Today, the Holy Land still lives in a context of debilitating conflict, rife with resentment and injustice. This has a decisive impact on local religious, social, and political dynamics, confining each person in his own pain and fear, making it difficult to listen to and understand others, their history, aspirations, and suffering. The Israeli and Palestinian education systems—except for some commendable but limited coeducational experiences—unfortunately remain separate, and this affects the meanings that are attributed to being citizens in this extraordinarily complex reality and the image one strives to convey of one's own identity, both individual and national, and that of others, whether Jewish or Palestinian. Yet there are many people, Israelis and Palestinians, who meet and, despite having been affected by the conflict, are not afraid and continue to dialogue and to believe in peaceful coexistence, working practically to give hope for the future of this land.

Here, the search for peace remains a challenge for everyone. While recognizing the fundamental role of political and legal institutions—which are responsible for the common good and for determining the foundations for coexistence and social growth—promoting the adherence of individual consciences and social groups to the values of peace, participation, and citizenship remains essential. Educational action can, therefore, do much by recovering the centrality of the integral human dimension, which synthesizes the ethical, cultural, spiritual, and religious components of the person. In many cases, political problems find no adequate solution through the use of merely political means; the foundational and inspiring role of the moral and cultural dimensions with regard to the civil, social, and political spheres therefore deserves to be further enhanced. The challenge of a new education, which is inspired by man's striving to realize himself fully in truth and justice, and which expresses the regenerative potential contained in the values of intellectual and moral creativity, is one of the more promising opportunities to outline new models of citizenship in the Holy Land and to nurture a culture of peace and reconciliation in which young people, on both sides, can truly be protagonists.

The purpose, therefore, is to promote more and more the transition from a mentality and a citizenship that reproduce conditions that fuel mutual distrust to factors that foster an inclusive environment that is capable of introducing the elements of change necessary for peaceful civil coexistence. For this reason, it is necessary to abandon all forms of indoctrination to violence and its justification through the construction of stereotypes, the mystification of truth, the reproduction of forms of segregation that affect even the youngest. To foster trust in others and the creative impulses for peace, we must help the new generations to understand and to internalize democratic values and the foundations of common existence, while protecting diversity.

This orientation is based on confidence in the power of

education to transform society while preserving its essential founding principles. Teachers, educators, and intellectuals must resist the weakening of the public sphere by creating a sphere of active democratic life and by giving voice to a variety of questions, viewpoints, and interests that would otherwise run the risk of being excluded because of the demands of security in society. The fundamental task of educators and intellectuals then becomes to include the questions of recognizing the "other", to promote human rights and children's rights, to admit mistakes, to request forgiveness and offer it, and to broaden public debate within a model of democratic education.

The new conceptualization of citizenship, patriotism, and national affiliation, understood as sharing a common destiny, should also be inspired by the needs of mutual recognition and acceptance, justice, peacemaking, forgiveness, and the effort to create a new shared space.

The goal of promoting democracy and achieving peace, which is pursued by education, also consists in deepening the moral understanding of citizenship and rights, cultivating multiple ways of being good citizens and fresh approaches in interpreting rights. It must also encourage the acceptance of complexity by the new generations. Education, as an opportunity to foster open-mindedness, relies in fact on the appreciation of diversity.

In order to foster the values of diversity and openness, especially in times of tension and conflict, the education system must become inclusive with respect to orientations, problems, persons, and their rights. This implies two essential, interconnected elements: first, growth must be achieved through the exercise of numerous personal faculties. It is necessary to combine attention to cognitive factors with attention to the individual's emotional and social dimensions, because all these components—psychological, cognitive, emotional, affective, social—can interact both in the formation of conflict-oriented perceptions and attitudes and also in the growth of the same in a democratic sense. Secondly, education for citizenship must also be understood as a political commitment, which in practice combines the demands of diversity, knowledge, understanding, recognition, and acceptance of others, encourages their development, and consolidates political exchange among a multiplicity of opinions, viewpoints, and expectations, as an effective pedagogical tool and an opportunity to grasp, in practical circumstances, the universal essence of the law.

Religious Pluralism and Dialogue in the Holy Land

Dialogue, and especially interreligious dialogue, can be considered a pilgrimage, an invitation to step outside one's own certainties to encounter the other and his or her experience of faith. It therefore represents a process, a journey of consciences in their diversity toward an ideal and shared point on topics of major importance. We are all on the path toward consensus: neither already arrived nor at the starting point, but in a situation in which dialogue between cultures is both necessary and possible, indispensable and feasible.

Dialogue requires the distinction and integration of two moments: on one hand, the determination of a common basis, and on this foundation the work of political, legal, and religious institutions proves to be essential; on the other hand, the search for consensus among consciences, to bridge, through educational commitment, the gap between the institutional level, which is gradually maturing in many contexts, and the level of lived consciousness, which in many cases remains highly uncertain. What is important, however, "is the conviction that there is no culture (religious or secular) that cannot make a positive contribution to the writing of this ideal ethical code, and on the other hand, there is no culture that can be considered its integral locus."[1]

The reality of the Holy Land is that of a land currently divided by a wall, of two peoples, Israeli and Palestinian, who for more than sixty years have been seeking a path of peaceful coexistence, and of three religions—Judaism, Christianity, and Islam—which are also internally fragmented into different spiritual currents, traditions, and cults. Christians, who currently constitute a minority compared to a huge Jewish and Muslim community, can, however, fulfill the important task of being a "bridge" with the Islamic world on the one hand—thanks to the many Christians of Arab origin, who share the language and numerous cultural factors with the Muslim majority—and on the other hand with Judaism, thanks also to the presence of a small Christian community of Jewish origin.

Although this is the vocation of the Christian world, it is nevertheless evident that the difficulties, sufferings, and traumas that traverse the history of these peoples often sap energy and motivation from commitment to dialogue. Religion is particularly connected to individual and social identity; it is an affirmation of the self, but it is also a channel for expressing the sense of personal vulnerability and the feeling of being under pressure. In the Middle East this phenomenon is particularly intense: everyone feels fragile and threatened, and therefore it is often more difficult to open up to others and to affirm our common humanity, not only by acknowledging the fact that every human being is

[1] Armido Rizzi, *Laicità. Un'idea da ripensare* (Villa Verucchio: Pazzini, 2006), 59.

created in the image of God, but also thanks to the fact that all monotheistic religions uphold the value of peace as an ideal of human society and consider violence an undesirable manifestation. The different faiths, therefore, are bearers of resources for reconciliation and almost never are the sole or main cause of misunderstandings and conflicts, nor, in themselves, a risk factor in this sense.

In the Holy Land, there are also many initiatives for interreligious dialogue, conducted at various levels; each has its own meaning, and even those implemented at the official and institutional level must be supported by extensive grassroots work. As Rabbi David Rosen points out: Interreligious dialogue in the Holy Land "serves as a testimony: it presents the vision in which religion is not seen as just part of the problem, but is seen to be part of the solution. . . . Political leadership must take religion seriously as a constructive part and parcel of a process of reconciliation, precisely in order to affirm that it is only through being respectful of our own traditions and toward those of others, that we will be able to create a climate in which peace can actually succeed and flourish."[2]

In the Holy Land, both in Israel and in the Palestinian Autonomous Territories, religion is crucial in a structural, historical, cultural, and human sense. It is rare to find traces of secular elements, in the sense introduced in the West by modernity, where State and Church are distinct and where faith is only one more or less important aspect of social reality. In the Holy Land, where all cultural and religious souls are represented, religion enters all aspects of daily life, both public and private, deeply permeating it. Thus, the majority

[2] David Rosen, "Faithfulness to Tradition and Peacemaking in the Middle East", paper presented at the first annual conference of the International Council of Christians and Jews, Riga University, Latvia, May 2002.

of the population continues to regulate and articulate their life based on a consolidated religious ethos, typical of the various groups to which they belong and deeply internalized by the members of each community. The religious component almost always constitutes an essential element in the construction of personal identity and tends to express itself in some specific and recurring traits, including, for example, active participation in ritual prayers and celebrations, the way of dressing, the choice to display and wear objects and symbols of one's faith, and the names chosen for children. Furthermore, each person receives an identity number on their birth certificate, next to which is an acronym that defines their faith affiliation. Faith thus becomes an integral part of their civil identity: everyone is defined and considered Christian, Jewish, or Muslim regardless of whether or not they practice their faith.

Finally, many aspects of the country's life are delegated to religious authority. A significant example is marriage. Civil marriages do not exist—either in Palestine or in Israel. Marriage is solely religious, with significant social consequences; just think of the dramatic impact of mixed marriages in such a context: marrying a person of a different faith is considered an abandonment of one's own community.

Paradoxically, religions, if understood in light of their profound vocation, which consists in putting man in intimate contact with God and in sincere communion with others, are bearers of resources for reconciliation, of a heritage of values thanks to which an understanding of diversity becomes possible, and of nonviolent tools for resolving conflicts, also through a humanly and morally sensitive hermeneutics of religious texts and traditions. This prerogative is proper to all religions, especially the three great monotheistic religions, which clearly express the need to ensure conditions of equal freedom and dignity for each individual, even if he is of a different faith.

Martin Buber writes about Judaism:

> Precisely in the religion of Israel, it is impossible to make an idol of the people as a whole, because the religious tendency toward community is primarily critical and controversial. Whoever attributes to the nation or community the attributes of absoluteness and self-sufficiency betrays the religion of Israel. What, in any case, does it mean to become a "people of God"? A shared faith in God and service to His name do not constitute a people of God. Becoming a people of God means, rather, that the attributes of God revealed to it—justice and love—are made effective in its own life, in the lives of its members with one another: a justice that is materialized in the indirect mutual relationships of those individuals; love in their direct mutual relationships, rooted in their personal existence. However, of the two, love is the higher, the transcendent principle. This becomes unmistakably clear from the fact that man cannot be just toward God; however, he can, and should, love God. And God's love is what is transferred to man; "God loves the stranger," we are told, "so you should love him too."[3]

Judah L. Magnes, one of the intellectuals who founded the Hebrew University of Jerusalem, stated in a 1939 letter to Mahatma Gandhi: "Jewish literature, in many ways, is the literature of martyrdom . . . accepting martyrdom rather than giving in to 'idolatry, immorality, bloodshed.' . . . If ever there was a nonviolent people throughout the ages, it was the Jewish people."[4]

[3] "Secondo Discorso," in *Martin Buber*, ed. Clara Levi Coen (San Domenico di Fiesole: ECP, 1991), 141–42.

[4] Judah L. Magnes, "Lettera al Mahatma Gandhi, Gerusalemme, 26 febbraio 1939," *Micromega* 1 (1991): 178.

So, just as there are authors, including Rabbi Marc Gopin,[5] who have highlighted the nonviolent potential and the wealth of peacemaking resources inherent in the Jewish religion, also with specific reference to the complex dynamics of the Middle East, there are scholars such as Abdul Aziz Said,[6] Mohammed Abu-Nimer,[7] and Chaiwat Satha-Anand[8] who have worked similarly within the Islamic religion, developing reflections on nonviolence, on dialogue with other cultures and with the Western world, on the hermeneutics of Qur'anic texts, and on the redemptive value of suffering in light of those universalistic values strongly emphasized in Islam.

Intercultural and interreligious dialogue, therefore, has a philosophical and soteriological significance whenever it represents the assiduous and shared search for truth, but it must also help strengthen the legacy of human values (wisdom,

[5] See Marc Gopin, *Between Eden and Armageddon: The Future of World Religions, Violence, and Peacemaking* (New York: Oxford University Press, 2000); Marc Gopin, *Holy War, Holy Peace: How Religion Can Bring Peace to the Middle East* (New York: Oxford University Press, 2002); Marc Gopin, "L'Ebraismo e la costruzione della pace nel contesto del conflitto Medio Orientale," *Quaderni Satyagraha* 5 (2004): 61–102.

[6] See Abdul Aziz Said, Ayse S. Kadayifci, Nathan C. Funk, *Peace and Conflict Resolution in Islam: Precept and Practice* (Lanham: University Press of America, 2001); Abdul Aziz Said, *Cultural Diversity and Islam* (Lanham: Rowman & Littlefield, 2003); Abdul Aziz Said, "La nonviolenza come metodologia del cambiamento sociale nell'Islam," *Quaderni Satyagraha* 5 (2004): 103–21.

[7] See Mohammed Abu-Nimer, *Dialogue, Conflict Resolution, and Change: Arab-Jewish Encounters in Israel* (Albany: State University of New York Press, 1999): Mohammed Abu-Nimer, *Reconciliation, Justice, and Coexistence: Theory and Practice* (Lanham: Lexington Books, 2001); Mohammed Abu-Nimer, *Nonviolence and Peace Building in Islam: Theory and Practice* (Gainesville: University Press of Florida, 2003); Mohammed Abu-Nimer, "Azione diretta nonviolenta in Israele e Palestina: possibilità e sfide," in *Quaderni Satyagraha* 5 (2004): 127–174.

[8] See Chaiwat Satha-Anand, *Islam e nonviolenza* (Turin: Edizioni Gruppo Abele, 1997).

solidarity, compassion) common to all religions, in order to help defend some important civil, religious, and cultural rights, to reach shared solutions to universal problems, to develop human relationships, to exercise active and responsible citizenship, and to enhance the human component of politics.

In order to build a culture of peace, especially in the Holy Land, it is therefore necessary for the "children of Abraham" to work actively to create a genuine citizenship of peace. The *Dabru Emet* document, which concerns relations between Christianity and Judaism, was signed by over two hundred rabbis and Jewish intellectuals and was published in *The New York Times* in September 2000; it emphasizes the importance of interreligious collaboration in order to promote the moral and spiritual values that are founded in faith convictions:

> Jews and Christians must work together for justice and peace. Jews and Christians, each in their own way, recognize the unredeemed state of the world as reflected in the persistence of persecution, poverty, and human degradation and misery. Although justice and peace are finally God's, our joint efforts, together with those of other faith communities, will help bring the kingdom of God for which we hope and long. Separately and together, we must work to bring justice and peace to our world.[9]

Unfortunately, all religious expressions carry the risk of fundamentalism, that is, an attitude that tends to absolutize one's own truth and is expressed in ultraconservative, fundamentalist, and rigid orientations in the interpretation of religious sources and traditions, is suspicious or closed to exter-

[9] "*Dabru Emet*: A Jewish Statement on Christians and Christianity," *The New York Times*, September 10, 2000.

nal influences, and is sometimes intolerant even of internal alternative currents. The danger of fundamentalism always exists whenever a believer or religious group maintains that it holds the truth and must fight against those who seem to be able to challenge this belief. Therefore, it is clear that fundamentalist positions are in serious conflict with the motivations of a citizenship that aspires to be structured openly on multiple levels of action, appealing to the truly ethical consensus achieved through dialogue between different cultures, within the dynamic process that unfolds between the recognition of the original pro-social ethical demand and the eschatological attainment of a horizon of values shared by all.

In conclusion, given that the Palestinian National Authority and the State of Israel present different dynamics regarding the function of the religious component and the development of intercultural and interreligious dialogue, citizenship, and social participation, the analysis of the two contexts will be kept separate.

The Territories of the Palestinian National Authority

The conflict in the Holy Land consists not only of physical violence between Israelis and Palestinians; it is also a way of thinking, an attitude that penetrates the culture and conditions people's mentality. For example, in Palestinian geography textbooks, seemingly the most objective and neutral of disciplines, the conflict is expressed by the fact that Israel is absent from the maps. Similarly, in Israeli textbooks, Palestine does not exist, or, for example, the 1967 war is called the "War of Liberation". The violent aspect of the conflict is therefore only the last link in a process that arises deeper within society: at the cultural, educational, and formative level.

In recent years, the conflict has also taken on a religious character. Hamas is not only a liberation movement from Israeli occupation, but also a movement with a religious pedigree: indeed, it also considers the Islamic faith the instrument though which to achieve the goal of liberation. While the official imposition of Islamic law, *Sharia*, is unthinkable, especially because the Palestinian Authority has close ties with the West, Islam nevertheless permeates Palestinian social life through customs: for example, in Christian schools, women do not wear veils, but social pressure remains, sometimes manifesting itself in stone-throwing at windows or similar provocations. There are therefore some movements that support the spread of Islam and its traditions; these reiterate, without rancor or anti-Christian intentions, that this is an Islamic land, but generally, they wish to have good relations with Christians.

For Muslims, it is a given to think of the Holy Land as Islamic. There is no overtly anti-Christian intention, although there are hotbeds of tension in "hot" spots like the Gaza Strip; fundamentalism is expressed rather in the increasingly evident tendency to make sure that the principles of Islam influence all of society. This directly affects the life of Christians, of the Church, and of the Churches, and poses a new, or rather ancient, challenge—for centuries the Church in the Middle East has existed within an Islamic context—in new ways.

Another worrying aspect concerns the attempt by Muslims to eliminate, or at least to make less visible and understandable, the external signs of Christianity. In Bethlehem, for example, Christian homes are identified by large crosses; Muslims consider these signs inappropriate and provocative.

In Nazareth—a city that is not part of the Palestinian Authority, but fits in some ways into the logic just described—a few years ago, plans were proposed to build an imposing mosque right next to the Basilica of the Nativity, and possibly taller. Something similar happened in Beirut, in Lebanon, a country that presents problems similar to those of the Palestinian Autonomous Territories: in the past, what caught the eye of those entering the city was the great Maronite cathedral, a monument that expressed the fact that, in Lebanon, the Maronites are an ancient and important presence. Today, however, someone entering Beirut first sees an enormous mosque, built right next to the cathedral. Examples like these show how the conviction that they live in an Islamic land leads Muslims to assert the Islamic element even through exterior signs.

Within the Christian world itself, there is a current of thought that maintains that Arab Christians are culturally Muslim. This thesis is based on the fact that Islam has influenced the life of society over the centuries and has therefore shaped its culture regardless of the religious affiliation of individuals: therefore, between Muslims and Christians there is supposedly a religious distinction but a cultural identity. In this view, Christians have their own faith, but culturally they are completely tied to the Islamic world: they are similar to Muslims, with whom they should therefore work and dialogue. This position contains some truth, but it is important to make the necessary distinctions. Belonging culturally to the same people does not eliminate the differences between Christians and Muslims: religious affiliation is not limited to the observance of precepts, but constitutes a mindset, an attitude that conditions a person's entire life, and the Christian faith must be able to express its uniqueness.

This should lead us to reflect on the influence that cultural and religious approaches have on attitudes in everyday and civil life. The real challenge is that Jews, Christians, and Muslims, as believers and citizens of a civil society, can share among themselves, and with nonbelievers, responsibilities and tasks for the common good. Although born from the single Abrahamic tradition, the three communities have predominantly maintained, over the millennia, an attitude of mutual distrust and exclusivity, developing doctrinal systems and schools of thought that are sometimes very different.

Aside from a few examples of authentic dialogue, only since the twentieth century—thanks to leading figures such as Louis Massignon, Jules Isaac, and Pope John XXIII—has a real turning point occurred, which found its highest and most significant expression in the Second Vatican Council, thanks to the declaration *Nostra Aetate*.[10] After the Council, Muslim-Christian dialogue underwent notable development, continuing on the path opened by theologians such as Piero Rossano and Hans Küng.[11] Some fundamental areas of this dialogue are the need for mutual understanding and esteem, as an indispensable premise; the recognition of religious values, whether common to the revealed monotheistic faiths or specific to each of them; a common religiously

[10] On relations with Islam, see David Pinault's *The Crucifix on Mecca's Front Porch: A Christian's Companion for the Study of Islam* (San Francisco: Ignatius Press, 2018). See also Augusto T. Negri, "Relazioni e dialogo tra cristiani e musulmani," in *L'Islam. Storia, dottrina, rapporti con il cristianesimo*, ed. Centro Federico Peirone (Turin: Elledici, 2004), 269–95.

[11] See F. Serri, "Cristianesimo e teologia delle religioni," in Peirone, *L'Islam*, 249–67. For an initial overview, see Giovanni Rizzi, *Cristianesimo e Islam alle soglie del Duemila* (Milan: Centro Ambrosiano, 2000); J. Jamie, "Dialogue christianisme-islam," in *Dictionnaire des religions* (Paris: Presses Universitaires de France, 1984).

grounded ethical tension, and a shared responsibility in social and civil life.

In 2008, a Catholic-Muslim forum was established; among the participants were the Pontifical Council for Interreligious Dialogue and a delegation of the 138 Muslim signatories of the letter "A Common Word Between Us and You" addressed to Pope Benedict XVI on October 13, 2007. The goal is to increase shared awareness of transcendent values and of the importance of moral and religious education, while respecting cultural and religious pluralism.[12]

The State of Israel

Although the context is very different from the previous one, a kind of religious fundamentalism exists in Israel, too, that of Jewish settlers who go to settle in the Palestinian Territories, not for practical or economic reasons, but for political convictions supported by a clear religious mindset. Therefore, whatever the specific context may be in which fundamentalist impulses tend to manifest themselves, they are almost always based on a close connection with political reasons and interests, which exploit certain religious positions and take them to extremes, making them a threat to constructive coexistence. They interpret intransigently the three distinctive elements of Judaism—Torah, people, and land—intrinsically endowed with a significance that is both historical and messianic. According to these positions, God gave the Jewish people that land, and, therefore, the settlers

[12] See G. Biccini, "Cattolicesimo e Islam. Verso uno storico incontro: Intervista al cardinale Jean-Louis Tauran, responsabile del dialogo interreligioso," *L'Osservatore Romano*, December 30, 2007, 8; "Dichiarazione finale del Forum," *L'Osservatore Romano*, November 8, 2008, 6.

fulfill the task of redeeming it, that is, conquering it, taking possession of it so as to live there and transform it, making it entirely their own.

In this context, the convergence, starting in the 1920s and 1930s, of the secular-national type of Zionist movement with religious-messianic influences has led, on one hand, to the characterization of Israel as a Jewish state, in which the goal of a democratic foundation inspired by freedom, justice, and equal social and political rights for all inhabitants coexists with a Jewish definition "satisfied both by integrating a religious component into its own administrative structures and by 'symbolically' excluding other elements, starting with the constitution (replaced by the presence of a certain number of fundamental laws), which might have appeared 'competitive' with the presence, at least implicit, of the Torah as the supreme norm of Jewish collective life."[13]

On the other hand, especially after the Six-Day War in 1967, a radical form of territorial messianism has also consolidated. This form, in its exaltation of the bond between people and land (ethno-messianic movements), conceives the relationship with the land in terms of inalienable and state-guaranteed possession, working toward the complete Judaization of "symbolic Jewish places". It is clear, therefore, that territorial messianism constitutes "a factor that objectively secularizes religion, transforming it into a political ideology. The nontransferability of the land, supported by religious motivations, therefore appears to be a phenomenon characterized by fundamentalist connotations. In fact, it presents itself as an attempt to re-conquer a secular space, that of state legitimacy, seen no longer as the product

[13] P. Stefani, "Il fondamentalismo e l'ebraismo," in *Fondamento e fondamentalismi: Filosofia theologia religioni*, ed. A. Ales Bello, L. Messinese, A. Molinaro (Rome: Città Nuova, 2004), 393–94.

of international recognition, but rather as exclusively guaranteed by pseudo-religious motivations."[14] However, the settlers are a small portion of the Jewish population, a few hundred thousand.

Israel can be counted among the secular and democratic states, but it also has a clearly Jewish imprint: it is the Jewish state, the state in which the Jewish character has been publicly affirmed and becomes evident in social life. This does not imply that all citizens must be practicing and observant, but it does mean that the state's primary purpose is to allow Jews to live as Jews in their own context. Religious practice is secondary: in Israel, there are many atheists, just as in Western societies, but they are still Jews. Even if they do not believe in God, many observe Yom Kippur and celebrate Passover to express their membership in the people of Israel.

The Church that lives in Israel, therefore, faces a challenge that is completely different from the one experienced in the Palestinian Territories. Indeed, while the Church has been accustomed for centuries to living in the Islamic world and maintaining relations with it, through its institutions as well—especially the schools, which play a very important role not only in preserving Christian identity but also in developing dialogue with the Muslim world—it is almost totally absent within Israel, for two reasons. First, Israel, unlike the Arab world, does not need the Church's institutions, and therefore the Church's role is objectively more complex. Building and managing schools, hospitals, and retirement homes is, in fact, a concrete way of engaging in dialogue with society, of creating culture. Secondly, the situation of conflict must not be forgotten: the Church in

[14] Ibid., 395–96.

Israel is almost entirely Arab-Palestinian and therefore remains rather alien to the Jewish world.

All this makes a constructive relationship of cultural dialogue difficult, although it would otherwise be of great interest. In fact, the Church has much in common and to share with Israel and its society. For example, Christian sacred music is highly appreciated by Jews, who flock to organ concerts much more than Christians do; furthermore, some Jewish universities offer courses in the New Testament, because Jews are aware that knowledge of Christianity is indispensable in understanding Western history, art, and literature. In the East, both Jews and Muslims are highly aware of Europe's Christian roots and traditions and thus know that its history is profoundly indebted to Christianity. From a cultural perspective, therefore, the scope for work is quite vast and almost entirely undeveloped.

The Role of Christians in the Holy Land

Living as Christians in the Holy Land means having a particular vocation and a universal one. The Latin Church here is essentially composed of three groups: the community of local Arab Christians (the Palestinian group representing the traditional Christian presence in these places); the Hebrew-speaking *kehila*, a new, vibrant Church, which brings together Evangelicals, Messianic Jews, and Catholics with its own specific characteristics and which celebrates the liturgy in Hebrew; the international community, which includes many foreign workers, especially Filipinos, South Americans, and Indians, who reside permanently in the Holy Land, and several other groups of various origins who, for different reasons, spend more or less long periods here. Alongside the Latin Church, other important Christian groups operate, the principal ones being the Greek Orthodox Church, the Armenian Church, and the Coptic Church. Even within the Catholic world itself there are, finally, groups with rites other than the Latin one.

This complex and fascinating world, where different cultures, languages, and traditions meet, is at the center of the faith of the three great monotheistic religions; here Christians experience the hardships and contradictions faced by a small minority in a context characterized by a huge Jewish and Muslim majority. Sometimes, then, the fragmentations within the Christian world itself also make it difficult to bear witness to one's faith coherently and serenely.

In the particular situation of the Holy Land, which has long seen the Jewish and Palestinian peoples divided by conflict and seeking a peaceful path of coexistence, Christians, as mentioned, can be a leaven of unity between the Muslim and Jewish worlds. At the same time, the movements of Christian and Jewish pilgrimages to the Holy Land seem to open onto the vision of Isaiah, who looks to Jerusalem as the Holy Place that will gather all the peoples of the earth to itself (Is 2:1–4). Through concrete gestures, pastoral and social initiatives, educational and academic activities, the international Christian community that gathers here, and especially the consecrated religious who work in the Holy Land, seek to bear witness to the prophetic face of the Church and the universality of Christianity beyond local tensions, overcoming distances, cultural and linguistic diversity, discrimination, and various forms of nationalism. In the Holy Land, too, the Church seeks to remind people that they are all brothers and sisters, united in one family while respecting individual values.

The history of the Church of Jerusalem, from her very

beginnings, has been marked by tensions and divisions, but she has always aimed to pursue her universal calling. Saint Paul writes: "For when one says, 'I belong to Paul,' and another, 'I belong to Apollos,' are you not merely men?"(1 Cor 3:4). Saint Paul denounces on many occasions the incompatibility of Christianity with particularisms: "There is neither Jew nor Greek, there is neither slave nor free, there is neither male nor female; for you are all one in Christ Jesus" (Gal 3:28). The witness of universal love makes us authentic signs of Christ—"For he is our peace, who has made us both one, and has broken down the dividing wall of hostility [through his flesh]" (Eph 2:14)—even to the love of enemies that annihilates every division. This, then, is the horizon of the Mother Church of Jerusalem, whose motherhood can only be universal.

Jerusalem and the Christian Holy Places remain to this day a fundamental sign of faith: the witness to the life, death, and Resurrection of Jesus. In the Holy Land, one can learn to look, listen, meditate, and savor the silence so as to grasp the profound meaning of Jesus' passing. The environment reminds us of the same places, customs, colors, and scents that Jesus knew when He revealed Himself to the world. The Church of the Holy Land also draws from this priceless heritage the strength to continue to nourish her universal motherhood and to support the small local Christian communities, communicating to them the passion for Christ, developing their talents, preserving their hope even when so many unfulfilled promises bring feelings of disappointment and despair.

In this Land, Christians are called to give a lofty witness of faith, to be a living presence, in love with their own history and ideas. They are called not to fear changes and encounters with diversity, but to be open, serene, free, positive, and, at the same time, well-rooted in their own sense of identity and belonging, proactive, and active in guarding the Holy Places.

Conclusions

The Abrahamic religions, especially when they embark on the journey of dialogue, have much to offer to the construction of new horizons of citizenship and peaceful coexistence, within increasingly complex national and international communities. This is also the case in the Holy Land and the Middle East.

From the radical Abrahamic, Mosaic, Christian, and Qur'anic affirmation of the one God comes the primary commitment to care for the world created by God. The traditional Jewish perspective expresses this responsibility as a *tikkun olam*, a "caring for creation", with authority and loving kindness, to prepare or bring about the Kingdom of the Most High.

Christians also recognize social justice and civil rights for every human person because, according to the biblical teaching received from Jewish tradition, all humans are created in the image of the one God and are endowed with a rational soul, having the same nature and origin. Man therefore finds his foundational and supreme meaning in God, and this acquires a meaning of relationship, freedom, and co-responsibility, both between persons and in communion with God. The Incarnation of the Word enriches human reality with meaning and makes the human experience of God concrete.

For Muslims, in accordance with the "five pillars" of Islam—profession of faith, prayer, almsgiving, fasting, and pilgrimage—obedience to God implies a commitment to a concrete brotherhood within the *umma*, the Islamic community, without discrimination of any kind, with particular regard for the weak and needy. Among non-Muslims, preference is given to those who profess a biblical religion (Jews and Christians, known as "people of the Bible") or in any case a monotheistic one.

Education in citizenship is therefore an essential component within the intercultural and interreligious perspective. The concept of citizenship must be understood in the depth of its meanings, not only political, but also legal, ethical, social, cultural, and religious.

The new citizenship, nourished by the practical orientations of nonviolence, interreligious dialogue, and responsible action, must therefore involve:

1. a recovery of the *prophetic and educational* significance of religious experience;
2. a reflection on the concepts of *personal and socio-cultural identity* and *cultural and religious belonging*, for the purpose of developing a complex, procedural, and dynamic interpretation, and on the concept of *citizenship*, unpacking its dense profile of legal, political, ethical, social, and cultural meanings and clarifying its connection with the dimensions of identity and belonging on the one hand and, on the other hand, with the exercise of the rights and duties acknowledged as belonging to all citizens equally, as well as with their political, civil, and cultural participation in shared life;
3. a new formulation of the *relationship between religion and politics*, where the different religious experiences are understood in light of their cultural foundations and basic values, and not from the perspective of fundamentalism and exploitation, which fuel forms of misunderstanding and intolerance;
4. an in-depth exploration of issues concerning *the global dimension of coexistence*, which calls us to work for openness, peace,

nonviolence, and constructive encounter between different peoples, based on the idea that contact between the West and the East cannot be limited to the economic, political, social, and cultural levels, but is also a religious problem that requires a synthesis of the living elements of the different traditions;

5. *a comprehensive reworking of ethics*, capable of combining rational and practical achievement with elements of trust, sympathy, empathy, and emotional openness to others, to the point of developing an ethics of service, responsibility, and gratuitousness;
6. a reconsideration of the values of *openness and interdependence*, which concern not only individuals, values, peoples, and states, but also the approach to the problems of our time;
7. a rethinking of the *categories of history, memory, guilt, justice, and forgiveness*, categories that place the religious sphere in direct contact with the moral, social, and political spheres of citizenship;
8. a reformulation of the *role and position of Christianity's cultural and religious pluralism*, which has, among other things, in the dialogue with other faiths, an essential task of demystifying the link between religiosity and violence and reevaluating the Jewish and Islamic contribution to reflection on nonviolence and on the search for peace.

The contemporary situation makes it timelier and more urgent to conduct the broadest possible debate, linked to the changing meaning and application of the traditional categories of citizenship, the need to introduce a sense of a multiplicity of affiliations, the need for individuals to develop a dynamic and inclusive identity and a "competent" and responsible citizenship at multiple levels of participation. This debate must offer equal opportunities not only to Jews, Christians, and Muslims, but also to other believers or non-believers, based on rational, ethical, and legal arguments, to which all can refer both as a shared point of departure and as an ideal to be achieved together, in fraternal collaboration. And this in the light of an ideal that aims to welcome increasingly distant individuals and peoples into a common project, involving them in the dialogue around those values—summarized by the philosopher Tzvetan Todorov in the six cornerstones of rationality, justice, democracy, individual freedom, secularism, and tolerance—which, despite having local interpretations, convey a universal appeal.

Francis of Assisi Between Contemplative Spirituality and Apostolic Life

Talk at the Tau Center, Salerno, Italy

October 16, 2012

In order to understand Saint Francis' experience of faith, it is necessary to state in advance that, unlike the characteristic feature of other institutes of apostolic life—especially the ones that arose between 1800 and 1900, which were founded for the purpose of accomplishing something specific, that is, very effective and necessary initiatives—"doing" is not the saint's primary aim. His first experience is, in fact, the encounter with Jesus. Francis' point of departure is a faith that becomes concrete experience and will manifest itself also throughout his spiritual journey: from this encounter, then, all the rest is generated. First of all, then, the encounter with Christ; this, transforms his existence by activating mechanisms of preaching that are in the first place the proclamation of a lived experience.

What struck me about Francis' faith is the fact that it is integral, the point that synthesizes his whole life; everything was involved in it: his existence, his heart, his affections, his thought.

There are some aspects of the life of this saint that as a youth I did not manage to understand; they "irritated" me, so to speak. One example is when Saint Francis wept and,

Talk given on October 16, 2012, at the Tau Center in Salerno, as part of a conference entitled: "Saint Francis of Assisi in the Year of Faith".

when someone asked him the reason, he replied, "Because Love is not loved." As a youth it took me some effort to accept these rather romantic expressions, but today, after years of experience, I have managed to understand them better. Expressions like this show precisely that Francis' faith is integral; it is not an intellectual activity: for him faith is experience, and knowledge always comes by way of experience.

His faith, moreover, is always trinitarian: for him, faith in God passes through faith in Jesus Christ, and only the Spirit can give the ability to open one's eyes to the encounter with Christ.

In his first admonition, Francis uses another, somewhat peculiar expression with respect to the faith: he speaks, indeed, about faith in the Church and in priests. In his 1226 testament we read: "The Lord gave me such great faith in the Churches that I used to pray simply this way and say: 'We adore you, Lord Jesus Christ, in all your Churches throughout the world and we bless you.'"[1] For this reason he has faith in the priests also, those specific priests, with all their humanity. Indeed, he used to say, "If I were to meet an angel descending from heaven to bring me the most dazzling announcement and, on the other hand, a sinful priest, I would stop first to kiss the hands of the sinful priest because, through his hands, even though he is a sinner, that priest delivers Jesus to me in the Eucharist."[2]

Another significant feature of Francis' faith is that for him this experience is a "seeing, touching, and believing": it testifies to a tremendous love for the humanity of Jesus. Just think of Greccio, where he decided to relive the nativity of Jesus, or else, at the height of his faith experience, in

[1] Francis of Assisi, "Testamento", in *Fonti francescane* (Milan: EFR, 2008), 111.

[2] See Tommaso da Celano, *Vita Seconda*, in *Fonti francescane*, 790.

Verna, where he was willing to relive, even in his flesh, the experience of the crucifixion. In Verna, Francis composed that very beautiful prayer: "May I feel in my heart the same love that You felt when You were on the Cross and [may I feel] also in my body the same pain that You felt when You were on the Cross."[3] Before receiving the stigmata, therefore, he had this deep desire, and for us friars in the Holy Land, this desire is very important, because without a place there is no incarnation and, therefore, no humanity: without Bethlehem there is no Greccio, and no La Verna without Calvary.

For a Franciscan, staying in the Holy Land is an integral part of Francis' charism: it means not only guarding the memory of the incarnation of Jesus, but also reliving the experience of it. It is no accident that, when the popes speak about the presence of the Franciscans in this Land, they always refer to a providential plan.

Saint Francis, therefore, is a very concrete man, and the place to encounter Christ is the Church: there is no other way for him, because the Church, through the sacraments, gives us the opportunity to have an experience of Christ, especially in the Eucharist. We need, then, to be able to see not only according to the flesh, but also according to the spirit. Returning to the example cited by Francis, according to the flesh that priest is a sinner and therefore a priest who should be avoided, but according to the spirit he is the one who delivers the person of Jesus, and this is what matters more.

Today this is not taken for granted: certainly the scandals that affect the Church are indefensible, but an experience of faith can go beyond the scandals of the flesh to the es-

[3] See *I fioretti di San Francesco*, in *Fonti francescane*, 1919.

sential thing, to the encounter with Jesus through the Eucharist and the sacraments. Communion with the Church is essential for Francis; think of the time of the Cathar or the Waldensian heresy: he wanted his friars to be absolutely Catholic. In his "Letter to a Minister"—a hymn to mercy that I reread continuously because it deals with poverty and human weaknesses—Saint Francis writes: "You must forgive everything." He has such great freedom that he declares: "Do not demand that that sinful brother become a better Christian. Love him as he is! It does not matter."[4] On one point, though, he never compromises: the friars must be Catholic, in other words, in full communion with the Church, and not the ideal Church but the real one, because if you are not in communion with the real Church, you cannot have an experience of Christ, it is not possible to touch him, to go to Holy Communion.

Saint Francis, then, wanted to begin, not with preaching, but with living as Jesus lived. There was surely an intimate aspect of his faith, but also a very strong communitarian aspect, which is evident, for example, in his "Letter to the Rulers of the Peoples".[5] Francis left very important writings, and his letters would be unthinkable today. He appears as an illiterate, but he also writes letters to the leaders of peoples, to those who hold power, and he does this not so that these persons might work for peace, justice, and coexistence among the nations: instead, he asks them to convert, to do penance, to go to Mass, to promote devotion to the Eucharist. Very concrete gestures, connected with the life of faith and of the Church. Today it would be considered inappropriate, it would be interpreted as an attempt on the

[4] See Francis of Assisi, "Lettera ad un ministro", in *Fonti francescane*, 234–35.

[5] See *Fonti francescane*, 210–13.

part of the religious sphere to invade the civil and secular sphere. It was a very different and distant world then, but I think that I understand Francis' reasons correctly: the experience of Jesus impacted his whole life, and consequently everyone must know this experience, particularly those who have responsibilities.

Francis does not care about what we today would call political correctness; if he had cared, he would not have traveled to the Holy Land to meet a sultan and would not have gone there together with the crusaders. He would not have spoken then with the sultan about Christ, but rather would have asked him to make peace or to set the crusaders free. During their encounter, Francis and the sultan dialogued for several days about the figure of Jesus, and yet the sultan was our enemy at that time, the heretic. But Saint Francis was not reckless; he was a man attached to his experience and so enamored of it that his passion drove him to do things that reasonableness would never contemplate. From that experience sprang a desire for communion, truth, communication, and freedom.

The Franciscans were to become known for their poverty and their way of life without ownership, which means not just having no property, but also repeating the experience of Abraham—our father in faith—with the sacrifice of Isaac (Gen 22). At first, God calls Abraham, telling him to follow Him and in return he will receive a great reward: the land and descendants as numberless as the stars. Abraham follows Him, awaiting this reward that is late in arriving, and at the moment when he asks God when it will arrive, behold—while now there is no longer any hope, because Sarah was thought to be sterile—God causes him to have a son; then, when all his hope is still placed in the son, God asks Abraham to kill him. In this experience, God takes away everything:

the encounter with the Lord deprives a person of all that is not dependent on the fundamental relation with God.

This is also the experience that Francis goes through, and as in Abraham's case, it is his greatness: he renounces the reward, the promises, but not God. At that point God tells him, "Now I know that you fear God" (Gen 22:12), in other words, that his faith is firm and that he is ready to renounce everything in order to preserve his relation with the Lord. This is the greatest freedom and, at the same time, a responsibility.

All this is typical also of the story of Francis: to live without anything of one's own is to live not simply in poverty, but also with nothing—in one's relations, heart, or faith life—that could get in the way of having a full relationship with the Lord. From this, then, springs the experience of the Holy Land: the experience of faith. This also involves some risks. When faith becomes dependent on an identity, it becomes self-closed or runs the risk of being closed off. If it becomes a "religion", it can become an element of conservatism and may set boundaries. In the Holy Land this is very obvious: the faiths and the identities coincide, civil registers are divided by religious affiliation, and whether or not one is a believer, one is nevertheless Christian, Jewish, or Muslim.

In this land, full of walls and divisions, the religious element runs the risk of setting up barriers, turning into an instrument for preserving identities; in Europe, too, it runs this risk. The true experience of faith, in contrast, leads to encounter: faith is first of all an encounter with Jesus, and through Jesus with God, and this encounter with Jesus and with God leads to a relation with the other, because every human being is created in the image and likeness of the Lord. This is also the experience of Saint Francis. At that time, eight hundred years ago, there were no Geneva or United Nations Charters on fundamental human rights and religious freedom. And so, when Saint Francis sends his friars among the Saracens, in the *Regola non bollata* [the first Franciscan Rule, not approved by a papal bull] he gives an important instruction for those times, which was also in part the reason for the destiny of the Franciscans in the Holy Land: "When you go among the unbelievers, there are two ways to stay there: first, stay there, subject to every human creature, simply showing and saying that you are Christians; second, when the Spirit prompts you, go and proclaim that Jesus is Lord."[6] Therefore the experience of faith leads also to a respectful, free encounter with the other. It is not true that the faith is an element of conservatism or a cause of war: when it becomes an instrument of identitarian needs, that risk exists, but if it is authentic, it gives the freedom to encounter the other without denying anything.

In conclusion, a brief note about the Hebrew language: the word *shalom* is commonly thought to mean "peace", but in reality that is not the case. *Shalem*, the root of *shalom*, does not mean "peace" but "integrity", "completeness", "entirety". When, for example, Jesus said on the Cross, "All is finished; all is accomplished," he used the passive voice of the verb *shalem*. Or, to take another example, the Hebrew verb "to pay" is derived from the same root, *shillem*: one person offers something, the other pays, and this brings about a kind of completeness in the relation between the two.

Therefore true peace is born when the person and the relations are integral, complete, full: this is the cry of expectation that is experienced in the Holy Land, which the Franciscans seek, in their humble way, to hear and to put into practice, while knowing that they cannot affect the course

[6] See Francis of Assisi, *Regola non bollata*, in *Fonti francescane*, 43.

of macropolitics in the Middle East in a very important way. What we are called to do as Franciscans is simply what Saint Francis did and asked us to accomplish: to remain in the Holy Land so as to affirm that in these places Jesus spent His own life, so as to touch those stones and to relive the experience that this Land enables us to go through again. And then "to open the eyes" of the man who lives there, whatever faith he may belong to, and to love him, in other words, to respond to his needs—therefore to build a school, a house, to have an encounter, a conference, and so on—in order to weave a dialogue. All these things, though, spring up as a consequence: the first mission, in the Holy Land as everywhere, is to stand always with our eyes turned to the Lord and, by looking at Him, to open the world's eyes and to perceive, in the world, a reflection of that love that has touched us forever.

The Power of the Heart

Seekers of Truth

Speech at the Rimini Meeting for Friendship Among Peoples

August 24, 2014

It is not easy to relate the tragic situation in the Middle East today, which is marked by violence and is undergoing a radical, dramatic transformation, to "the power of the heart". We might wonder what the heart is capable of doing about the humanitarian tragedy that we have been witnessing for months. I maintain, on the contrary, that it is a mistake to limit ourselves to a political, social, and historical analysis, even a professional one, without a religious, redeemed view that helps us to interpret events without being overwhelmed by them. The two spheres are mutually necessary: we need experts who help us to understand from the political, economic, and social perspective the major changes that we are facing, but we also need a broader vision that is free of fears and complexes.

In recent months, numerous requests and proposals have arrived in Jerusalem from altogether secular international associations and movements that, alarmed, propose to get involved in different sorts of initiatives, in the media, cultural,

---

Speech given on August 24, 2014, at the Rimini Meeting for friendship among peoples, promoted by Communion and Liberation. The title of that year's meeting was: "To the Ends of the Earth and of Existence. Destiny Has Not Left Man Alone."

political and even military spheres, in order to "save Christianity and its culture" in the Middle East, and not only there. These are legitimate fears, but they lack the faith perspective of someone who not only trusts in his own abilities to act, but also *en*trusts—that is, surrenders—his own life to an Other, in another way. This "other" way means by working, praying, and listening to every suggestion of the heart, letting the passionate, free search for truth point out unexpected paths, ready to take responsibility for embodying our personal commitment to and with others.

The Middle East Being Radically Transformed

The Middle East that we knew in the twentieth century—born from the ruins of the Ottoman Empire, from the end of various colonial projects, and from the birth of nation-states—no longer exists. A new period is starting, and we cannot yet tell what direction it is taking: Egypt, Israel and Palestine, Libya, and above all Syria and Iraq are at the center of a profound change, and it is not possible right now to foresee the outcomes.

The process, set in motion by the so-called Arab Spring, a phenomenon that initially raised many hopes, has been hijacked, so to speak, by religious movements and parties, which have distorted the nature of this "spring", transforming it into a veritable power struggle among the different religious and social elements of the Middle East, in particular in the struggle between Shiites and Sunnis. Obviously, this power struggle is not unaffected by different sorts of interests: political, economic, energy-industrial, and so on. Obvious signs of this involvement are the persecutions that have victimized Christians and other religious minorities in recent months, along with the consolidation of Islamic movements and parties, some of them rather extremist. A serious crisis in relations with the minorities has been brought on by forms of persecution and exploitation.

In the Middle East—the only region in the world that has always been the site of religious differences—attempts at coexistence over the centuries have never been easy, and there has been no lack of persecution, but never has the region witnessed a "religious cleansing" of the sort that we see today.

An example may help us to understand better the type of coexistence that exists among Judaism, Christianity, and Islam, in their internal variations. Although in Italy, or in general in the West, we are experiencing a moment of dialogue with persons of other faiths and religious traditions, it is generally within a framework that "smooths down the rough edges", emphasizing the strengths of the various participants: each wants to offer its best to the other and to see what is best in the other. In the Middle East, on the contrary, when a Jew, a Muslim, a Copt, and an Armenian meet, each one remains himself. They come in contact in a daily routine that is not a "special" moment in life, but rather they experience together the same problems, each with its own culture, faith, and traditions. Usually there are the everyday difficulties, or else what is deliberately excluded in the West. This is coexisting: living-with-others, without prevarications, impositions, or a spirit of conquest. This form of interreligious coexistence—something different from integration, which, in turn, is a Western challenge—has characterized the Middle East for centuries, although never in a simple, linear manner, and it is the essential character thereof; this is the reason why Christians of different confessions, Sunni and Shiite Muslims, Yazidi, Kurds, Alawiti, Druze, and others are in this region to this day.

The main concern at this time is precisely the fear about a rise to power, especially in Syria and Iraq, but not only there, of fundamentalist Islamic movements, in particular the so-called Islamic State, or caliphate, which has targeted not only the non-Islamic minorities, but also the Muslims themselves who do not share their doctrine.

Within the Christian communities, in view of these movements, we witness a growing tension, perhaps regret about lost securities, and the temptation to go away, which sometimes has become an absolute necessity, as in Iraq. What was done to the Christians and Yazidi on the plain of Nineveh is shameful.[1] The disgraceful "religious cleansing" currently being engineered by the Islamic State, yet present also in other parts of the Arab countries, is in the first place contrary to the history and the character of the Middle East and cannot be ignored: it is necessary for all religious communities to raise their voice against this abomination. The Islamic world has finally started to react, but the denunciation has been rather timid and the Arab media have not given much coverage to the declarations by various Muslim religious leaders.

The interreligious dialogue currently cannot fail to issue a strong common denunciation. It is required by the seriousness of the moment and the need for continued coex-

[1] In June 2014, with the capture of Mosul and all the surrounding centers by the Islamic State, thousands fled from the plain of Nineveh in northern Iraq. That period marked the first wave of a major exodus that involved Christians and Yazidi. To date, over a million refugees have fled into the autonomous region of Iraqi Kurdistan.

istence and dialogue. It is clear, moreover, that this type of fanaticism must be stopped, if necessary even forcibly, with all possible guarantees. The use of force, nevertheless, will resolve nothing without a prospect of reconstruction at all levels. Force stops and destroys, but unless rebuilding follows, the void created by the use of force will give rise to greater extremism.

This is true also about the Israeli-Palestinian conflict: force, without the prospect of social, economic, and political rebuilding, will lead to nothing but the further exercise of force, in a sort of vicious circle. How can we speak about peace or the prospect of peace if we do not build some hope, if nothing but hatred, rancor, sorrow, and revenge has accumulated in the heart because of the violence that has been endured? There is not one family that has not lived through violent experiences. Force is never the way; sometimes, if necessary, as now in Iraq, it can open a way, but it can never build one.

The Middle East, starting with the Holy Land, Israel and Palestine, urgently needs to identify a new process for outlining its own future, which can only be prepared together, with all the different souls that make it up. Christians, Muslims, Kurds, Jews and all the other religious and ethnic communities are an integral part of the life of these countries and will not disappear; to presume that they can be canceled successfully is a sheer illusion, and to ignore their existence is blindness.

Besides the betrayal of the historic coexistence among the different religious communities, which is the sad chronicle of several Iraqi cities now occupied by fundamentalists, there are nevertheless also forms of solidarity worth noting. In a recent visit to Syria, in the martyred city of Aleppo, I observed how it is possible for some foreigners to join forces to confront the common needs and emergencies; I will mention just a few examples that I learned about first-hand.

For months the city of Aleppo has been without water, and the only way to get any is from the private wells, but, obviously, they are not available to everyone. Moreover, since there is a lack of electricity, too (which is rationed for no more than two hours per day), for people without a generator it is impossible to obtain one; gasoline for the generator is almost nowhere to be found and very expensive. It is therefore extremely difficult for almost the entire population that remains, made up mostly of the poor who do not know where else to go, to supply themselves with water; it is up to the main institutions (mosques, churches, hospitals, etc.) to make water available. I saw Christians and Muslims lined up in church to get water, and Christians bringing water to their Muslim neighbors and vice versa.

Another example: in the convent of Holy Land College in Aleppo there is no generator, but the Muslim neighbor has one; the other neighbors, all Muslims, then take up a collection for the gasoline, the neighbor runs the generator, and the friars obtain the water for the neighborhood.

Moreover, thanks to the Jesuit Relief Service, the Jesuits have utilized a building belonging to the Franciscan Sisters of Aleppo to set up a kitchen for entire districts of the city. Every day, more than ten thousand meals are sent out from that convent, for everyone. The foodstuffs arrive from Islamic organizations, the sisters organize the preparations and several volunteers, Christians and Muslims, deliver the food to the needy. Keep in mind that moving about in the city is dangerous, and no one ever knows, when he goes out, whether he will return home. Despite this, there are also many people who risk their life every day touring the city in order to do something for others, and not only for those who belong to their community.

Finally, during my stay in Aleppo, the Syrian Catholic cathedral and the bishop's residence, our neighbors, were hit not once, but twice. First the cathedral was attacked and destroyed by the rebels; then the bishop's residence was targeted by the governing forces. In both cases, everyone, without distinction, made great efforts to help, support, encourage, but also just to be neighbors: very often, indeed, nothing can be done except to witness the tragedy helplessly. The examples and the testimonies could continue.

In the Middle East, then, the ancient forms of coexistence seem to have disappeared, while the new ones are not sufficiently clear. We are facing contradictory phenomena: betrayals of ancient friendships, the birth of new ones; rejections of the other, the search for the other. Besides the heart that has betrayed, there is the heart of someone who has loved by spending and devoting himself. The gestures just described and those of many, many other people are the secret force that is needed in order to keep going and not to stop at the darkness of the moment. The neighbor who, though confronted by so much death, performs an act of friendship, offers the "respite" needed in order to believe that it is still possible to continue staying in the Middle East and to live together, different and united.

The Power of the Heart

As we recalled, the tragic problems cannot be denied: the betrayals and the cruel acts that probe everyone's conscience challenge the Islamic world in particular and ask us to be firm in demanding from that world a position that is equally clear against so much violence. I also think, though, that it is not enough to stop there; it is necessary always to have a clear vision: rebuilding, life. It is not enough to denounce; it is necessary to show a way forward.

The evil that confronts us must not frighten us; it challenges us as Christians and asks us to be even more so, deep down. These are precisely the circumstances in which we are called to live out our Christian vocation completely, without excuses.

> To remain in perfect tranquility. Not the Stoic *ataraxia* and impassibility in the face of worldly ruin, but the assurance that mankind and the world are in God's hands. No destruction, however great, can jeopardize the fulfillment of his will; no ruin can take man away from his loving omnipotence. The Christian's life is always the same. God does not spare you some difficulty or trial; God seems to abandon you to the destructive force of evil, but if he lives in you, evil is the one that is destroyed.[2]

We often hear hopeless statements and analyses of the situation; apparently we are near the end of it all. Perhaps old, exhausted models are on their way out, but the world is not, nor are we, although not uncommonly we hear words of discouragement and resignation among our people, even from our religious. Then there is talk about a "clash of civilizations" and, not indirectly, about a sort of call to arms to defend ourselves; all of this has nothing to do with the Christian faith. Christianity springs from the Cross and cannot leave it out of consideration; Jesus becomes king of the world on the Cross, not after the success of the multiplication of the loaves. Christianity springs, in other words, from a human failure and from a pierced heart. When we

[2] Divo Barsotti, *L'attesa. Diario: 1973–1975* (Cinisello Balsamo: Edizioni San Paolo, 2014).

speak about "the power of the heart", that is the heart to which we must look. It is the measure of God's love and consequently of ours: our activity as Christians must be measured by that heart. Often we forget this aspect and fall into the temptation of thinking that our deeds are what will save us.

For a Christian, therefore, an analysis of any reality is not complete unless it is conducted in reference to Christ also. The truth of an event is not understood except in reference to Jesus—not to an ideology, but to a person, who becomes a model of one's own activity and thought. It is enough to cite the episode narrated in the Gospel of Mark (4:35–41) about the disciples' boat, tossed by the waves, the panic of the disciples, and Jesus' rebuke: "Why are you afraid? Have you no faith?" (Mk 4:40).

Political prospects must be sought urgently, but they will not save Christianity in the Middle East. The bark of Peter will always be in danger, and there will always be someone within it to dictate solutions, but only the Lord's command will be able to calm the storm. Our presence will be salvaged by the little ones, by those who courageously risk their own life, defying death in order to love their brother with no thought of repayment.

The images that are broadcast from the Middle East leave us alarmed; it is legitimate to wonder what we must or can do, and we are obliged to make a concrete commitment to put an end to this tragedy. But our action must be accompanied by the serene conviction that, in order for it to bear fruit, our activity must be united to Christ's.

> All solidarity and union with men continues the solidarity of Jesus with all humanity, but if the latter were finite, it would be proof of the supreme failure, because this solidarity is itself consummated and becomes perfect in His

> death on the Cross. His death on the Cross is the way to the Resurrection, and the Resurrection is no longer the solidarity of Jesus with human beings, but rather the union of human beings with the risen Jesus. All solidarity with men, all union with them is the means and the necessary path to the union of men with God; if it does not lead to it, it is in vain; it does not save, it only makes us sharers in sorrow, poverty, and death: it does not give us life.[3]

In conclusion, I present two images connected with the Middle East from several months ago, even though they now seem quite distant in time because unfortunately they are distant from the current situation.

The first has to do with the meeting on May 25, 2014, in Jerusalem, between the Patriarch of Constantinople, Bartholomew I, and Pope Francis at the Holy Sepulcher. That basilica, which preserves the memory of the death and Resurrection of Christ, but also of the sad divisions among us Christians, witnessed, for the first time in its history, the meeting between two institutions, Orthodox and Catholic, which for centuries fought one another. The divisions certainly remain, and everything seems now to have gone back to the way it was before, but that is not so: those signs are powerful and oblige those who give them. The two Churches have committed to confront one another in a different, positive way; there is still a long road ahead, but it has been marked out.

The second image is connected with the moment of prayer—planned by Pope Francis and Patriarch Bartholomew—that took place in the Vatican on June 8, 2014, with Shimon Peres and Mahmoud Abbas, the Israeli and Palestinian presidents of two countries that have always been hos-

[3] Ibid.

tile. In this case, too, from the political perspective, the two presidents could not and cannot do much, and the pope still less. Immediately after that meeting between the two parties, unprecedented and inexplicable violence was unleashed,[4] which seems almost like an effort to negate that historical moment, but, once again, the signs have been posted, and the path is open. The images of death that we have seen to this day, the bombardments, the missiles, but especially the deep hatred that is nourished by all this violence, must not be separated from the image of the two presidents who are praying together for peace: that historic event tells us that it is possible, by helping us to lift up our eyes and to warm our heart.

In the Middle East we need everything: financial, military, and political assistance, mediations, support, but we need above all to believe that it is still possible to wish each other well. The testimonies remind us that, despite everything and thanks to the little ones, this force still lives.

[4] A few days after the meeting, in an already tense atmosphere between Israel and Hamas, the kidnapping of three Jewish boys in the West Bank (subsequently found dead) and then the killing of a Palestinian youth led to an escalation of violence and armed conflict.

Risks and Opportunities for the Future Middle East

Address at the Installation of the Captains Regent, San Marino

October 1, 2014

Today the Middle East is the center of attention for the media, but above all a source of apprehension for the whole world. It is tragic to see how the barbarity perpetrated by ISIS and its satellites and imitators, which only appears to reflect religious values, can kill and overturn the most elementary human rights of believers of different faiths and of entire peoples. The atrocious power struggle under way in the Middle East is changing its appearance from the political and religious perspective, but above all it runs the risk of destroying forever a unique heritage of traditions, relations, and cultural cross-fertilization that for centuries has characterized that part of the world. It is everyone's duty to stop this tragedy, because we are all involved.

We have to take an interest in the fate of peoples and nations, of faiths and cultures, that are now threatened by this war: this interest must not arise only because globalization, the media, and the social networks, as well as the emigration of millions of people in the world, have made all countries even more connected with one another from the cultural,

Official address delivered in San Marino on October 1, 2014, on the occasion of the installation ceremony for the new Captains Regent, San Marino's heads of state.

economic, and social perspective. The fates of everyone today are interwoven with those of others in all areas of life: we observe this, in a negative image, even in the context of the Middle Eastern tragedy, with the enlistment of many Westerners in this senseless war, which thus runs the risk of overflowing its boundaries. Participation in what is happening must spring above all from a common moral rejection of the threats to human coexistence perpetrated by these terrorists. It is no longer possible today for persecutions to exist on the basis of ethnicity or religion; international conventions on human rights and the common awareness no longer allow the possibility of committing crimes of this sort.

Faced with so much violence, we see different reactions.

The Risks

The first risk is indifference, maintaining that this is just one of the many wars that have always existed and exist today in the world; thinking that the Middle East is a context too complicated to meddle in, a complex reality that is difficult to understand and to help, because of the economic crisis, too. These are only a few of the recurring assessments; after the initial reaction, one becomes accustomed to everything—and it is easy to get used to the tensions in the Middle East—while limiting one's own participation, in the best case, to economic contributions.

The second risk is the exact opposite: the call to arms and to the clash of civilizations. This position denies any form of critical and positive dialogue with the moderate souls of the world that it confronts, simply because it maintains that such souls do not exist. Therefore, it denies that there are nuances, too, or else it ignores the variegated spectrum of forms of coexistence, movements, and presences in the Middle Eastern world, which therefore is identified *sic et simpliciter* [simply and per se] as fanatical and hostile to the Western world. This position, in my opinion, is unrealistic.

The third risk is that of an approach that is sincerely interested and involved, yet partial. The partial approach is the one that maintains that it already has clear ideas about the situation and rejects a critical analysis of the characteristic complexity of the Middle East. This is typical especially in the context of the Israeli-Palestinian conflict, where each side has its own opinion: the Palestinian victims and the Israeli executioners, or vice versa. One's interpretation of events is elaborated through the filter of positions that have already been assumed; there is no room for other evaluations: faced with the conflict, you just need to choose what side you are on, what cause to espouse.

Another partial approach is the one that tries to address or seeks to interpret what happens from an exclusively political, military, or solely religious perspective. The Middle East is unfamiliar with this distinction: entering into the current political dynamics without understanding their religious background, or vice versa, is a serious error and does not help to identify possible solutions.

Finally, another partial approach is the one that foresees a discussion of possible solutions to the problems with only some of the countries in the Middle East, or with only some religious and social elements. The problems between Sunnis and Shiites, to mention one example, are not resolved by dialoguing only with the Sunnis. Confronting the complex knots from only one of these perspectives, without putting them in their context, has led to many errors.

Therefore it is necessary to intervene. A common awareness, between East and West, is important in order to stop the barbarity in progress, especially in Syria and Iraq. If necessary, we must resort to the use of force. Nevertheless, if this is not situated in a political prospectus for reconstruction at all the levels of those populations and of those countries, without a clear plan for the aftermath, the umpteenth approach to the problem will remain partial and will not be able to offer a lasting solution. Without an integral view, one leaves room for integralism, for fundamentalism.

The Opportunities

This dramatic situation, however, can also become an extraordinary opportunity. The tensions, the war, and the tragedies in which we are involved oblige everyone—religious persons of the different faiths, politicians, intellectuals—to take a common position and to react together in a new way.

Interreligious and intercultural dialogue is necessary now more than ever. We must call the different civilizations in East and West to a common position against the barbarity of ISIS and similar groups. Fundamentalist movements threaten all civilizations, not only ours; initiatives to meet, to become acquainted, and to overcome mutual distrust are therefore all the more necessary.

We face a religious conflict, and we must not give in to the temptation of those who want to take us back to the times of the wars of religion. On the contrary, today it is necessary more than ever, precisely because of the threat of these integralist or fundamentalist movements, to foster dialogue between believers of the different faiths; this dialogue can have a remarkable influence on politics, especially in the

Middle East. Indeed, it is appropriate for politics to fashion a synthesis of the social and religious dynamics and to translate them into concrete actions on the ground. Even a nonbeliever can acknowledge that it is necessary today, not only in the East, to understand the complex religious phenomenon, without denying it, in order to identify shared solutions of encounter.

True interreligious dialogue is the kind that starts from reality, does not deny the problems and the mutual fears, yet does not let itself be overwhelmed by them; it rejects all forms of violence; it seeks at all costs to understand the other, without necessarily sharing his opinion; it tries not to convince or to convert, but to respect and to be respected. It neither affirms nor presupposes that we are all equal: the different religious and cultural identities are not denied. Denying the differences is typical of fundamentalist movements: interreligious dialogue, in contrast, acknowledges the differences, which it does not consider threats, while seeking to understand them. To summarize, it is configured as the encounter of religious communities and of their leaders, local and otherwise, in order to discuss common, concrete problems. One cannot undertake an interreligious dialogue on problems of faith, but it is necessary to have a dialogue between religious believers on common problems, starting from our common humanity.

The path to serene, peaceful relations among the different religious souls in the East, and between East and West, is still a long one. This tragic moment is an invaluable opportunity to coordinate and bring closer together all those religious and lay persons who otherwise would not have been moved or have met each other. Christian and Muslim leaders who act together against ISIS, Christians, Jews, and Muslims who meet to pray and to demonstrate against the war are the image that the fundamentalists want to destroy, an image that is now still more necessary for precisely this reason. The testimony of Pope Francis, in this context, is exemplary: from his journey to the Holy Land in May 2014, to the day of Invocation for Peace in Rome (June 8, 2014), to the numerous calls to reconciliation, he is summoning the faithful not to give in to the temptation of conflict, but to continue to believe and to pray for dialogue, encounter, and reconciliation among peoples, cultures, and religions.

Sons of Abraham in Prayer for Peace

Speech for the Anniversary of the Interreligious Meeting for Peace, Assisi

October 26, 2014

Before reflecting on the invocation for peace that was held in Rome a few months ago,[1] which apparently was hastily shelved by the tragic events that followed it, I maintain that a preliminary remark on the pope's visit to the Holy Land is important.[2] The two events are interconnected. Indeed, it was in the Holy Land that this idea matured and the day of prayer in Rome was announced. The invocation in Rome, therefore, has its heart in Jerusalem.

Pope Francis' Pilgrimage to the Holy Land

The pope's brief but intense journey to the Holy Land moved on two distinct but interrelated levels. The ecumenical level is the better known and more obvious one. It accented the meeting with all the Christian communities, and in particular with Patriarch Bartholomew, with whom

---

This speech, addressing Pope Francis' visit to the Holy Land and his subsequent invocation for peace, was given in Assisi on October 26, 2014, on the twenty-eighth anniversary of the Interreligious Meeting for Peace, which Pope John Paul II sponsored in 1986.

[1] As noted above, Pope John Paul II held an invocation for peace in the Vatican on June 8, 2014, in the presence of the Israeli President Shimon Peres and the Palestinian President Mahmoud Abbas and the Ecumenical Patriarch of Constantinople Bartholomew, guests of Pope Francis.

[2] May 24 to 26, 2014.

there is a special relationship, confirmed also by the important journey to Turkey, to Constantinople/Istanbul.[3] The principal purpose of the pilgrimage was to commemorate the historic meeting between Pope Paul VI and the Patriarch of Constantinople Athenagoras. That meeting changed irreversibly, after centuries, the relations between the two "lungs" of the Church, the Eastern and the Western.

The other aspect of the papal journey was inevitably connected with the Israeli-Palestinian conflict: the stop at the separation wall, a symbol of the wound inflicted on the Palestinian people, and the one near the Israeli monument to the victims of terrorism, and in particular the meeting with the two presidents, representatives of the respective peoples, with whom the pope remained for a long time.

These two levels, the religious level with the meeting at the Holy Sepulcher and the "political" level with the two presidents, are connected. In both situations, the pope wanted to "touch" the wounds created by the deep divisions that the Holy Land has always known: those between the Churches and those between the two peoples.

The two moments were on the same track, heading in the same direction; in order to understand this, it is necessary to go back to the day on which the pope announced his journey to the Holy Land, on the Vigil of the Solemnity of the Epiphany (January 5, 2014). On that day, the pope communicated the fact that he would travel to the Holy Land on a "pilgrimage of prayer". This was the Supreme Pontiff's intention, and in my opinion, it is the key to understanding the papal journey: prayer. The pope, indeed, did not give speeches of a political sort. He said almost nothing in that regard. He did not go into the questions by adding his own

[3] November 28 to 30, 2014.

proposal for a solution to the thousands that already exist and are now almost useless. He only intended to bring his personal solidarity and especially his prayer, while inviting everyone to join him, without expressing judgments. He invited them to pray that the Lord might give the strength to make peace to those who do not have the ability. That's all. This is the context, then, in which we must interpret the journey of Pope Francis to the Holy Land and, shortly thereafter, the prayer meeting in Rome.

This approach had and still has now a great impact. If the pontiff had elaborated a proposal or a call to find a solution to the problems, everything would have been shelved immediately as the umpteenth point of view; there would have been supporters and detractors, and it would have brought further divisions with expectations that were satisfied or frustrated. By making himself available, not to mediate but rather to pray, and by inviting others to join in his prayer, the pope instead brought the discussion to a completely different level. He "neutralized" the expectations and the fears of politics and invited people and politicians to take a wider view and to give a different and perhaps new perspective to everyone's vision. He intended to become present with his humanity, without judging, condemning, instructing, or making a point. He replaced no one, thus calling off almost completely the mutual prohibitions.

Who can deny the desire to pray for peace? How can anyone reject a public, authoritative invitation, like the pope's, to join together, not to discuss boundaries or percentages, but to pray to God, the one God, that He might enlighten everyone and give the strength to build peace seriously? The pope brought politics onto a new and different terrain: he led his interlocutors to take off the garments of current politics and to put on those of a poor human being who turns to God. Because this is what we all are.

But in the first place, it is a good idea to return to the journey to the Holy Land and, in particular, to the prayer meeting at the Holy Sepulcher.

The Ecumenical Meeting at the Holy Sepulcher

It will take a little more time, perhaps, for us to realize how important that meeting was. Fifty years ago, Paul VI and Patriarch Athenagoras met on the outskirts of Jerusalem, on the Mount of Olives, in their respective residences. No more could be done, then, and nonetheless that was an extraordinary historical event. That meeting, as was anticipated, marked a turning point in the relations between the two Churches.

This year, in contrast, the commemorative meeting was held in the heart of Christian Jerusalem, at the Holy Sepulcher, which preserves the memory of the death and Resurrection of Christ and, unfortunately, is also a reminder of our divisions. It was not a diplomatic but rather a prayerful meeting. For the first time, the head of the Catholic Church and the head of the Orthodox Church, in Jerusalem, joined in prayer, not just personally, but also with their respective Churches. Anyone who knows firsthand the life of the Churches knows very well that this is by no means to be taken for granted. There can be religious leaders who, as guests, join in the prayer of another Church. But two Christian religious leaders who, at the same moment, in the same place (and not just any place, but rather Jerusalem, in the Holy Sepulcher), pray together with their respective communities: that is something absolutely new. In that moment, an enormous bastion tumbled down, one of the great buttresses that hold up the wall of division between the two Churches, and this made it increasingly fragile.

Besides the moment in itself, which was intensely moving, the preparations for that meeting were important; they were conducted exclusively in Jerusalem, the work of the local Churches. Therefore, this was not an event that was merely hosted, but rather a moment of prayer that was organized, prepared, and desired by the local Churches, which joined with their respective pastors.

Discussions were held on all the details, even the smallest ones: about who would do what and where, on the responsibilities, the precedents, the division of tasks, who would be in attendance, the guests. And then the readings, the chants, the gestures. Everything was new. The Status Quo,[4] which has reigned as sovereign over the Holy Sepulcher for decades, did not foresee that there would ever be an event of this sort; therefore the organizers needed to interpret the Status Quo in the light of this absolute novelty. Never had the Latin and Greek choirs sung together. Never had Patriarchs and Custodes met to choose together a passage from the Bible (generally they meet to discuss "condominial questions", without going further). Never had they met to establish the chants best suited to a common event. Everyone wanted to contribute his best vestments, only then to reach the shared conclusion that there was nothing to vest, but that everything should remain simple and sober.

After the initial difficulties in understanding the nature of the event, little by little, unconsciously, we found ourselves

[4] A regulation from the Ottoman era that establishes the norms of conduct and the rights of the various Christian confessions who share ownership of the Basilica of the Nativity and [the Basilica] of the Holy Sepulcher.

discussing and preparing the liturgy together, as one does in any ecclesial institution: Scripture passages, hymns, gestures, and so forth. Trivial things, if you will, but, if done for the first time in centuries, they take on an extraordinary value of newness and renewal. Only afterward did we realize that we had toiled and worked for months to construct together a simple liturgy, whereas generally our usual preoccupation, in Jerusalem, is to mark the distinctions between us. We did the opposite of what we do routinely, and we met each other again, re-encountered one another in a new way. In our "condominial" meetings, we generally discuss how to preserve our rights from the others. For this meeting, instead, the main concern was how to share responsibilities: a novelty and an important methodological sign.

It must be noted that it was by no means simple and that the past was not canceled at all. There were prohibitions and various limits, for sure! Difficulties were noticeable and, at several moments, the desire the make the whole thing unsuccessful. There was no lack of intricately "Byzantine" complications, on both sides, nor of strong opposition to the initiative. What created more tension was the impossibility of having greater involvement on the part of the other Churches. The disappointment of the other communities over not being able to participate actively was intense. I think that this, too, is important to note. The disappointment, of course, was also an expression of the desire for visibility, which was denied; this must be acknowledged. But we need to add that there was also, however, a sincere desire on the part of all to be there, to be part of this new and extraordinary embrace, to be an active part of that historic moment.

Fifty years ago, the meeting was held on the peripheries. Today important progress was made: meeting at the Holy

Sepulcher, with a common liturgy. Who knows whether someday it might be possible to extend that meeting to others, in another stage of this long, irreversible journey of reconciliation. Neither of the two protagonists, Paul VI and Athenagoras, could have foreseen fifty years ago the impact of their gesture. Nor can we today, then, understand how this gesture, made in Jerusalem, will have repercussions in the next years of the life of the Church, but we know that it is and will remain a fundamental step in the process of reconciliation.

The Invocation of Peace in Rome

After touching the wound of division between the Churches in Jerusalem, it was necessary to touch the other painful wound: the division between the two peoples, Israeli and Palestinian.

The approach was the same. No political discussion or generic calls for peace, to which no one has paid attention for a long time now. Only an invitation to prayer. And, as at the Holy Sepulcher, in this case, too, the invitation surprised many people, who were unprepared for a "novelty" like that. Institutional circles in Jerusalem, whether religious or political, are indeed accustomed to conducting a "peace proposal", but not an invitation to prayer for peace. So they wondered: "What is done in such cases? There is no protocol for events like that!" Of course, there was no lack of opposition, on the part of both politicians and religious leaders. Time constraints, technical difficulties, and the intense local conditions made it impossible to carry out this proposal in Jerusalem. But the idea was not abandoned. The invitation, once made official, met with a positive public response from the two presidents, who accepted, going beyond their official mistrust and requiring their respective staff members to resolve their hesitations and make themselves available for the initiative. Thus it was decided to hold the meeting; each one changed his own calendar to make this a priority. And they said to themselves, if it is still difficult in Jerusalem because of the conditions connected with the tangle of political and religious tensions, then we will pray in Rome. Therefore not only *with* the pope, but also "in the house" of the pope. Impossible to refuse. Once again politics and politicians were brought out of their own terrain and, in this case, also outside of their own house. Indeed, Pope Francis expressed himself this way: "I wish to invite you . . . to join me in heartfelt prayer to God for the gift of peace. . . . All of us want peace. Many people build it day by day through small gestures and acts; many of them are suffering, yet patiently persevere in their efforts to be peacemakers. All of us—especially those placed at the service of their respective peoples—have the duty to become instruments and artisans of peace, especially by our prayers. Building peace is difficult, but living without peace is a constant torment."[5]

The request to help organize that moment of prayer was made to me in Gethsemane, the place of Jesus' *fiat*, anticipating the sufferings that can never be eliminated from the horizon when we speak about the desire for peace in the Holy Land.

The common thought was that such a moment would be postponed to the following months. We received a communication, though, stating that it should be held right away, within a few days. The initial assent to the initiative was thus replaced, immediately, by a concern about carrying it

[5] Regina Coeli, Bethlehem, May 25, 2014.

out. However, even the choice of times then turned out to be providential. If we had not seized the occasion of grace connected with the pilgrimage to the Holy Land, after the crisis that broke out during the summer, probably it would no longer have been possible to celebrate that encounter and we would find ourselves now with no sign, with no image at all of possible peace between the two peoples, but only with the ruins left by the war.

The frantic, intense weeks following the announcement were taken up by an endless series of meetings, first with the political staffs, then with the religious, separately and together, mediating between the parties, overcoming the fears and sensitivities, defining the common criteria for the preparation of the texts, the topics, the limits, the composition of the delegations, their distribution (in other words, whether the delegations should be divided by religious or by national affiliation), and identifying a place that would take into account the different religious sensibilities associated with the presence or absence of symbols. This was a novelty not only for the two national delegations, but also for the Holy See and for the Vatican staff. It could not be a mass event, and therefore the delegations had to remain numerically restricted, yet representative of the different religious compositions of the respective countries. Not all the religious leaders were willing to participate, not all of them were ready to recite the chosen texts or to accept those of others. Each delegation had to choose its texts autonomously, with respect to the set topics. All had to approve the texts of all, which therefore had to be reviewed, and possibly revised, in time.

The religious leaders who had agreed then had to confront also, within their respective communities, the opposition of those who were against the initiative, for religious or political reasons. If for the Christians it was difficult to accept the idea of praying together in Jerusalem, it is easy to imagine what sort of reaction was provoked by the idea that, at such a high level and with worldwide visibility, the religious leaders of the three faiths, which do not meet often in the Holy Land, would not only pray beside one another, but also together with their respective political presidents, in a context—that of the Holy Land—where politics and faith not infrequently coincide. To summarize, this was a meeting that publicly tasked religious and political leaders with an authentic call for peace. Even the terminology was important: to pray for peace or to call for peace? The choice of the term "invocation" mitigated the difficulties but did not do away with them. At the political level, too, there were misunderstandings. Many persons in the respective delegations did not understand the meaning of the initiative, which was totally separate from their ordinary field of activity. Others, in contrast, were decisively against it, because the gesture was not in tune with their political agenda, which pits one against the other or blames the other for the political stalemate, the misunderstandings, and so on. The image of the two presidents who not only shake hands but pray together twisted their narrative, and therefore it was necessary to prevent it somehow from becoming a reality. Others, again, had prepared texts that were veritable political agendas and had nothing to do with a prayer addressed to God. Or else religious texts were composed, but with clear political references. In conclusion, taking off the political robes and thinking outside of the ideological box was more difficult than one might think.

There were many difficulties, then, but the desire to move

forward prevailed, despite everything. In the moments of stalemate, it was not always clear how planning could continue, but everyone was aware of the fact that they could not stop. The two presidents, at times, intervened personally to resolve dilemmas, fears, or difficulties.

As with the meeting at the Holy Sepulcher, the determination of the two political leaders to participate in the invocation obliged their respective staff members to fall in line and to put their own expectations, agendas, and different objectives in second place. They all saw themselves obliged to adapt, to seek to review their own texts so as to meet with the consensus of the other, and vice versa. In this case, too, not only the event in itself was important, but its preparation was also. It was obvious that, when there is strong motivation, people can meet with one another, overcoming obstacles of all sorts. Until the end, the discussion of the texts was lively, candid, and fair. Some also assumed the responsibility to continue despite the opposition of their own party. Peace also requires taking clear, decisive positions.

The presence of Patriarch Bartholomew was closely connected with the meeting in Jerusalem; the rendezvous in Rome was the prolongation of it. The prayer involved not only the head of the Church of Rome with the two presidents of Jerusalem, but both the heads of the Eastern and Western Churches, who embraced in Jerusalem. The second embrace was the direct consequence of the first.

There was no dishonesty, and the meeting was not a farce. In composing the texts and in choosing the gestures to perform, the delegations not only listened to one another, but also sought to remain faithful to their own identity. They wrote or chose no passages that were not clearly connected with their own tradition. Words and gestures had to be true, first in themselves, and then for the others, without sentimental rhetoric that would be crowd-pleasing but not significant for the community to which one belonged. What emerged in the diversity of choices: Jews, Christians, and Muslims, addressing the same topics (creation, forgiveness, and invocation), expressed themselves in very different ways that were not always entirely understood by the others. Basically, though, there was never a lack of respect; everyone was aware of the fact that it was not possible always to understand the other group's text in depth and that therefore it was necessary also to trust. Everyone expressed himself to the best of his abilities. The Muslims composed texts strongly inspired by the Qur'an that were created specifically for the occasion, with the chanting of a surah added at the last moment. The Jews chose passages from the Bible and from Jewish tradition. The Christians selected Scriptural passages, prayers that were well-known, and others composed *ad hoc.* Everyone with full autonomy and according to his own sensibility. It was not an interreligious prayer meeting, but a moment of invocation by the two presidents, with representatives of the two peoples who were Christians, Muslims, and Jews.

Could it have been done better? I do not know. But it was the best that they could do. In order to understand the meaning and the impact of the event, we certainly must consider the texts and the gestures together. But we also need to take into account the choice to be there, to participate firsthand in the gesture itself. Not one of those present was obliged to come, but each one, accepting the invitation, declared his own intention to work and to pray for peace, despite the opposition from one's own party. No one could expect to have everything picture-perfect and in order, with clear, distinct ideas. The delegations, their gestures, and texts could not be "weighed" solely on the basis of their own expectations and their own criteria. They met together in the truth of each one, seeking, for once, to set aside the obstacles, and at the same time without denying themselves, without deceiving themselves that they would attain who-knows-what objectives or meet expectations that were too high and beyond the reach of reality. While acknowledging and respecting also the difficulties and the efforts of everyone, his times and perspectives, without ceasing to wait for him: this, too, is an important methodological sign.

The Fruits of the Meeting

Much has been said about the fruits of the meeting. Or better, commentators have talked at length about its "failure", given that immediately afterward unprecedented violence was unleashed: "The prayer did not serve or gain its purpose, it was a farce quickly contradicted by reality."

Bishop Sorrentino[6] wrote an important page on this subject. Here are a few excerpts from it:

> The visit of Pope Francis to the Holy Land and especially the moment of prayer that he shared in the Vatican with Shimon Peres and Mahmoud Abbas roused many hopes. Perhaps too many. There could be no greater disappointment, with the explosion of the conflict that occurred shortly afterward between the two peoples, once again resulting in casualties and ruins. Politics, as always, was powerless to prevent the unscrupulous attack by Hamas and to restrain the abnormal reaction by Israel. The triumph of hatred. The defeat of reason. The defeat of prayer also? . . . But why "invest" in prayer, in a place where it seems that it fails punctually? One might give the facile answer: even be-

[6] Domenico Sorrentino, bishop of the Diocese of Assisi-Nocera Umbra-Gualdo Tadino.

> fore prayer, the political initiatives fail. . . . Turning to God is an act of truth and humility: ingredients without which no peace is possible. . . . It would be far too convenient if a single prayer, even one by a pope, should magically resolve such a knotty problem that borders on hopelessness. . . . Where reason is blinded and feelings are embittered, only the Spirit of God can enter. If the initiatives of politics have a task to complete—and they do!—they must be accompanied by much prayer. Therefore the initiative of Pope Francis, without being a substitute [for politics], is decisive. It was not only an "event": it was a great methodological sign. The "spirit of Assisi" remains more alive than ever.[7]

I think that this quotation already says it all. One must not have a "consumerist" approach to prayer, which does not produce results, and never immediately. Prayer leads to an attitude, a condition, a relation. Prayer does not produce or generate; it does not replace human work, but rather illumines it. It does not exempt us from traveling down the road, but it does show the way. And in this sense the meeting in Rome was and remains a powerful, mighty, binding sign. It is the image to which we can refer, which gives hope to anyone who is not resigned to the sad realities of our days.

No one was ever under the illusion—and this was said clearly—that peace would suddenly break out; peace can be made only together and over a long time. Certainly the power of Satan, who breeds division, could not remain inert. But we know that one day this will end, and we will need a sign that brings us back to the common desire for peace; we will need to rediscover the road through a different way of standing together and acknowledging one another.

[7] Address for the Feast of the Pardon of Assisi, 2014 (dedicated to prayer for peace in the Holy Land).

That image of the presidents together with the pope and the patriarch has another function: it cannot be canceled. Together with the image of the physical and moral ruins left by the last war in Gaza, there is also the image of the common prayer to the one God and Father of all whom no one, not even Satan, can cancel.

The political interpretations and analyses that followed the visit to the Holy Land and the event in Rome are irreconcilable with the gestures of Pope Francis, with his personality, the substantiality of his teaching, with a simplicity that is an expression of lucidity. But it seems that they do not reflect the respect due to the figure of the pope, even aside from the figure of Francis, the pope who came from the end of the earth. The pope is a religious figure: his speech must reach us in the place where we cannot pretend to ourselves. If we do not start from there, we invalidate our expectations, our judgments, the actual bottom line of the prayer meeting and of his visit to the Holy Land. A land that suffers already from too many superficial analyses, a land that is wounded by partisan judgments, and land that is contested and violated when we forget that it is a Land of salvation, a Land of God. These interpretations are unfair also with regard to the many Israelis and Palestinians, both religious and secular, who make a commitment every day, going against the current, and fight to continue to wish one another well.

Therefore I like the pope's ambitious, "high-flying" approach: his embrace of all the faiths in the Holy Land, expressed in the embrace of his two friends; the fact that he kept Israelis and Palestinians united in his heart, principally addressing human beings; the fact that he puts the poor first, underscoring the different needs of these peoples.

Pope Francis wanted to fly high, far from the routine difficulties, so as to be immersed in the heart of everyday life with reasons that make it livable in different ways—to be outside the tangle of insuperable obstacles so as to discover, and to risk, a new way of life. To fly high is not to conceal the problems but rather to be liberated from fear, to dare, to accept the challenge, to trust in the future.

The fatherhood of Abraham brings us—Christians, Jews and Muslims—to brotherhood, the most beautiful gift that peace can bring on this Earth, the cradle of humanity, which has been desperately torn in its irresistible impulse toward justice and in the reciprocal need for forgiveness.

The "spirit of Assisi" has not exhausted its calling, then. The day of prayer in Rome was not useless. There are many people in the world, even in the Holy Land, who need, more than bombs, a sign, some encouragement, an impetus to keep looking each other in the eye and to raise their sights to the one Father of all, thus acknowledging one another as brothers.

It may seem like a dream to declare this now. Rather, it is the truest thing to look at, the most beautiful reality of the Holy Land, and the meeting in Rome is its most powerful, unforgettable, and consoling sign.

A Witness Stronger Than Evil?

Speech for the Spanish Bishops' Conference, Madrid

October 27, 2015

In the first place, a general preliminary note on what is happening in the Middle East. Every day we receive updates on the situation, almost in real time: the internecine war between Shiites and Sunnis, the energy issue, the persecution of the Christians and other minorities, international interests that are now obvious and immediately comprehensible, civil war, and so on. Moving on specifically to the problems of the Holy Land, that is, of Israel and the Palestinian Authority, the situation is no better: we are probably at the start of another long and painful period of tension and clashes. For the moment, everything still seems to happen at the level of individual initiatives, but the fear is that sooner or later someone will "hijack" this movement, identifying it with an extremist, fundamentalist movement.

What is new compared to the preceding *intifadas*—I do not think that it is possible to speak, for now, about just one *intifada*—is that the religious element is prevalent, while the political element remains secondary. The religious element existed before, too, but it was less important: the central topics were the occupation, the settlements, etc. Now, though, reporters speak about the liberation of Al-Aqsa,[1] about the uprising of the Muslim people. Indeed, the tension is no

Speech given in Madrid on October 27, 2015, as part of the twenty-fifth symposium on interreligious relations for the Spanish Episcopal Conference. The theme was "Christianity and Islam: 1400 Years of Difficult Coexistence".

[1] The mosque on the Temple Mount.

longer limited to the Palestinian zones, but also involves all the Muslims present in Israel, whereas in the past this phenomenon was more restricted. It is still too early to draw conclusions, but these seem to be the premises. In this context, therefore, it is possible that some extremist movement or local group imitating the extremist movement, such as *jihad*, ISIS, and the like, might turn these frustrations into a vehicle for itself.

We are witnessing today a continual barbarization of social relations. If we consider only Syria and Iraq—without examining the front of the various wars in progress, with the barbarities that we unfortunately know too well—with regard to the life of the rest of the population, we can say that all the reference points of common, everyday community life have gone missing: in many parts of these two countries, security, schools, courts, and various sorts of public services no longer exist. In short, everything that regulates a normal social life, with its inevitable network of relations, seems to have disappeared definitively. The little everyday assurances have been suspended, things connected with human relations of any sort seem to have been blown up because of this senseless war: from the difficulties in normal telephone conversations to the civil administrations, where they are still present but now paralyzed; from the schools that are in session only for a few periods, and only in certain zones, to the near-impossibility of transportation.

In Iraq and Syria, at least two-thirds of the Christians—and this is true of the whole population, also—have evacuated and now find themselves abroad or in other parts of their respective countries. They have fled to localities where they are homeless; they are often without work or prospects and have lost their religious bearings as well. This implies that most of the faithful are far from their own churches and church-affiliated institutions, which in turn have remained empty and unused.

In the Holy Land, in the everlasting Israeli-Palestinian conflict and as far as the dialogue between the two parties is concerned, the scenario is no better. The daily news reports leave us alarmed. All this is creating in the population, and therefore among the common folk, a sense of frustration, abandonment, and disorientation that is reaching unheard-of proportions. In recent months in the vicinity of Bethlehem, various Christian families have decided to leave definitively; the number is even higher among the Muslim families. These families are not poor, but middle-class, with children: they feel that they cannot leave their own children in this apparently hopeless situation.

In recent weeks, in Jerusalem but not only there, the deep distrust between the two elements seems to grow more and more. If an Israeli Jew happens to be in an entirely Arab zone, he will probably be, at the very least, the target of stone-throwing.

What is worrisome is not the conflict in itself: this is not the first time that there is war in the Middle East, and we know that all this will pass sooner or later. The cause for concern, rather, is the burden of frustration, hatred, and deep distrust that poisons the atmosphere. It will take a lot of time and energy to overcome this situation: there is hatred and distrust between Palestinians and Israelis, distrust between Christians and Muslims; the Muslims, in turn, feel that they are being attacked by everyone, and so do the Israeli Jews.

The era that we knew, on which the sun has now set, was the era in which the Middle Eastern Christian communities flourished again and developed, built churches, hospitals, and various institutions, and therefore were at the center of political and social life in those lands, only to become, little by little, increasingly isolated, and now the heart of their activities has been struck. The network of relations that characterized Eastern civilization in this past century has been broken up, and consequently we are experiencing the present moment with inevitable disorientation.

To use religious language, one would say that Satan seems to prevail and that the image of God, which is man, is seriously disfigured and offended by the barbarity and the rejection of all forms of relationship, so much so that it is difficult to find even marginal examples of functioning social relations. When one cannot manage to communicate and every form of dialogue seems to be ruled out, even the smallest problem becomes insurmountable and man is alone and, therefore, disoriented. Reality is built on relationship, and if that is absent, man is lost, because he is unable to confront reality adequately. The greatest difficulty today is precisely this: communication as a whole appears to be impossible.

As I spoke recently with the various Christian communities in the martyred city of Aleppo, what clearly emerged was their sorrow and frustration over the destruction of entire Christian districts and of their churches. The constant refrain that we heard was that the Muslims had shown very little solidarity with the Christians who were killed, or that they had not spoken in their defense. On the other hand, while dialoguing with the leaders of several Muslim communities and questioning them on the reason for their silence, the reply was that the Muslims who had been killed were much more numerous than the Christians, and so were the mosques that were destroyed; moreover, it was emphasized that this has been going on for a much longer time, and yet not one of the Christian bishops ever spoke up in their defense. Why, then—they asked—should they take any action as Muslims?

The Christians, moreover, are sometimes viewed by the Muslims as a Western presence that has made its way into their midst and therefore should handle its own problems by itself. The Christians, again, feel that they are the object of persecution, while those in the Muslim communities perceive themselves as the object of the world's hatred. Each group interprets reality exclusively from within its own perspective, without knowing that of the other side. What is obvious is the absence of adequate communication between the different communities, and this aspect accentuates the current drama. Each one is blocked off in a vision that often does not go beyond the boundaries of one's own community of affiliation. Each party forms its own perspective without or against the other: in other words, the other is excluded or is the enemy.

In order to overcome this crisis, in conclusion, and in order to be able to speak about the future, it is necessary to reestablish the ties of the relations between the various communities and to seek to identify at least some common traits, so as not to give rise to narratives that are completely distinct, if not antithetical.

Muslims, Christians, and Jews, indeed, will remain in the Middle East. The current crisis will not destroy the different communities; their destiny will not change: they will be compelled once again to confront one another. The Christians will necessarily have to actualize their future together with all the other religious communities, particularly with the Islamic ones, with which they will continue to coexist. The dialogue with Islam is not a "luxury" for intellectuals, but a necessity.

The future of the Christians, therefore, cannot be separated from that complex social and religious context: rather, it is closely connected with the future of all the other social and religious elements of the Middle East. It is not enough, therefore, to say that we need to stop the persecution of the Christians: it is not only necessary to stop the present course of cancellation of all the existing differences in the name of a religious and social "purity"—that is, in the name of a particular model of Islam—but it is also indispensable to modify the climate of distance, suspicion, and prejudice that is being created among the many religious and social elements of the Middle East.

At the same time, the Muslim leaders must understand that the Christian communities are an integral part of their territory and that the relation with these minorities is an indispensable part of their internal process of reform. In other words, they must become aware of the fact that the relation with the other, with the outside world—with its cultural, social, religious, and economic spheres—is not an irrelevant challenge, and that their future, essentially, cannot do without these considerations.

What I just said seems unrealistic and utopian in the current situation. In facing such a tragic context, then, what attitude should we take?

First of all, I will cite these words, written recently by Father Ibrahim Alsabagh, one of our pastors in Aleppo:

> With this [pastoral] assignment there is in us the certainty that God is present even today, even here among the ruins of Aleppo, that "the gates of hell shall not prevail" and that, for those who love him, the Lord always makes a "greater quantity" of good spring up, even from evil. We continue to encourage our people to "hope against all hope", carrying their cross courageously every day. . . . In our diligent prayer, we find the energy to continue to see with the eyes of the heart that there is something beautiful and luminous that belongs, after this storm, to the Eastern Church: it is

the expectation, and not a vain one, of a new time for witness to the Kingdom of God and for the expansion of it.

Let me add two more similar testimonies. A year ago, Father Hanna Jallouf was abducted by the jihadist rebel forces in Syria. A few months later, another confrere, Father Dhiya Azziz, was abducted by another jihadist group and taken far from his parish. Both were liberated in a daring manner.

After those episodes, however, the two friars, although they had valid reasons to go away, insistently asked to return to their parish, to the place from which they had been abducted, so as to continue to stand by their people, without condemning anyone, and to resume their work of rebuilding what had been destroyed. The walls of the convent and of the parish church had to be repaired, but the spirit of the community, although now considerably reduced in numbers, was more steadfast than ever.

It is necessary, then, to consider this fact: most of the Syrian population has been displaced or has emigrated, including the Christians. In other words, they no longer live where they did before the war. In recent years, our friars have renovated all our churches and parish centers, the oratories and the various structures; now these spaces are completely empty, and where the Christians are now, on the other hand, there are no buildings—there is nothing. And yet the Christian community in those zones is more vital now than ever. The Christians go looking for the priest for the sacraments and for the Mass, even risking their lives, because traveling is dangerous; they organize catechism sessions to help one another. This upheaval of their life has reawakened their thirst for God.

Hope is a Christian virtue, the smallest, perhaps, but it is the one that keeps the other two joined: faith and charity.

Hope is the ability to see, in faith, that which does not yet exist and to bring it about concretely in love: it is the life of many witnesses, from the first pages of the Bible down to today's martyrs.

Abraham wandered all his life in the land that had been promised to him, without ever possessing it; so it was with the prophets: they announced the deliverance of Jerusalem when the city was still destroyed or occupied. The first Christians proclaimed the Kingdom of God when they were being killed in the Colosseum; Bishop Oscar Romero was assassinated without witnessing what he cried out for every day at the altar; today's martyrs are slaughtered by a fanatical hatred never seen before. Therefore, if we look at history with our own eyes, we see only a series of defeats and deaths, of irremediable failures. But if we observe it from another perspective, that of the believer, we see "something more", as Father Ibrahim writes, which in a different way cannot be explained. In other words, there is a limit that evil cannot go beyond or conquer: the freedom to do good, to believe, despite everything, in man's goodness and to love him passionately.

Moreover, we must free ourselves from the presumption of trying to deliver the world from evil. This is a serious error. To deliver the world from evil is the program of the Antichrist, not of the believing Christian. How, indeed, can the world be delivered from evil, if at the same time man is not deprived of the freedom to commit evil? Do not forget the parable of the wheat and the weeds (Mt 13:24–30): the Christian believer, naturally, rejects evil without hesitating, but he does not presume to annihilate it; he does not let himself be overwhelmed by it, he does not accept its dynamics, he does not allow it to threaten his own freedom. The Christian does not overcome evil, in the sense that he cannot and will not annihilate it; he acts in order to build up the good, conscious that evil cannot deprive him of his own freedom: it may kill him, but when confronted with freedom, evil is powerless.

The examples of Father Ibrahim, Father Hanna, and Father Dhiya are the sign of the approach that we want to adopt in this tragic situation: we do not presume to defeat evil, but we desire to be a little sign of freedom.

A real risk, finally, is to lament the "onions of Egypt" (see Num 11:5), that is, the lost securities, the world that accompanied us for such a long time and in which we grew up in the Middle East. Everything is changing; nothing will be as it was before. At first this frightened us, but now it is clear that we must enter into this perspective with the freedom that springs from faith, the certainty that, despite everything, our presence will remain alive.

In conclusion, I mention two models on which we apparently built our civilization: the models of Abraham and Ulysses. Ulysses heroically overcame a large number of trials and temptations, vicissitudes and difficulties, but his purpose was to go back home, to Ithaca, to rebuild his own "nest"; to recover certainties and securities, to revive them. Ithaca is for him the place to which he makes his return. The adventure, for Ulysses, is to overcome the obstacles so as to go back home, and to stay there: to leave what is uncertain for what is certain.

Abraham, in contrast, has the diametrically opposite prospect: to set out, to travel toward a place that he does not yet know, to abandon what is certain for what is uncertain, to live without seeing what he believes in, in other words, the fulfillment of the promise. It is a continual departure without ever going back. In Abraham there is one certainty: God.

Indeed, Abraham loses everything—house, fatherland, family, son, inheritance—but he does not renounce God. On the contrary, in that faith, he already "sees" everything, even without ever having experienced it. When we lament our past and its lost securities, we are like Ulysses. Our model, on the contrary, is Abraham: to depart, without fear, because the Lord is our shield (Gen 15). And to enter into this reality with the freedom that springs from our faith, from our relation with God.

A New Ministry, at the Service of All

2016–2020

On June 24, 2016, after accepting the resignation of Patriarch Fouad Twal, Pope Francis appointed Father Pizzaballa as the apostolic administrator—that is, the interim archbishop—of the Latin Patriarchate of Jerusalem, until the appointment of a new patriarch. This vast diocese spans Israel, Gaza, Palestine, Jordan, and Cyprus. He served in this deputy capacity until October 24, 2020, when he officially became the Latin Patriarch of Jerusalem. Collected in this section are his most compelling responses to his new role as the spiritual shepherd of the Holy Land.

Sufficit Tibi Gratia Mea

Speech in Bergamo upon His Consecration as Archbishop of Jerusalem

September 10, 2016

I spent the last few days before the episcopal consecration at the Shrine in Caravaggio, where all of us have been at least once; my memories of it go back to my earliest childhood. From there I tried to retrace the journey of grace that has accompanied me through all these years. As you know, I chose as my motto *Sufficit tibi gratia mea*, "My grace is sufficient for you." I tried to see how this grace has intervened over the course of my life, even in ways that I was unaware of. Grace has the features of faces and names of people through whom I have received so much. Obviously I will not recount here the whole story of my life and I will not say all the names.

I think first of all about my family: about my parents, who gave me life, the siblings and that first vital nucleus that has accompanied me to this day, I must say in a way that has always been very discreet. Every time I return, I always remember my first years as a child. I left home early, but I remember very well those years in the countryside around Cologno al Serio, in Liteggio. Perhaps few people are acquainted with that forsaken little town.

The episcopal consecration of Father Pizzaballa was celebrated in September 2016 in Bergamo, his native province. (He was born and raised in the little town of Cologno al Serio, not far away.)

Those were the last years of a simple rural life, with farms that already were starting to become depopulated but that still were experiencing the final moments of a world that has now disappeared. I remember the visits to the cow-sheds, where Mama sent me to fetch the milk. I had fun riding on the cart drawn by the horse. Then someone also used to take me on the cart to make hay . . . then the simple country games, and so forth. It was a simple, natural life, and a sober, happy life. Only with the passage of time did I understand how that world influenced me by its frugal ways and its demand for sincerity.

I was attracted above all by the figure of the priest, who used to come in from the countryside on his bicycle: Don Pèrsec (Father Battista Persico). How they looked forward to seeing him! How they loved him! And how he loved his people. I left home early, but I remember those years well, and they were decisive in giving a face to my first calling.

I wanted to be like Don Pèrsec.

Then the years of minor seminary, in the Emilia Romagna Province of the Friars Minor. I think of Father Giovanni, Father Francesco, Father Gregorio, Father Candido, Father Davide and many others. In that little seminary at the Convent of Grace in Rimini, I learned from the passion and the discipline of those friars that the Church has no boundaries. At that time we had a missionary museum that we had to keep open for the visitors (and had to clean rather painstakingly). It had rooms for Papua New Guinea, the Holy Land, China, and so forth. It told the life story of many missionaries who returned from those lands and brought back memories, which were preserved in the museum. Every object had a story. I was struck most of all by the rooms about China, which were full of treasures. Especially the relics of the martyrs from 1900, victims of the Boxer Revolution.

And then the visits of the missionaries who arrived from afar, especially from Japan and Papua New Guinea, where they had gone after being expelled from China; they always used to stop by the seminary to tell about their experiences, which were always very inspiring. Then there were missionaries who had returned from China and lived among us.

Each of us seminarians had to correspond with a missionary. I was assigned to write to Father Gaetano Orlandi in Papua New Guinea. It was made clear to our childish minds, without our even noticing, that the Church speaks all languages, that she thrives in all cultures, and that when you say yes to the Lord, you can go anywhere. You could even think of leaving and going far away. There are no borders. I, too, wanted to go to mission lands. To China.

Strangely enough, the room dedicated to the Holy Land was the one that interested me least.

Then in Ferrara as a boy in high school, with my first parish assignment. I was in charge of the choir and also the organist. There I was clothed in the Franciscan habit.

Entrance into the Franciscan Order was for me a natural choice which concretely expressed my desire for simplicity and a radical choice of frugality.

The formators and superiors at that time were very patient with me, and I thank them for that patience and also for their severity, when it was necessary.

My departure for the Holy Land was another important lesson. I did not want to go to the Holy Land. I did not like the room dedicated to the Holy Land and did not want to go down there. But the provincial, who was old-school, said: "I am the provincial. You obey, take your assignment, and go. No fussing!"

A yes to the Lord passes through very concrete and human yeses. It is not an abstract, vague sentiment.

The departure under obedience for Jerusalem taught me to make the vital synthesis between spiritual insights and real life. A lesson that then became more important as I matured in the following years.

I arrived in the Holy Land, where I have spent more than half of my life. I can summarize my experience in the Custody of the Holy Land under two headings: love for the Word, through the years that I spent at the Studium Biblicum Franciscanum and Hebrew University, and then accepting the complexity of reality as a way of life. The Custody's own complexity, with people coming from all over the world and its complicated internal organization, is a sign of a greater complexity of which Jerusalem is the symbol: in relations between the Churches, between the monotheistic faiths, in the vexed and ever-difficult political and social question, and so on. It is a reality full of complications. Accepting all this does not necessarily mean participating in it, but accepting it as a reality in which to immerse yourself and from which to start building the Kingdom, and then to intercede patiently while looking at things with freedom and detachment. Looking at things from above, as Saint Paul would say, and not only with an earthly perspective (Col 3:1).

My thanks to all those faces and names (and I certainly cannot mention them all) through which so much Grace passed.

And now the Latin Patriarchate and, more generally, the entire Church in the Holy Land, to which I dedicate my life and what I am in a new, comprehensive way.

I thank you, the many people here present. Your voluntary and desired presence encourages me in the ministry that I am about to begin. I thank in particular the Patriarch Emeritus Fouad Twal and the auxiliary bishops, almost all of whom are present.

A special word of thanks to the priests of the Patriarchate present here, who are now my priest "sons", the primary object of my attention.

Now I come to the present—to this ceremony that once again changes my life and my service to the Church of Christ, and to those who have brought me thus far.

My thoughts go to the Holy Father, Francis, for the confidence that he has shown in me with this new ministry, and for his friendship.

To Cardinal Sandri: Thank you, Your Eminence, not only for having agreed to come up here to consecrate me, but also for your service and your presence to the Eastern Churches. Together with you, my thanks also to all the members of the Congregation for the Oriental Churches, whom I see very well represented, and to all the bishops here present. There are a lot of you; I was not expecting so many. It is a beautiful sign of solidarity, not only with me, but with the Church of Jerusalem. Through the prayer and the imposition of hands, you introduced me into the episcopacy. I thank in particular the nuncios present here: the papal representative in Jerusalem and in Israel Archbishop Giuseppe Lazzarotto, Archbishop Alberto Ortega Martin, Apostolic Nuncio to Jordan, and Archbishop Antonio Franco. There are other nuncios: Archbishop Gabriele Giordano Caccia, Nuncio to Lebanon, and bishops from various parts of the Middle East, such as Bahrain, Turkey, and other countries.

Special thanks to Bishop Francesco Beschi, who personally represents the whole beloved Church in Bergamo, which welcomed us here with joy, making everything available for this ceremony, which is certainly beautiful yet not easy to prepare and conduct. My sincere thanks, Your Excellency. In a certain sense, today the Church in Bergamo, which fathered me in the faith, is handing me over to the

Church in Jerusalem, where I will carry out my new ministry. I also thank the Eastern-rite archbishops who are members of the Assembly of Catholic Ordinaries of the Holy Land (Assemblea degli Ordinari Cattolici di Terra Santa, AOCTS) present here: Archbishop Moussa el-Hage and Archbishop George Bacouni.

I wish to make a special mention of my Minister General, the Minister General of the Friars Minor, Fra Michael Perry, who honors me with his presence, knowing very well how busy he is traveling throughout the world to organize the Order, and also of the many confreres who have arrived from all over Italy, particularly from the former and the new religious province to which I belong.

To the Custodian of the Holy Land I send my congratulations, and I offer prayers for the ministry that he has just started, the complexity of which I alone know. In his person I greet the confreres of the Custody, thinking especially of those who for years have been in a war zone, giving an exemplary witness.

I also see a few sisters: Sister Maria Chiara, Sister Ines Yaakoub, General of the Sisters of the Rosary, with whom we collaborate in serving our Church, Sister Paola, and many sisters present.

Thanks also to Archbishop Nektarios of Anthedona, whom we heard speak, a representative of the [Greek Orthodox] Patriarch of Jerusalem, whom I thank for this exquisite gesture of neighborliness. I certainly confirm my commitment to guard jealously this special relation that is not only between the two of us but also between our respective Churches. The Gospel asks us, our people ask us, the Christian community of Jerusalem asks us to work in harmony and in communion.

Thanks to our Jewish and Muslim brothers and friends,

not present here today, who in recent days have nevertheless expressed their joy, assuring us of their prayers and collaboration.

To the Knights of the Holy Sepulcher, with their Governor General Agostino Borromeo, and the various delegations present: I assure them of my complete availability and that of the Patriarchate for collaboration, in full, sincere, and honest confidence.

To the representatives of the civil authorities in Jordan, Palestine, Cyprus, and also in Israel, who excuse themselves because of the Sabbath. I see also the civil and military authorities of the Province and of the Commune of Bergamo, whom I thank, excusing myself for the inconvenience that I may have created.

To the Mayor and to all the citizens of Cologno, I will be happy to express my sentiments tomorrow, but already here and now: thank you. Your reception has moved me.

And all you friends, present and absent, near and far.

I know how many of you are praying, and I feel the strength of your prayer and friendship, which are my greatest comfort at this time.

Now, looking ahead—a very brief look, so as not to weary you too much.

The awareness of grace does not exempt us, but rather impels us to be zealous, so that we will have enough resources to work in God's field, which is the Church.

Here I state with confidence and conviction my desire to be for everyone. If what I am comes from so many, I can only live for many! For those who are entrusted to me, first of all, for those who share my love and concern for the Middle East, for Jews and Muslims, for the poorest, for the whole Church to which my ministry consigns me in a special way.

On the coat of arms that I chose, I wanted to put only two things: Jerusalem and the Word of God. I want the Word to be the starting place and foundation of the ministry that has been assigned to me. I will not start from the problems, the needs, the troubles, the fears. Rather, I wish to start from the Word of God, which must shed light on the needs, the troubles, and the fears that are here and are only human. It is normal for them to exist. But they must be illuminated by a Word that forms us, as it has done from the beginning through generations of believers, a Word that illuminates our choices, our relations, and also our cities, in which the life of us all is immersed. May this light be shed above all on Jerusalem, which summons us all.

And Jerusalem. Psalm 122, verse 6, is normally translated: "Pray for peace for Jerusalem." In reality we ought to translate it: "Pray for the peace of Jerusalem." I, together with many people, pray for peace for Jerusalem; but the peace of Jerusalem exists unexpectedly: it is the peace offered in the Cenacle of the Last Supper and of Pentecost: a peace that is not a suppression of the differences, a canceling of the distance, but neither is it a truce or a non-aggression pact, guaranteed by agreements or partitions.

I pray for a peace that is cordial and sincere welcome of the other, an unyielding desire for listening and dialogue, open roads on which the existing fears and suspicions yield the right of way to acquaintance, to encounter, and to confidence, in which the differences are opportunities for companionship and not a pretext for mutual rejection. I will commit myself so that, thanks also to my service in this land, the peace of Jerusalem may arise for the whole Church and on the people of this land.

Thank you! I await you all in Jerusalem.

Service in the Light of Easter

Speech in Jerusalem upon Installation as Apostolic Administrator

September 21, 2016

Dear brothers and sisters,

I thank you for coming here in such great numbers from the different parts of the Holy Land.

I have already emphasized on different occasions my surprise and gratitude for what is happening to me personally and to the Church in Jerusalem, through this decision of the Holy Father.

Sufficit tibi gratia mea: "My grace is sufficient for you" (2 Cor 12:9). I have chosen to live out the new service that has been asked of me in the light of this biblical passage. All is grace, said a famous writer. The daily awareness of my weakness and my limitations is especially a grace, a true open door through which to this moment the mercy of God has passed.

And despite my weaknesses, I am astonished to see how the Lord nevertheless proceeds, visits, and acts through me with His work.

I started my service on the day on which the Church commemorated the birth of John the Baptist, and taking my inspiration from that great figure, I thought of the beginning of my ministry as an opportunity to "prepare the way . . . [to] open, smooth paths, free of all that impedes the encounter with Him and between us." And I added: "I would like a new grace to set out again from Jerusalem . . . for us and for the whole Church, the ability to meet one another and to welcome one another, by building roads and bridges and not walls."

I can only emphasize this intention once again. To welcome, to listen, to discern and, together, to guide the journey of the Church through the next few years.

I know that it will not be easy. I am not naive. After the joy of the Transfiguration, there is the descent from the mountain, into ordinary, everyday life, with its cargo of joy, certainly, but also of problems, sufferings, and divisions. And in Jerusalem and more generally in the Holy Land, there is no lack of divisions. And they are hard, a wound in our everyday life. We observe it continually: in political and social life, with a political conflict that is consuming everyone's life, in offended human dignity, in the lack of respect for basic human rights; we see it also in the intra-religious relations, between our Churches and also not infrequently within our respective Churches. The devil, who is at the origin of all divisions, seems to have taken up residence in Jerusalem.

Well, then, precisely in this very difficult context, which does not allow us to have any illusions, we are called to be Church, that is, to give our witness of unity. Here, in this torn and divided context, after all, the first proclamation to give is unity, which begins with us, within our own house.

In this context, I thank the Greek-Orthodox Patriarch of Jerusalem for his participation, through a delegate, in my episcopal consecration, and from now on I assure him of my desire to work for communion and mutual harmony. Indeed, we cannot venture to give the world lessons about dialogue if divisions and mistrust reign between us!

Jerusalem recalls Easter. At the Holy Sepulcher it is always *Pascha*. Pasch means Passover: from death to life, from darkness to light, from the discouragement of the apostles on the road to Emmaus to the impetus of the apostles on Pentecost. We can and must, then, become experts in a life that comes from the Cross, which is not resigned to death but conquers it with love.

I wish to carry out my service as a bishop, therefore, in the light of Easter. Given so many signals of death within and around us, I wish to accompany this Church of ours to reinterpret her own history, as Jesus did with the disciples on the road to Emmaus, in order to discover a Presence that never abandoned us and is the source of life everlasting. We should ask ourselves whether we truly believe this. Whether we truly think that Christ is the source of strength and light.

Indeed, our human strategies, which are often short of breath, are not what will save the Church and her institutions. Our greatness is not measured by the number of enterprises that we manage to start, nor by the degree of consensus that we obtain. All of that passes quickly. And perhaps we will have to ask ourselves whether we have spent too much energy and attention on something that, on the contrary, is only secondary. *Sufficit tibi gratia mea.* First of all we must seek and receive God's grace.

We must start from an awareness of Christ's presence in our midst. This awareness must be at the origin of our choices and projects. All the rest comes afterward.

I ask all of you to help me in this service.

To the lay people, to the families, to the men and women religious who perform such an important service in this Church of ours, to the priests and the bishops, and especially to the young, who are our future: I ask you to support me and to accompany me. I ask you to help me by your prayers, first of all, but also by joining me in finding the direction for the next phase of our community's journey.

I want the different souls that make up this Church of ours, which is one yet multiform, to collaborate more and more, and better and better. For this purpose, I wrote a few days ago to the priests of the Patriarchate:

> The Church of Jerusalem has a wealth of initiatives, institutions, and prestigious centers of theological and biblical scholarship (I am thinking of the Universities of Bethlehem and Madaba), men and women religious, movements, numerous schools that perform an important service and are a decisive pastoral sphere; we have unique and special relations with other Christian Churches, not to mention the necessity of coordinating with the Eastern Catholic Churches; the interreligious relation with Muslims and Jews is our daily bread, although it is never easy; the arrival of foreign workers and refugees has brought new dynamics into our Church, both in Jordan and in the Holy Land; in all our territories it is becoming difficult to offer care and follow-up to families, which are distancing themselves more and more from the Church; the presence of hundreds of thousands of pilgrims from all over the world then puts us in contact with the universal Church that continues to meet in Jerusalem as on the day of Pentecost; furthermore we cannot ignore the fact that we are in the Land where the Word of God was written and was fulfilled.

Look: for me, to be Church means to feel that we are all part of one body and sharers in one another. I hope that this sentiment is shared by you, too.

I want to be the bishop of all and for all. I hope for the full collaboration of all.

I thank you for having accompanied me this far with your prayers and participation. I have experienced very beautiful, intense moments that have comforted and consoled me. You have been God's comfort in recent months.

May God sustain our journey toward Him, may He open our eyes to the sufferings of this Land and of its inhabitants and make us capable of consolation and comfort.

My prayer and blessing is upon you all.

Beginning Again from Nazareth

Speech for the Solemn Entrance into the Basilica of the Annunciation, Nazareth

October 16, 2016

Most Reverend Excellencies, dear fathers, priests, brothers, and sisters,

May the peace of the Lord be with you!

It is particularly significant for me to enter Nazareth once again, the House of Mary, our Mother, the place of the "Yes" that changed human history.

I have been here many times, as you know. I am not new to this holy place and to the Christian community that has always been here.

Yet today, here, something new is starting for me, and also for all of you, for our whole community. Many times in these recent days I have thought about Mary's "yes", which she pronounced in this place. I come here today to ask, through Our Lady's intercession, that the strength and humility will be given to us to live profoundly the will of God, for us, for our families, and for our Christian community. In short, to live out our "yes" to the Lord.

I do not want to repeat what I have already expressed recently in other visits.

As I have already said, I am not new in the life of the Church in the Holy Land, but nevertheless I enter into a new vital and ministerial context, and I realize that I have much to learn. The welcome that I have received so far comforts and encourages me on the journey that awaits us, which our Church will have to travel.

Today's Gospel invites us to constant prayer, to stay in our relation with the Lord, to live faithfully in expectation of His coming, certain and assured of His presence and of His interventions in history. And Nazareth is a concrete example of how this is possible. In coming here to Nazareth, we wish, therefore, to place into God's hands our life and our history, that of our families and especially of our ecclesial community. It is from Nazareth that we must begin again. Like Mary at the announcement of the angel, we do not understand everything, we do not know everything, but we trust in Him, in the assurance that "nothing is impossible for God."

In short, we must not look only at the problems and difficulties, at the divisions and tensions that sometimes seem to submerge us in our respective contexts of life: familial, social, political, and also ecclesial. Let us lift up our eyes to Christ, let us allow Him to illumine our choices and actions; may He change our way of living in this world that is sometimes so hostile. If we start from the problems, we will never emerge from the discouragement. If we entrust ourselves to Christ, we will be able to build a solid community. This is the lesson that comes to us from Nazareth: to have confidence that even in this world of ours, in this reality of ours, it is possible to build something beautiful and positive together by remaining in God's will and by being completely available for His plan.

In this spirit, I place myself completely and without reservations at the service of this ecclesial community, in the assurance of the Lord's providential support and of your help. Indeed, I know your generosity and your passionate desire to serve the Church.

May the Lord, through Mary's intercession, give us strength for the journey and support us all, so that at His return He may find a land rich in faith.

May the Lord bless you!

The Surprises of God

Christmas Press Conference, Jerusalem

December 19, 2016

I want to thank you for your presence today, here at the Latin Patriarchate, and in the name of the universal Church I wish you a Christmas full of blessings, joy, and love! In our region, which is surrounded by wars, violence, and injustice, the Infant God whose birth we celebrate has much to teach us.

Advent, the time leading up to Christmas, is a time to prepare for God's surprises. We know who is coming, and we want to be ready to welcome Him in our hands and in our wide-open hearts. Two thousand years ago, He surprised us when He came to us as an infant, wrapped in swaddling clothes and laid in a manger. We commemorate this incredible Christmas gift to all humanity. But this is not just a time to remember; it is also a time to prepare ourselves, since we know that He will return and that He will probably surprise us again.

We need God's surprises. With these surprises, God widens our horizons and offers us the newness that can change our world and our lives. The year that is about to conclude was difficult, and more than ever, we need our horizons to be open and our hope revived.

The situation of the Christians in Syria, Iraq, and Egypt is a real tragedy. In these countries, the cradle of our civilization, the spiral of violence seems desperate and endless. All of us have seen the images of Aleppo last week but also those of the whole region during the long years of the conflict. Syria and Iraq have been destroyed. The wars and the use of force have not been able to bring peace and justice; they have only resulted in an increase of violence, death, and destruction. These terrible wars are blindly guided by the arms trade, by the interests of powerful players, and by ruthless fundamentalism. Peace needs negotiations and political solutions. Armies can win the war, but in order to build there is a need for politics, and at the moment we see no trace of it. In these wars there are many interests in play, but the poor and the weak are the ones who pay too high a price for it.

In our diocese, in Jordan, we have welcomed thousands of refugees, Christians who have chosen to remain faithful to their faith and also Muslims. They all fear for their lives. Their anguish, their thirst for peace must become ours.

In Egypt the Christian community is constantly threatened, as we saw incidentally one week ago with the attack in a church in Cairo; twenty-five persons were killed during Sunday Mass. It is time to lift up our eyes toward the Only One capable of saving us. We have our share of responsibility in these devastating tragedies: we cannot continue to limit ourselves to speaking about dialogue, justice, and peace. Words are no longer enough. We must fight against poverty and injustice; we must give a serious witness by works of mercy so as to show the world the love and tenderness of God.

Our situation in the Holy Land echoes that of the whole world, which finds itself confronted by growing extremism and fundamentalism. What strikes us is the fact that fundamentalism has taken root in the younger generations. During this past year we have deplored several acts of vandalism against Christians, churches, or cemeteries. We do not intend merely to lift up our voice to denounce these acts; we wish to collaborate in searching for solutions, confronting the root problems, by offering a better future to the younger generations. From our perspective, education is fundamental. This is the seed of a better future for all. However, our schools in Israel are still going through an unprecedented crisis, and so far no concrete solution has been offered.

Our future seems hazy. We lack a perspective. The persistent obstacles to peace in Israel and Palestine and the absence of dialogue and the lack of commitment to a true peace founded on justice and security are obvious. Because of the lack of unity and the lack of vision on both sides, hatred and violence seem to prevail over reason and dialogue. The false pretexts and the selfishness must be abandoned, politicians must look courageously at their people, who suffer and aspire to peace and justice for all. In Cremisan (near Bethlehem), the wall was built after a long struggle despite our repeated appeals to the Israeli authorities. The expropriation of the land of Christian families is a confiscation of their patrimony, of their heritage.

In Israel, too, as the universal Church, we welcome and care for thousands of foreign workers, many among them Christians. We seek to rebuild hope, once again with particular attention to the little ones and the defenseless. We recently opened a new nursery school for the children of migrants in Jerusalem.

Confronted by so many problems, we must take up our responsibilities; we must keep working to create a mindset of peace. Our local Church here in the Holy Land recognizes her own need for spiritual renewal and is entering into a period of reform in terms of organization, administration, and pastoral work.

Here we can lift up our eyes and see some light on the horizon. Pope Francis guides us and preaches the Good News.

On the international level, in the current political confusion, the pope is the only clear, prophetic voice that we can listen to and in which to place our trust. We can truly recognize his voice as that of the Good Shepherd. His message is universal.

The Year of Mercy that he has offered for us to experience has once again brought into focus our mission to strengthen confidence in the mercy of God, of the One who never grows weary of forgiving. God is the Father of all; He always waits for us and comes to meet us. With the other Churches, we must continue to work toward unity.

The restorations of Jesus' Tomb in Jerusalem and of the Church of the Nativity in Bethlehem, carried out thanks to the cooperation of different denominations, have shown us that only together can we build with our foundations on the rock. As Church, we will continue unceasingly to work with people of goodwill—Jews, Muslims, and nonbelievers—to build bridges, to help the poorest of the poor, to educate our children, to welcome the refugees and the homeless.

In conclusion, I would like to emphasize that, despite everything, we still have hope. This hope is the light that guides us in the darkness and confusion of this region and of the whole world.

Our broken hearts must be prepared for God's surprises. And Christmas is in fact the moment to renew our faith in the God of surprises by going to Bethlehem to adore this apparently powerless God: the Baby Jesus. In our prayers, let us carry—and we will do so without growing weary—this wounded world.

His Tomb Is Our Mirror

Speech at the Aedicule of the Holy Sepulcher After Restorations

March 22, 2017

Your Holiness, Your Beatitudes, Most Reverend Father, Your Excellencies, distinguished guests, dear friends, it is an honor for me, and a great joy, to join with His Beatitude the (Greek-Orthodox) Patriarch of Jerusalem, His Paternity [the Custos], and His Beatitude the Armenian Patriarch in this celebration of the reopening of the Holy Sepulcher of our Savior.[1]

I think that most of the inhabitants of Jerusalem and all those who are familiar with life in the Basilica of the Holy Sepulcher and, more generally, with life in Christian Jerusalem thought that it would be impossible to arrive at this moment. Often, when the pilgrims asked whether or when the Aedicule of the Holy Sepulcher could be restored, the usual answer was: "We will never see that day." Even in the discussions of the various Ecclesial Committees, such as that of the Status Quo, this objective was considered "unachievable". But now, despite common opinion, we are here

[1] When he was still Custos of the Holy Land, Pizzaballa had been signatory to the agreement to restore the Aedicule of the Holy Sepulcher, which is jointly owned by three Christian communities: Greek Orthodox, Catholics, and Armenians. Otherwise, he would not have been welcome to speak at this event, since—according to the strict norms of the Status Quo—neither the Latin Patriarch of Jerusalem nor a substitute acting for him (such as the apostolic administrator) plays an official role in the management of the Holy Places.

to celebrate this event! In the Gospel of Luke, the Archangel Gabriel says to the Blessed Virgin: "For with God nothing will be impossible" (Lk 1:37). Yes, if we stand with God, nothing is impossible. What appeared to be a "mission impossible" [the restoration of the Aedicule of the Holy Sepulcher] became possible because we allowed God to enlighten our thoughts, our eyes, and our relations. May the Lord be blessed in all those who "hear the word of God and keep it" (Lk 11:28).

Indeed, things do not change by themselves. The reason we are here is that the different Churches and those responsible for them were able to listen to the Word of God, to change their perspectives, and with their guidance, to lead everyone to understand, accept, and realize the fact that the moment had come to build. To build a new model of relations among all of us, based on trust and mutual respect. This restoration signals not only an important technical finish line, the end of an important professional work, but above all a new phase in our relations; it is the visible result of this construction that has just been restored, which is the life of the Church of Jerusalem. The Holy Sepulcher, in which all Christians commemorate the death and Resurrection of Our Lord Jesus Christ, is the guardian of our faith, but also of our respective histories, of our identities. It is the mirror of what we are. And while we see in this building the wounds that our historical divisions have created, today we also want to celebrate and show our desire to heal these wounds.

Today the Churches of Jerusalem, with the restoration of this material edifice, are putting oil and balm on the wounds of the one Body of Christ, which is the Church of believers and of peoples, like the women in the Gospel who had come to the Sepulcher to see "the tomb, and how his body was laid" (Lk 23:55) "and prepared spices and ointments" (Lk 23:56) for the Body of Christ. This cannot be the end of the work. We are only at the beginning. My hope, for you all, Your Beatitudes and Your Paternity, is that we Churches of Jerusalem can continue to rejoice together in this new approach we share as we see the restoration continue for all the other parts of this unique basilica, and can continue to rejoice at the same time in this new spirit in our relations. I am confident that, thanks to your leadership, you can overcome the inevitable problems and continue to give to us all this important, long-awaited witness to the Risen Lord. May the Lord bless all those who have the courage to "hear the word of God and do it" (Lk 8:21), here in our beloved Holy City of Jerusalem. Thank you!

A New Creation

Holy Week Greeting to the Custos of the Holy Land, Francesco Patton

April 12, 2017

Very Reverend Father, may the Lord grant you peace!

In a little while we will enter into the Sacred Triduum, three intense days with a great wealth of liturgies, rites, and processions through the various parts of the Holy City, which, in turn, will be invaded by Christian pilgrims from the different Churches, who celebrate together this year, and by many Jews who go up to the Holy City precisely in this week for their yearly pilgrimage and for the priestly blessing: a swarm of activities and persons that will transform the Holy City into a great, complicated, confusing, and certainly also a bit wearisome City of Prayer.

But the opportunity to be here will also be a great joy and a grace, despite the understandable but also inevitable difficulties. It is a grace because we will enter into the very life of Jesus, we will enter into the mystery of His death and finally of His Resurrection; through Him and from Him we will receive the Spirit of God, who will make us a new creation this year, too. And how we need to be a New Creation in this city where everything seems to repeat itself and to become crystallized, where fears of what is new, of what is different, and of the other person prevail over trust and giving; where, in short, the hardening of positions is a safe refuge and therefore also an excuse not to accept the challenge of trust and friendship, which instead could resolve many of our problems. We see this continually also in our little everyday initiatives, in our relations with the civil authorities, with the religious authorities, but also among our people and perhaps sometimes even among ourselves. "Why does he want to do it that way? What could be behind it?" How many times we hear these questions. To be new creatures, capable of newness of life—in order to do this, we also need to be able to die, to hand over our life, to surrender the old man that is in us. And perhaps this is the biggest difficulty: our little everyday securities, feelings of power, great and small, feelings of possession and belonging; it is troublesome for us to let them go. How much work we still have to do!

My hope, therefore, is this. That through our life of faith, and therefore also through our humanity and the service that we are all called to perform, we may have the courage to hand our life over to Christ and to let ourselves be enveloped by the strength of His love. For the Custody of the Holy Land, the Sacred Triduum is the climax of a liturgical service that starts much earlier, from the week preceding this one. I thank you in the name of the whole Church for your invaluable service of prayer and intercession that, day and night, is lifted up by the Holy City for the whole Universal Church to the Father of mercy, as the psalm says: "His delight is in the law of the LORD, and on his law he meditates day and night" (Ps 1:2); thanks also for your service to the pilgrims of the world who travel here with joy to draw water from the wells of salvation (see Is 12:3). May our spiritual Father, Saint Francis, who exactly eight hundred years ago sent his first companions here, intercede and support the friars today who in the Holy Land and in many other localities in the Middle East offer their service to the Church. May the Lord bless you!

Do We Believe?

Homily for Easter Sunday at the Church of the Holy Sepulcher

April 16, 2017

Dear Brothers and Sisters,

May the Lord's peace be with you!

Here we are gathered on the day so long awaited: the Lord's Passover and ours! Like Mary Magdalene and the Apostles John and Peter, today, we have also arrived at the Tomb of Christ to bow down before this mystery of His Resurrection, to welcome this extraordinary gift that is His life in us. During the entire week we have celebrated the beautiful and ancient liturgies that also intended to retrace even physically the human experience of Jesus in the same Places, especially in this very Place where He was buried.

And now that all these wonderful liturgies are about to end, it yet remains for us to ask ourselves what we have understood and what the many and meaningful gestures that accompanied us in these days have left with us. For many of us here present, perhaps, they have become moments that we take for granted, being by now used to the years of repetition of very familiar liturgies. For many pilgrims, though, they are exciting new experiences, precious memories to take home and share with their families and keep in their own heart. The joyous and exhausting confusion of these days, on which all the Christian communities celebrate the Paschal Mystery at the same time in this very Place according to their respective traditions, creates a festive and exceptional atmosphere. In short, everything tells us of something different and special, joyous and unique. Surely, the Paschal Mystery in Jerusalem is also this.

But also in Jerusalem, as in any other part of the world, today the mystery *par excellence*: the Resurrection, the core of our faith, is placed before our minds. The apostle Paul reminds us of it: "If Christ has not been raised, then our preaching is in vain and your faith is in vain" (1 Cor 15:14). Today, Jesus also addresses us with the same question that He put to Martha, which we heard a few days ago: "I am the resurrection and the life. . . . Do you believe this?" (Jn 11:25–26).

What have we understood of this mystery? Christ is risen, and He lives in us; how much has this awareness changed our lives? How crucial is it for our existence? We will soon proclaim around the tomb, at the restored Holy Aedicule, the Resurrection Gospels: four times, in four different locations (representing the four points of the compass), to signify the proclamation of this extraordinary event to the whole world, which has gone out from Here, from this Place, from Jerusalem, and has reached everywhere. But how much of what we are proclaiming is consciously lived?

Perhaps we have become accustomed to the idea of the Resurrection, to the point where we do not realize how shocking the significance of the empty tomb is. But speaking about it to our non-Christian neighbors among whom we live would be enough to make us realize what madness it is, according to a human way of thinking, to believe that there can be a resurrection.

And we still have today various modern forms of the Areopagus (see Acts 17:32), the various contexts where we Christians are welcomed, heard, and in demand, where our works and services are appreciated and desired. Where, in a word, what we do is a source of consolation and sharing, where our proclamation of solidarity with each person, our desire for peace, is shared and welcomed with joy. At the same time, though, wherever the Risen Christ is neither understood nor wanted, all that is of no interest and perhaps even annoying.

Yet this is our faith. This is our message: "He is not here; for he has risen, as he said. Come, see the place where he lay" (Mt 28:6). "Do not be amazed; you seek Jesus of Nazareth, who was crucified. He has risen, He is not here; see the place where they laid Him" (Mk 16:6).

It is a mystery that our minds cannot understand or explain. It can only be received and kept in the heart, with trust and love. It is an experience. "Then the other disciple, who reached the tomb first, also went in, and *he saw and believed*" (Jn 20:8, emphasis added). In the Gospel of John, to see means to experience. This kind of seeing involves all the senses, not sight alone. We see with the heart, too. And with a heart full of trust, bending our knees before the mystery of the empty tomb, we say, together with the evangelist Mark, "Lord, I believe; help my unbelief!" (Mk 9:24). Here we declare, despite our limitations and insecurities, "Yes, we believe!"

We believe that the Paschal Mystery is God's final, definitive intervention in history, for all. The most unexpected and most surprising one. We believe that after having saved us from nothingness, from slavery, from exile, God had to save us again from one last enemy, which is death, in other words, sin. We believe, and today we announce, that death is every place in life where God is absent, where man is unrelated to Him. This is the real failure in life. Life, in fact, is without meaning not when something is absent, when we experience pain or weariness, but rather when the Lord is absent, when we are alone, without Him. Death is found where God is not Father, where He is not the source of life. Where we are unable to make room for Him.

And today, we believe and announce that God the Father has made room for Himself in the life of each one of us, forever. The Resurrection is His life breaking into ours.

We believe that there is no longer any place where the Father is not present; not even death is such a place now. Death cannot hold Jesus, because Jesus belongs to the Father, because this relationship is stronger than everything and remained alive even in death.

The bandages and the face cloth are not wrapped around Jesus, but are folded by themselves, because Jesus is not shrouded by death: He is enveloped by the life that the Father gives Him. For this reason, today the disciples go to the sepulcher but do not find anything, except the now useless bandages (see Jn 20:6–7). In John, there are no explicit prophecies about the Passion and Resurrection, as in the other Synoptic Gospels. But Jesus had said repeatedly that the "place" of His life is the Father, that He came from Him and was returning to Him; that the final stage would not be the sepulcher, but the life of the Father. With this certainty, Jesus enters into death. He enters into it with this trust, a dramatic trust; in Gethsemane and on the Cross we saw that it was the result of a very hard struggle. But Jesus never fails to turn to the Father; this relationship remains steadfast even when He is betrayed and left alone, even when life is slipping away. Even when the Father seems to be absent, Jesus remains confident and goes all the way in giving life, in doing the Father's will, in making His own life, His own will coincide with His Father's.

At the same point where man had sinned and had believed that God was giving Him death and not life, there Jesus believes that the Father is giving him life and not death.

For Jesus, death is entrusting His life to the Father. It is not entrusting it to nothingness, it is not throwing it away, it is not despising it, but rather returning it completely to the One who gave Him this life, Who is its infinite source, Who guards it, and Who finally restores it.

Today, we are saying that we believe all this.

But what does this faith actually mean for us, little believers of today? What does the Paschal Mystery say to us?

It says that the fullness of relationship that exists between the Father and the Son, from that Easter morning, is also ours. Before then, this was not possible, because death remained the place where trust in the Father had not yet entered, where the man was still alone. Now we, too, are enveloped by the life of the Father, because Jesus, in giving the Spirit, gives us this relationship between Him and the Father.

So, really, there is no place in our existence, in our history, that cannot be potentially a dwelling place of God, a place of encounter with Him. There is no place in the life of each of us where He cannot be present. Because this relationship, the fact that we are His children, is our salvation.

This knowledge does not exempt us from the experience of trial, pain, and darkness. All of this remains, but is no longer a condemnation: an ingredient in each of these situations can be trust that God is with us, that He can draw life even from them. That even there He will give life, not death.

Think for a moment about all the situations of death that surround us: indeed, it is enough to look around, and we will have reason to worry and to feel overwhelmed by death, by its victories and stings (see 1 Cor 15:55). Without going too far, think of the terrible situations in which neighboring populations find themselves: Syria, Iraq, and Yemen. The life that we celebrate here today is cynically and arrogantly despised and humiliated there every day.

Allow me to say a word here and a reminder to our Coptic brothers who, once again, a week ago, were dreadfully massacred in Egypt—in Tanta and in Alexandria. It is a deadly situation, a desire for death, for which many people in our countries seem to thirst today; in those circumstances it seems that in social and religious relations hatred and contempt prevail over everything, and so human, religious, and civil respect have become empty words: the other is the enemy to be destroyed, there is no place for him. Even before being a physical death, it is a moral and spiritual death. Woe to us if we surrender to all this! But precisely in these circumstances with gratitude we see the strength of life. Those Christian brethren of ours have not embraced the same death wish, and they remain open, with serene confidence, to every collaboration. With all. No word of hatred and contempt. No violent reaction, but only the serene and rightly steadfast desire for justice. The death of those martyrs has not erased the strength of that community's life! Palm Sunday for them was already Passover!

But even here in our Holy Land, the shadow of death is not absent: the wounds in the geography of the country and in the life of our people are too many to count. Justice and peace have become slogans devoid of all credibility. Our families are divided. Talking about hope seems like talking nonsense; it seems to be detached from reality. Overall, there is fear and mistrust: between members of different faiths, between the different communities, within our own communities and families we see continual divisions of all kinds, based on the fear of others, on the fear of losing something, on the fear of dying or of giving life. And when we act like this, we hand ourselves over instead to death and to its power.

But if we really believe in the Resurrection, if we believe in the power of the Spirit, in the power of the Word, if we entrust all these situations to Him, if we make them become a request, a prayer, a cry, then these same situations will become a way of life.

The experience of the Resurrection cannot be understood unless this same experience is shared, unless it becomes a life that is lived, experienced, and proclaimed.

In today's second reading from the Letter to the Colossians (3:2), there is an expression that is difficult to translate, and it is translated in different ways in different languages. "Think on the things that are above," our version reads; others say, "Set your heart on the things above," and so on. I like the Latin translation of this verse: "*Quae sursum sunt sapite*." *Sapite! Taste* the things that are above. It tells us that we need to be rooted here in this land, immersed and totally embodied here, passionately loving this world that God has handed over to us and the human beings who inhabit it, but at the same time we must have a different taste. The taste of the Resurrection, of those who do not belong to death, but to a freedom that cannot be taken away from us, from those who belong to the Father of life, before whom death is powerless.

Therefore, let us not retreat or shut ourselves away in our fears. Let us not allow death and its subjects to frighten us. That would be to deny, by our way of life, our faith in the Resurrection!

And let us not restrict ourselves either to venerating this empty tomb. The Resurrection is the proclamation of a new joy that bursts into the world and cannot remain locked up in this Place, but from here must go forth to everyone even today.

"Go, tell his disciples and Peter that he is going before you" (Mk 16:7).

"Where? Everywhere. In Galilee and on the mountain, in the Upper Room and along the road to Emmaus: on the sea and in the deserts, wherever man pitches his tent, breaks his bread, builds his cities, crying and singing, sighing and cursing: 'He is going before you.'" (Don Primo Mazzolari).

This is my sincere wish for all of us. That it may be granted to us to celebrate in everyday life the Easter that we celebrate today in this Eucharist.

Christ is Risen! He is truly Risen, Alleluia.

No Jerusalem Without Christians

Speech of Welcome to Israel's President Reuven Rivlin, Jerusalem

April 19, 2017

Dear Mister President,

May the peace of the Lord be with you!

It is with great joy that we welcome you to our house.

It is a longstanding custom, now part of the official Status Quo, that the President of Israel receives in audience the leaders of the Christian Churches in his residence toward the end of the civil year, during the Christmas festivities, so as to offer his greetings to the Christian communities. It is always an important and interesting occasion, during which we have the opportunity to meet also representatives of the communities that otherwise we would not see so frequently.

In the last three years, you started a new tradition. You decided to return our Christmas visit and to meet all of us in our respective houses. I want to thank you for this sensitivity to the Christian presence in the Holy City and in Israel in general. It is nothing new for us to observe your interest in the Christian presence in Jerusalem. We know that you belong to a family that has its own roots in the Holy City and that it is familiar with the different local traditions and their respective communities, including ours. Moreover, we have appreciated your solidarity and your clear words about the Christians on various occasions. To mention just one, the twofold visit to the Tabgha site in Galilee, after the sad incidents a few years ago.[1]

[1] The reference is to the arson in June 2015 that damaged the Benedictine Church of the Multiplication of the Loaves and Fishes.

It is important to meet the Christian communities, especially here in Jerusalem. It is true: numerically we are not very large. But we are nevertheless an integral part of the identity of this city; without our presence, Jerusalem could not be the same city. Jerusalem is that "house of prayer for all peoples" (Is 56:7), and without this little but deep-rooted community, it would lose its universal character.

During Holy Week, the days leading up to Easter, almost all the Churches walk through the streets of the Holy City from one end to the other: from the Mount of Olives to the wall of the old city; from the Cenacle to Gethsemane; along the Via Dolorosa to the Holy Sepulcher, and so on. This year, moreover, all the Christian communities celebrated Easter on the same day. In a joyous confusion that is typical of Jerusalem, we saw simultaneously our local communities mixed in with people coming from all over the world, from Egypt to the island of Mauritius, from Europe to the Far East, from the Americas to Russia. Jerusalem was a collection of persons of different colors, customs, languages, traditions, and liturgies that is impossible to find anywhere else in the world. Furthermore, this year Easter almost coincides with the Jewish Passover. The Christian processions during Holy Week very often went through the streets together with thousands of Israelis who had arrived in the Holy City for their pilgrimage. Despite some inevitable logistical problems, it was amusing, and at the same time fascinating, to see the Israeli policeman—who had come here to help the local force keep public order during the Jewish feast days—who was trying to bring order to the processions of Christian pilgrims in the old city. To watch the agent when he tried to guess what for him must be a great mystery: distinguishing a Catholic from an Orthodox so as to decide then in what direction to send him. Without forgetting, at the same time, to direct the Jews to the Kotel and the Muslims to the mosques, all of them astounded and impressed by our strange liturgical vestments, which they had never seen before. These colorful scenes of life in Jerusalem are unique and must be preserved. Yes, it is important to preserve and to safeguard in Jerusalem the presence of the Christian Churches, communities, and traditions.

The fact that you decided to call on us, despite our small numbers, as I said, makes your visit even more appreciated. We count on your support.

This is not the moment to speak about our problems. We will have other opportunities to speak about our concerns. Not here. Not now.

At Easter, on this occasion, we want to celebrate, like the Jewish Passover, the feast of feasts, the feast of the deliverance from Egypt and from slavery. You teach me that the liberation from Egypt for the people of Israel and also for us Christians has become the image of deliverance from any form of oppression. For us it is the definitive deliverance from the power of sin and death, through the Resurrection of Jesus.

It was not easy to tell our people, after the massacre in Tanta and in Alexandria, Egypt, right at the beginning of this Holy Week, that Jesus conquered death and its power over mankind. And it was not easy to speak about deliverance from slavery, when we see the images of Syria and of other neighboring countries and in general the many difficulties that our communities are experiencing today.

But this is our faith. There is no faith without hope. And Christian hope is already an assurance. Yes, today we are free. Despite the violence and the persecutions, we are free. The freedom that I speak about does not come from outside; it is not granted to us by others. Without disregarding the importance of the social dimension of freedom, during the Easter season we celebrate the freedom that God granted us as Son of God. It is an attitude, it is a heartfelt assurance that no one can take away from us. Not even death has a power so great. This is what we celebrate and will continue to celebrate, despite the death that is around us.

Mister President, once again, thank you for your visit and your support.

May the Lord bless you in your effort to be an element of unity among the different souls of the country that you represent so well. We will continue to pray for you, for your mission, and for your important service to the whole community.

Christ is risen. Truly He is risen.

APPENDIX
We Must Not Be Afraid
2020–2025

On October 24, 2020, after four years as apostolic administrator, Pierbattista Pizzaballa was consecrated as Latin Patriarch of Jerusalem. He was installed as a cardinal on September 30, 2023, just a week before the October 7 attacks took place in Gaza, a part of his diocese. The militant group Hamas killed some 1,200 Israelis and took around 250 hostages, provoking what is now known as the Gaza War. According to Reuters, one week later, Cardinal Pizzaballa offered his own life in exchange for the release of the hostages. "There is total willingness on my part," he said. The war has radically transformed life in Israel.

Letter to the Patriarchate of Jerusalem After the October 7 Attacks

October 24, 2023

Dear Brothers and Sisters,

May the Lord give you peace!

We are going through one of the most difficult and painful periods in our recent times and history. For over two weeks now, we have been inundated with images of horrors, which have reawakened ancient traumas, opened new wounds, and made pain, frustration, and anger explode within all of us. Much seems to speak of death and endless hatred. So many "whys" overlap in our minds, adding to our sense of bewilderment.

The whole world views this Holy Land of ours as a place that is a constant cause of wars and divisions. That is precisely why it was good that a few days ago, the whole world joined us with a day of prayer and fasting for peace. It was a beautiful view of the Holy Land and an important moment of unity with our Church. And that view is still there. The pope has called for a second day of prayer and fasting on October 27, so that our intercession may continue. It will be a day that we will celebrate with conviction. It is perhaps the main thing we Christians can do at this time: pray, do penance, intercede. For this, we thank the Holy Father from the bottom of our hearts.

This letter was issued to the faithful of the Latin Patriarchate of Jerusalem two weeks after the October 7 attacks by Hamas in Israel's Gaza Envelope, 2023.

In all this uproar, where the deafening noise of the bombs is mixed with the many voices of sorrow and the many conflicting feelings, I feel the need to share with you a word that has its origin in the Gospel of Jesus. That is the starting point from which we set out, and to which we return, time and time again: a word from the Gospel to help us live this tragic moment by uniting our feelings with those of Jesus.

Looking to Jesus, of course, does not mean feeling exempt from the duty to speak, to denounce, to call out, as well as to console and encourage. As we heard in last Sunday's Gospel, it is necessary to render "to Caesar the things that are Caesar's, and to God the things that are God's" (Mt 22:21). Looking to God, we therefore want, first of all, to render to Caesar what is his.

My conscience and moral duty require me to state clearly that what happened on October 7 in southern Israel is in no way permissible, and we cannot but condemn it. There is no reason for such an atrocity. Yes, we have a duty to state this and to denounce it. The use of violence is not compatible with the Gospel, and it does not lead to peace. The life of every human person has equal dignity before God, who created us all in His image.

The same conscience, however, with a great burden on my heart, leads me to state with equal clarity today that this new cycle of violence has brought to Gaza over five thousand deaths, including many women and children, tens of thousands of wounded, neighborhoods razed to the ground, lack of medicine, lack of water and of basic necessities for over two million people. These are tragedies that cannot be understood and that we have a duty to denounce and condemn unreservedly. The continuous heavy bombardment that has been pounding Gaza for days will only cause more death and destruction and will only increase hatred and resentment. It will not solve any problem, but rather create new ones. It is time to stop this war, this senseless violence.

It is only by ending decades of occupation and its tragic consequences, as well as by giving a clear and secure national perspective to the Palestinian people, that a serious peace process can begin. Unless this problem is solved at its root, there will never be the stability we all hope for. The tragedy of these days must lead us all, religious, political, civil society, international community, to a more serious commitment in this regard than we have had so far. This is the only way to avoid other tragedies like the one we are experiencing now. We owe it to the many victims of these days and to those of years past. We do not have the right to leave this task to others.

Yet, I cannot live this extremely painful time without looking upward, without looking to Christ, without the faith that enlightens my view and yours on what we are experiencing, without turning our thoughts to God. We need a Word to accompany us, to comfort and encourage us. We need it like the air we breathe.

"I have said this to you, that in me you may have peace. In the world you have tribulation; but be of good cheer, I have overcome the world" (Jn 16:33).

We find ourselves on the eve of Jesus' Passion. He addresses these words to His disciples, who will shortly be tossed about, as if in a storm, before His death. They will panic, scatter, and flee, like sheep without a shepherd.

Yet, this last word of Jesus is an encouragement. He does not say that He shall win, but rather that He has already won. Even in the turmoil to come, the disciples will be able to have peace. This is not a matter of theoretical irenic peace, or of resignation to the fact that the world is evil and we can do nothing to change it. Instead, it is about having the assurance that precisely within all this evil, Jesus has already won. Despite the evil ravaging the world, Jesus has achieved a victory and established a new reality, a new order, which after the Resurrection will be assumed by the disciples who were reborn in the Spirit.

It was on the Cross that Jesus won: not with weapons, not with political power, not by great means, nor by imposing himself. The peace He speaks of has nothing to do with victory over others. He won the world by loving it. It is true that a new reality and a new order begin on the Cross. The order and the reality of the one who gives His life out of love. With the Resurrection and the gift of the Spirit, that reality and that order belong to His disciples. To us. God's answer to the question of why the righteous suffer is not an explanation, but a Presence. It is Christ on the Cross.

It is on this that we stake our faith today. Jesus in that verse rightly speaks of courage. Such peace, such love, require great courage.

To have the courage of love and peace here, today, means not allowing hatred, revenge, anger, and pain to occupy all the space of our hearts, of our speech, of our thinking. It means making a personal commitment to justice, being able to affirm and denounce the painful truth of injustice and evil that surrounds us, without letting it pollute our relationships. It means being committed, being convinced that it is still worthwhile to do all we can for peace, justice, equality, and reconciliation. Our speech must not be about death and closed doors. On the contrary, our words must be creative, life-giving; they must give perspective and open horizons.

It takes courage to be able to demand justice without spreading hatred. It takes courage to ask for mercy, to reject oppression, to promote equality without demanding uniformity, while remaining free. It takes courage today, even in our diocese and our communities, to maintain unity, to feel united to one another, even in the diversity of our opinions, sensitivities, and visions.

I want, and we want, to be part of this new order inaugurated by Christ. We want to ask God for that courage. We want to be victorious over the world, taking upon ourselves that same Cross, which is also ours, made of pain and love, of truth and fear, of injustice and gift, of cries and forgiveness.

I pray for us all, and in particular for the small community of Gaza, which is suffering most of all. In particular, our thoughts go out to the eighteen brothers and sisters who perished recently and to their families, whom we know personally.[1] Their pain is great, and yet with every passing day, I realize that they are at peace. They are scared, shaken, upset, but with peace in their hearts. We are all with them, in prayer and concrete solidarity, thanking them for their beautiful witness.

Finally, let us pray for all innocent victims. The suffering of the innocent before God has a precious and redemptive value because it is united with the redemptive suffering of Christ. May their suffering bring peace ever closer!

We are approaching the solemnity of the Queen of Palestine, the patroness of our diocese. The shrine was erected during another time of war and was chosen as a special place to pray for peace. In these days we will once again reconsecrate our Church and our land to the Queen of Palestine! I ask all churches around the world to join the Holy Father and to join us in prayer and in the search for justice and peace.

[1] On October 19, 2023, the Orthodox Church of Saint Porphyrius was bombed in an Israeli airstrike, killing eighteen Palestinian civilians.

We will not be able to gather all together this year, because the situation does not allow it. But I am sure that the whole diocese will be united on that day in prayer and in solidarity for peace, not worldly peace, but the peace that Christ gives us.

Characteristics and Criteria of a Pastoral Care of Peace

Speech at the Pontifical Lateran University, Rome

May 7, 2024

Introduction

Thank you for your invitation, which is an honor. I am grateful to your venerable institution, with which we have been in collaboration for many years now, thanks to the fact that the Latin Patriarchate's theologate has been granted affiliation with your department of theology. I consider this link between Rome and Jerusalem of fundamental importance for the Church today. I also take this opportunity to extend my best wishes to the new Magnificent Rector, Msgr. Amarante, the new Pro-Rector, Msgr. Ferri, and the new Dean of Theology, Msgr. Lameri.

What is happening in the Holy Land is an unprecedented tragedy. In addition to the seriousness of the increasingly deteriorating military and political context, the religious and social context is also deteriorating. The dividing lines between communities are deepening; the few but important contexts of interreligious and civil coexistence are gradually disintegrating. Instead, an attitude of distrust is growing progressively by the day. A bleak landscape. There is certainly no lack of hope among the many people who still, despite everything, want to work for reconciliation and peace. But we must realistically recognize that these are niche realities and that the overall picture remains very worrying.

In addition to binding me even more to the flock I shepherd, this tragedy provoked countless reflections on peace. Today, can one still "think of peace" in the Holy Land? "Peace" seems to be a distant, utopian word empty of content, if not the object of endless manipulation. Not infrequently, the same people who are in favor of peace end their speeches by saying that to reach it, war is inevitable.

Our land is still bleeding, and our people are in the grip of fear and uncertainty of the future. Many, too many, have only rubble in front of them.

The theme you have proposed to me for this lecture—"Characteristics and Criteria for a Pastoral Care of Peace"—can only be briefly presented here, without exhaustive intentions. My task here, as I understand it, is not to make a discourse and propose general criteria for building contexts of peace or concrete paths of possible peace. The paths and criteria, as we know, are many: besides religious ones, there are economic, political, social, media, and educational ones. They are closely related to the concepts of memory, identity, and much more. That is to say, it is a very broad topic. This will not be the scope of my presentation, but rather an introduction based on my experience as a pastor in the Holy Land. Starting from my own experience, I will try to indicate some criteria on which the Church of the Holy Land should base her action for peace, in this specific context, which today has become the focus of attention throughout the world, as well as a source of division in many other parts of the world.

1. Looking at the Face of God

First, I think it is important to clarify why peace is a central theme for the life of the Church and her actions in the world.

The first peculiarity of peace is that it, before being a human project conforming to the divine will, *is a gift from God; indeed, it says something about God Himself: Adonài shalòm*, "The Lord is peace" (Judg 6:24).[1] As is well known, the Hebrew *shalom*, as indeed its Arabic counterpart *salaam*, indicates much more than a warless sociopolitical situation: it expresses the "fullness of life", which acts as an integral approach. It is thus not just a human construction or an achievement of human coexistence, but rather a reality that comes from God and a relationship with Him: it is the fulfillment of the Messianic promises (see Is 2:2–5; 11:6–9). Jesus Christ, the Messiah, is *Sar shalòm*, "Prince of Peace" (Is 9:6); he is "our peace", the one who has broken down the barrier between men, the wall of enmity that was between them (Eph 2:14–16).

From Jerusalem resounded the cry of the Risen One that reached to the ends of the earth: "Peace be with you" (Jn 20:19). Not by chance is this the first word of the Risen One to the apostles and women gathered in the Upper Room, and as new and risen men, it must also be our first and last word. It is not a "worldly peace"—Christ says—but "my peace" (Jn 14:27). Therefore, "our peace" comes from "His peace", for He gives us Himself, who died and rose again for us. The heart of peace is the Paschal Mystery of Christ. It is precisely by this mystery that peace, which is Christ, becomes at the same time reconciliation with God and between people. For this reason, it must be forcefully reiterated today that all pastoral action of the Church, as indeed all her social work, can never in any way be separated from evangelization:[2] the proclamation of the Gospel is the

[1] See *Compendium of the Social Doctrine of the Church* (Rome: Libreria Editrice Vaticana, 2004), no. 488.

[2] See *Compendium of the Social Doctrine of the Church*, no. 493

proclamation of the "gospel of peace" (Eph 6:15), and he who evangelizes proclaims peace even to his enemies, just as Peter did to Cornelius, who was—and we should never forget this in these times!—centurion of the military forces occupying his land (see Acts 10:36).

This first and exquisitely theological peculiarity of peace provides us with the first and basic criterion for peace: to look upon the face of God. This criterion was pointed out by Pope Saint Paul VI when, while he was busy concluding the Council, he wanted to call the people back to peace, not by chance, on the feast of Saint Francis of Assisi, on October 4, 1965, before the representatives of 116 nations, in the United Nations glass building in New York. The importance of this speech comes from the fact that no pope in history had ever delivered a peace speech in person before the diplomatic representatives of the world's highest assembly. At the end of his speech, the Pope, with great parochial and prophetic spirit, called the nations to base peace on faith and conversion to God:

> The edifice you are building does not rest on purely material and terrestrial foundations, for in that case it would be a house built on sand. It rests most of all upon consciences. Yes, the time has come for "conversion," for personal transformation, for interior renewal. . . . The real danger comes from man, who has at his disposal ever more powerful instruments that are as well-fitted to bring about ruin as they are to achieve lofty conquests. To put it in a word, the edifice of modern civilization has to be built on spiritual principles, for they are the only ones capable not only of supporting it, but of shedding light on it and inspiring it. And we are convinced, as you know, that these indispensable principles of higher wisdom cannot rest on anything but faith in God.[3]

[3] Paul VI, Address to the United Nations, October 4, 1965.

This implies two things, which always go hand in hand: being aware of one's weakness and seeing God's face. There is a passage in the book of Genesis, which I always like to recall, indicating how one recognizes God's face. I refer to the well-known episode of Jacob in his struggle with a mysterious personage on the banks of the Jabbok, on his journey to meet his brother Esau, with whom a reckoning is coming. In that singular struggle, Jacob recognizes the face of God, so much so that he calls the place of struggle Peniel, the "face of God". From that troubled night he emerges limping, but confessing, "I have seen God face to face!" (Gen 32:31). He emerges defeated but victorious, limping but leaning on God. Only by limping can Jacob go to meet his brother-enemy: Esau embraces him, and the two weep. At this point, Jacob addresses Esau with one of the most beautiful phrases in the Bible, sometimes inadequately translated and which I, therefore, render literally: "To see your face is for me like seeing the face of God" (Gen 33:10). Only when we have experienced our weakness and, in this, have encountered the face of God are we ready to go out to meet the brother-enemy. If we do not go to meet the other with a limp, we constantly risk opening scenarios of war, because the other is no longer a fellow man, but an enemy, to be feared or eliminated.

In the Bible, however, there is also the opposite, confrontational perspective. Indeed, the book of the prophet Obadiah describes the dark side of that relationship, declaring to Edom, the descendants of Esau: "For the violence done to your brother Jacob, shame shall cover you, and you shall be cut off forever!" (Obad 1:10) Hence, the same prophet's exhortation, as relevant today as ever: "You should not have gloated over the day of your brother, in the day of his misfortune" (Obad 1:12).

2. *Looking at the Face of the Other Person*

What we have just affirmed leads us to the second characteristic of peace: in addition to being a divine reality, it is a human and social reality, *a universal value, and an inescapable duty that calls all to act*, on the pain of man's self-destruction. However, peace on an anthropological level is not just a social convention, armistice, mere truce, or absence of war, the result of diplomatic efforts and global or local geopolitical balances, which in the Holy Land are unfortunately collapsing! Of course, under the current conditions, that would be eminent! Yet, peace is much more: it is based on the truth of the human, which alone can lead to an authentic *tranquillitas ordinis*, "the tranquility of order" (see Augustine, *City of God*, bk. 19, ch. 13, no. 1), because it is established according to justice and charity.

And here, then, is the second criterion: *put man back at the center, return to the face of the other, to the centrality of the human person and his unparalleled dignity.* When the face of the other fades away, so does the face of God and, thus, true peace. Only in the context of integral human development, with respect for human rights, can a true culture of peace be born and the "unarmed prophets, who are often the objects of ridicule",[4] arise as witnesses and pillars of peace. The world needs them more than ever, even at the cost of being persecuted and branded as utopians and visionaries. For peace, one must always take risks. One must be willing to lose honor, to die like Jesus.

Jewish philosopher Emmanuel Lévinas stated, "In the simple encounter of a man with the Other, the essential, the absolute is at stake. In the manifestation, in the 'epiphany'

[4] *Compendium of the Social Doctrine of the Church*, no. 496.

of the face of the Other I discover that the world is mine insofar as I can share it with the Other. And the absolute is played out in proximity, within reach of my gaze, within reach of a gesture of complicity or aggression, of welcome or rejection."[5] No one is an island: when we destroy the face of the other, we also dissolve our own, especially in the era of global interconnectedness in which we live. If we sink, we will sink together, in the same boat, because we are more than ever in a global village.

3. The Church's Mission

After this brief look at the theological and human aspects of peace, we must now come more directly to the topic you have proposed and ask how this dimension is expressed in the life of the Church. How is the Church called to give such proclamation and witness? As I said at the beginning, I will limit myself here to sketching a thought about the Church of Jerusalem, based on my personal experience, with no presumption.

For a long time now, our Church has been reflecting on this war-torn context of ours; a reflection that is constructive and at the same time true, real, and does not fall into discounted slogans or obvious platitudes. The conflict with its consequences involves the lives of everyone in our diocese and is therefore an integral part of the life of the Church, of her pastoral care. Everything we are and do has to do directly and indirectly with the conflict and its consequences, from the more practical aspects to the increasingly heated

[5] Quoted in "Includere per comunicare", in *Educazione, comunicazione e lingua dei segni*, ed. Elena Causa and Loredana Scursatone (Varazze: PM Edizioni, 2017), 14.

reflection on more complex issues: from closed borders and crossings, permits given and not given, to reflection on occupation and the possible Christian response to it. What I mean to say is that conflict is not a temporary and secondary issue in the life of our Church, but is now an integral and constitutive part of our identity as a church: conflict and division, with the consequences of hatred and resentment, are an ordinary reality with which we have to reckon and which requires on the part of the Christian community a continuous journey of reflection and spiritual, pastoral, and social elaboration. To speak of peace, therefore, is, for us, to speak not of an abstract theme, but of a deep wound in the life of the Christian community, which causes suffering and weariness and touches the human and spiritual life of all of us deeply.

I don't know if we have been able to arrive at a synthesis in the interpretation of this theme, probably not yet. I think that for us the reflection regarding the witness on peace will always be a work in progress; we will never have a complete and conclusive discourse, but we will have to reckon with the continuous developments of the various political frameworks that gradually form and unravel, and the consequences they have for the lives of the peoples of the Holy Land. Situations that question our faith, time and time again. And perhaps this is not even the time for synthesis, but rather for listening. Listening to the different voices, feelings, visions, labors, and hopes, and trying to read them in the light of the Gospel. However, striving to identify some common features, characteristics, and criteria that will still have to accompany our reflection permanently.

In fact, we cannot fail to ask ourselves how to live out peace in Jerusalem, a city called to be the custodian of peace, but continually torn and embattled.

For us, the Church of the Holy Land, set in the context of a multi-religious and multi-cultural society, rich in diversity but also divisions, the "peace of Jerusalem" of which Psalm 122 speaks, is not the suppression of differences, the annulment of distances, but neither is it a truce or a pact of non-belligerence guaranteed by pacts and walls. We are convinced that it is based on a cordial and sincere acceptance of the other, on a tenacious willingness to listen and dialogue, that our community is called to be an open road on which fear and suspicion give way to knowledge, encounter, and trust, where differences are opportunities for companionship and collaboration and not a pretext for war.

We will increasingly have to move away from the preoccupation with occupying physical and institutional structures and focus more on beautiful and good dynamics of life that, as believers, we can initiate. Of course, sometimes even for us the temptations of flight and resignation, easy compromise with power, or violent response may appear as the only possible reaction to the difficult time we are given to live in.

However, as believers and religious, we will be an "interesting" presence to the extent that our prophecy will be our daily witness, because in a social and political context where overwhelm, closure, and violence seem to be the only possible words, we will continue to affirm the way of encounter and mutual respect as the only way that can lead to peace.

Peace needs the witness of clear and strong gestures by all believers, but it also needs to be proclaimed and defended by spoken words.

For this reason, we often find ourselves at a crossroads, almost called upon to choose between the necessary denunciation of violence and abuse, always perpetrated to the detriment of the weakest, and the risk of reducing religion to a "political agent" or even to a party or faction, forgetting its true nature and exposing it to easy and superficial exploitation. Our being in the Holy Land as believers cannot be enclosed in devotional "intimism", nor can it limit itself only to the service of charity for the poorest, but it is also parochial, that is, it cannot refrain from expressing, in the ways proper to each religious experience, a judgment on the world and its dynamics (see Jn 16:8, 11). We know well how politics envelops ordinary life in all its aspects in the Middle East. Everything becomes politics, and this seriously questions all our religious institutions and our faithful, who await from us a word of hope, of consolation, but also of truth. What is required here is a truly difficult discernment that has never been achieved once and for all, requiring the ability to listen to all voices, but also to interpret critically, and therefore also prophetically, the present.

We cannot remain silent in the face of injustice or invite quietude and disengagement. However, the preferential option for the poor and weak does not make us a political party. Taking a stand, as we are often asked to do, cannot mean becoming part of a confrontation, but must always translate into words and actions on behalf of those who suffer and groan and not into slogans and condemnation against anyone. It may be easy and convenient at times to join the chorus of criticism and recrimination, and we may even gain applause and approval, but this may be a worldly temptation. In short, as believers we are called to love and serve the polis and to share with all concern and action for the common good, in the general interest of all and especially the poor, always raising our voices to defend the rights of God and man, but without entering the logic of competition and division.

Now that I have laid down these premises, the question

to be asked is this: How do we live like this, what are the needed characteristics and criteria, the elements on which to base this style of ours, this way of being in the Holy Land, as Christians and as a church? What are the elements that must stably accompany our Christian reflection on peace, the criteria that must support our interpretation of the present situation? What are the areas of action on which to base a solid and credible ecclesial pastoral for peace? Of course, there are many, and always evolving, as I mentioned earlier. What we call a pastoral ministry of peace is no different from any other pastoral activity: it needs people, it needs a specific methodology and clear spiritual foundations on which to base its action: on what, about what, and for what to work.

Leadership

In the context we have sketched above, the responsibility of religious leadership, especially in the Middle East, is essential. First, it is necessary to have guides, pastors, and leaders capable of listening and being the voice of their community and directing and guiding.

Instead of being the religious support of political regimes with little credibility, religious leadership should, first of all, cooperate with the best part of society in creating a new culture of legality and become a free and prophetic voice of justice, human rights, and peace. As we stated at the beginning, these values are not only human values, but first and foremost an expression of God's desire for man. As religious leadership, our contribution to resilience and innovation amid today's enormous local challenges is not to reinvent the wheel—that is, to find new and modern operational strategies—but to be credible, sincere, and passionate witnesses of God ourselves.

I wonder if in the actions and words I use, I fear God more or the reaction of people, politicians, the media . . . In addressing my community, do I have the "courage" of *parrhesia*, of guidance? Do I open new horizons? Or do I simply weigh my words so as not to be disruptive to anyone?

This is not a trivial issue. I would say it is central. Especially in these contexts of pain and disorientation, in a context where religion plays such a prominent public role, one must never stop asking oneself whether and how faith can orient one's community, to invite it to question itself, without settling down. Faith must be a comfort, a support, but also in a sense a disturbing element. If faith is based on an experience of transcendence, it must also lead thinking to transcend the present moment, open the boundaries of mind and heart, and go beyond.

In Deuteronomy 30:15, God says, "See, I have set before you this day life and good, death and evil." We must take note therefore that one can fail to choose life and good, and we see this every day. However, we must also ask ourselves how to stand before those who make those choices of evil and death, and what is the right attitude of a believer toward those responsibilities. How should religious leaders act and behave in those specific situations, what kind of guidance should they give to their communities regarding not some generic evil, but regarding who perpetrates this evil, and how to read those situations, objectively, in the light of God's Word?

Whether we like it or not, faith and politics have always had a close relation to each other on the social relations level. In the Middle East, faith and religion have a function for the life of national communities, and politics has always consequently had to deal with religion and its public function.

Moreover, each generation has always had to identify the criteria and forms for regulating the relationship between these two spheres of each country's social life. Our generation and those to come are faced with challenges that we can describe as unique since in these times it is also a matter of defining the relationship between the two spheres mentioned above, but also of rethinking the role of politics and religion, within themselves and not only in relation to each other. Not infrequently, national politics and religion find themselves in the same boat, accused of today's evil, incapacity, backwardness, and so on.

Moreover, religious faith plays a key role in the rethinking of the categories of history, memory, guilt, justice, and forgiveness, which directly bring the religious sphere into contact with the moral, social, and political spheres. Cross-cultural conflicts will not be overcome unless different and antithetical readings of one's religious, cultural, and histories are reread and redeemed. The wounds caused in the remote and recent past, as they can be assumed, processed, and shared, will continue to produce pain even after years or even centuries. In this regard it is so stated by Pope Francis:

> In many parts of the world, there is a need for paths of peace to heal open wounds. There is also a need for peacemakers, men and women prepared to work boldly and creatively to initiate processes of healing and renewed encounter. Renewed encounter does not mean returning to a time prior to conflicts. All of us change over time. Pain and conflict transform us. We no longer have use for empty diplomacy, dissimulation, double-speak, hidden agendas and good manners that mask reality. Those who were fierce enemies have to speak from the stark and clear truth. They have to learn how to cultivate a penitential memory, one that can accept the past in order not to cloud the future

> with their own regrets, problems and plans. Only by basing themselves on the historical truth of events will they be able to make a broad and persevering effort to understand one another and to strive for a new synthesis for the good of all. Every peace process requires enduring commitment. It is a patient effort to seek truth and justice, to honour the memory of victims and to open the way, step by step, to a shared hope stronger than the desire for vengeance.[6]

Nobody can take this path on his own. National communities, whether political or religious, need people who know how to promote, orient, guide toward that understanding of self and other, sometimes even at the cost of paying a high price in terms of loneliness, misunderstanding, and rejection.

Of course, peace is not the responsibility solely of the pastor and/or religious leader. I would not like to give the impression that peace is only made by leaders. They are, however, called to guide and accompany, as well as listen to, their respective communities, to create contexts in which communities can express themselves. The pastor alone does not make the community, but the community cannot exist without a pastor. In continuous dialogue, in listening to one another, and in sharing, a serious pastoral ministry of peace is born. The role of a leader, prophet, and voice of the pastor therefore remains inescapable.

Interfaith Dialogue

As Rabbi J. A. Heschel wisely said, no religion is an island. Therefore, the Church cannot presume to operate a peace

[6] Pope Francis, encyclical letter *Fratelli Tutti*, October 3, 2020, nos. 225–26.

ministry alone, as if it were the only reality in the land. There would be much presumption in that. As if the whole world is waiting for our word and witness. It is not. At least it is not so in the Holy Land. Like the whole world now, we live in a multi-cultural and multi-religious context. Without the collaboration of other Churches and other religious communities, no ecclesial peace ministry can have substance. Collaborating with others on peace will also help to heal the internal problems within our communities, for it is only in a sincere relationship with the other that we can best define ourselves in truth.

Different faiths, if understood in their genuineness and deep vocation, are bearers of reconciliation and peacemaking resources and are rarely the sole or main trigger for misunderstandings and conflicts, nor are they in themselves a risk factor in this regard. But if they become functionaries of political struggle, as is often the case in the Holy Land, religions become like gasoline thrown on the fire.

Interreligious dialogue has produced very beautiful documents on human fraternity, on being all children of God, on the need to work together for the preservation of an individual's rights. These are all fruits of an activity that I consider spiritual.

Yet, in our current context of war, all this in the Holy Land today seems to be a dead letter.

There is a great absentee in this war: the word of religious leaders. With few exceptions, no speeches, reflections, or prayers have been heard in recent months from the religious leadership other than from any political or social leader. I hope to be proven wrong, but one gets the impression that everyone is speaking exclusively within the perspective of his community.

Interreligious relations that seemed to be established now

seem to be swept away by a dangerous feeling of mistrust. Each feels betrayed by the other, not understood, not defended, not supported.

I have asked myself several times in recent months whether faith in God is really at the root and the formation of personal conscience, thus creating among believers a common understanding at least on certain central issues of social life, or whether our thought is formed and based on something else.

The Jewish world did not feel supported by Christians and expressed this clearly. The Christians in turn, divided as always on everything, incapable of a common word, were either divided in support of one side or the other or else uncertain and disoriented. Muslims feel attacked, seen as having connived with the massacres committed on October 7 . . . In short, after years of interreligious dialogue, we have found ourselves not understanding each other. It has caused me great sorrow, but has also served as a great lesson.

From this experience, we will have to start again, aware that religions also play a central role in orientation and that the dialogue between us will perhaps have to take an important step and start from our current misunderstandings, our differences, and our wounds. It can no longer be a dialogue only between those belonging to Western culture, as it has been until now, but it will have to consider the various sensitivities of the various cultural approaches, not only European, but first and foremost local. It is much more difficult, but we will have to start from there.

This war is a watershed in interreligious dialogue, which will never be the same again, at least among Christians, Muslims, and Jews.

And it must be done, not out of need or necessity, but out of love. Because, despite our differences, we love each other, and we want this good to find concrete expression in the lives not only of ourselves but also of our respective communities. Loving one another does not necessarily mean having the same opinions, but knowing how to express and appreciate them, and respecting and welcoming one another.

When it is sincere and addresses issues related to one's territory and respective communities, interreligious dialogue creates a mentality of encounter and mutual respect; it creates the necessary background on which subsequent political perspectives can then also be based.

Forgiveness

Having identified the indispensable responsibilities of religious leadership concerning serious pastoral care for peace, and the "open" way in which to operate, one must now ask what religious leaders must work on, both within their respective communities and in dialogue with each other. What should one work for, how, and with what style should one's communities live this central dimension of their faith?

I would say that the central theme is forgiveness. One cannot abstractly speak of peace, as if it were an idea. Peace is not something one has to do but is a way of being in life, an integral attitude of the person and the community, which in every context—personal and collective—must come to terms with the wounds caused by divisions, by attitudes of possession and exclusion, and by hatred. In sum, it must come to terms with sin. And in this context, peace is closely linked to forgiveness. I would say that they can be considered, if not synonymous, then closely necessary to each other.

Biblical revelation tells us that like peace, so too forgiveness has its root in God's love and requires first a personal journey, a path of understanding, of "taking on" the evil received or committed. It can never come about through inertia. The evil committed cannot be forgotten but requires a precise will to overcome, which is the fruit of a clear and definite desire. It does not erase the wrong done but wants to overcome it for the greater good. Trying to forget, waiting for time alone to heal the wounds, not taking on the evil committed, identifying it, looking it in the face, calling it by its name, means making forgiveness a banal gesture, which does not heal any wound, does not change people's hearts, and does not produce peace.

At the social and political level, reflection on forgiveness takes a long time. The paths to be taken are often enormously complex because they must take into consideration not a personal or context-specific relationship, but a social one. That is, one must consider the collective wounds, the pain of all, the necessarily different understandings of the events at the origin of common pain, and the different kinds of interpretations.

To look to the future with hope and at rest, it is necessary to go through a process of memory purification. Wounds, if not healed, create an attitude of victimhood and anger, which make reconciliation difficult, if not impossible. The wounds of the past will continue to be baggage to be carried on one's shoulders and a criterion for reading mutual relations. Until there is a purification of the common memory on everyone's part, until there is a mutual acknowledgment of the evil mutually committed and suffered, in short, until there is a reinterpretation of one's historical ties.

Faith naturally can open the believer to a relationship because it opens him up to an encounter with God, which then naturally also becomes a glimpse of the other from oneself.

But what is also needed is a human education in forgiveness, a cultural formation that enables man to look at events not exclusively from the perspective of one's wounds, which always has a limited and closed horizon. This will help interpret events on a both personal and collective level, with the future in perspective, which also considers the good of others, the social reality, and the need to reactivate life dynamics. Therefore, in this context, reflection on forgiveness can also be open to nonbelievers.

The first fruit of forgiveness is freedom from the emotional ties produced by resentment and revenge, which imprison any prospect of fostering a relationship within a circle of pain and violence. Forgiveness allows the healing of the human soul, reactivates the dynamics of life, and builds the future.

The necessary action must be taken in all spheres: political, religious, and civil, at the same time, including the various groups of aggregation and formation of thought such as schools, universities, and the mass media. Because people interact at all these levels. And forgiveness, in its function of healing the subject, can only act if it involves all the fibers of his being.

The Church, together with other faith communities, has a fundamental role in education for reconciliation, and in creating the context for an approach to forgiveness, but she cannot impose it. It is necessary to give time and respect to the pain of those who suffer, while also helping them to reread their history, allowing wounds to heal. Often in the Holy Land, it is a matter of knowing how to wait. The hearts of people and communities are not always ready and free to speak of forgiveness. The pain is still too strong. It is often easier to deal with anger than with a desire for forgiveness. It is therefore necessary to know how to wait, but at the same time to propose the Christian way of peace without tiring.

So far, all the peace agreements in the Holy Land have

failed because they were often theoretical agreements, which presumed to resolve years of tragedy without taking into account the enormous load of wounds, pain, resentment, and anger that still smoldered and exploded in an extremely violent manner in recent months. Furthermore, no account was taken of the cultural and especially religious context, which instead spoke a language exactly opposite (starting with the local religious leaders) to that of those who spoke of peace.

Therefore, in this context, the pastoral care of the Church cannot fail to have in its horizon of action the proposal of forgiveness and reconciliation, which takes into account wounds and pain but does not stop there. Pain can close us in on ourselves, but it can also open up new dimensions, it can turn into resurrection. Without this perspective, no political project can succeed in the Holy Land, and peace would remain just a slogan with little credibility. Hence, the task of the Church's pastoral work is to untiringly propose paths of reconciliation, to accompany efforts at healing, to propose languages that exclude no one, to patiently weave webs of relationships, to build trust within one's ecclesial community, and then with other religious communities, with concrete gestures.

Truth and Justice

Forgiveness, as I previously mentioned, is a central theme of the peace ministry. But in our context, forgiveness cannot be separated from two other words: truth and justice.

The suffering, the pain, the wounds that this conflict has caused are well known. I am not here to list the evils that are being done. That is not the theme of this meeting, and I think it is a theme known to all. And I do not intend here to enter the question of this phase of the conflict that is going on now, which began on October 7.

For decades in the Holy Land, there has been the Israeli occupation of the West Bank territories, with all its dramatic consequences on the lives of Palestinians and also Israelis. The first and most visible consequence of this political situation is the condition of injustice, of nonrecognition of basic rights, of suffering in which the Palestinian population in the West Bank lives. It is an objective situation of injustice.

As I said earlier, for our Church the conflict with its consequences is an integral part of ordinary life and is inevitably part of the thinking and reflection of the whole community. Not infrequently, as in this period, it is a matter of harsh and painful reflection and discussion. Maintaining communion between Palestinian and Israeli Catholics, in this torn and polarized context, is more difficult than ever.

Therefore, one cannot speak of forgiveness without speaking of truth and justice. Not to speak a word of truth about the life of a Palestinian, whose life has been a sum of decades of waiting for justice and dignity to be granted, would be to justify an objective situation of injustice.

As the Latin Patriarch of Jerusalem, I have found myself, since the beginning of this conflict, in a situation that requires a choice and a clear and precise stance. How do I reconcile this call to take sides with what I am and what I have just said about forgiveness? How to defend the rights of God and man in this context, how to speak of forgiveness, to be faithful to Christ, who on the Cross freely forgave, without giving the impression of not defending the flock entrusted to me, its rights, its expectations? How to preach love to enemies without giving the impression of unwittingly confirming one narrative against the other, Israeli against Palestinian, or vice versa? How to heal divisions with firm and just choices, but without creating more divisions, and always with mercy?

More concretely, I am often asked: "How can I think of forgiving the Israeli who oppresses me, as long as I am under oppression? Wouldn't that mean giving him the upper hand, giving him free rein without defending my rights? Before talking about forgiveness, is it not necessary that justice be done?" In turn, the Israeli may add: "How can I forgive those who kill my people?" These are questions behind which there is real, sincere pain to be respected.

I do not know if it is possible to answer these questions, but one cannot avoid asking them. A peace ministry cannot ignore the wounds of its community, nor can it delude it with easy answers that do not touch real life. Some situations have no immediate solutions and perhaps no solutions at all. But there is nevertheless a Christian way of being within a conflict. Peace can be experienced even in these circumstances. Often, this takes more than easy answers, which probably do not exist; instead, one must help identify paths and lifestyles.

I have tried to point out some of them, with a letter to the diocese sent a few months ago, which I would like to quote here:

> To have the courage of love and peace here, today, means not allowing hatred, revenge, anger, and pain to occupy all the space of our hearts, of our speech, of our thinking. It means making a personal commitment to justice, being able to affirm and denounce the painful truth of injustice and evil that surrounds us, without letting it pollute our relationships. It means being committed, being convinced that it is still worthwhile to do all we can for peace, justice,

> equality, and reconciliation. Our speech must not be about death and closed doors. On the contrary, our words must be creative, life-giving; they must give perspective and open horizons.
>
> It takes courage to be able to demand justice without spreading hatred. It takes courage to ask for mercy, to reject oppression, to promote equality without demanding uniformity, while remaining free. It takes courage today, even in our diocese and our communities, to maintain unity, to feel united to one another, even in the diversity of our opinions, sensitivities, and visions.
>
> I want, and we want, to be part of this new order inaugurated by Christ. We want to ask God for that courage. We want to be victorious over the world, taking upon ourselves that same Cross, which is also ours, made of pain and love, of truth and fear, of injustice and gift, of cries and forgiveness.

In conclusion, forgiveness alone cannot build peace. Truth and justice alone cannot build peace. The relationship between these words is never easy and is a source of great discussion, but also of beautiful reflection.

To speak only of forgiveness, disjoined from truth and justice, in our precise context, is to disregard the fact that man is created in the image and likeness of God; it is to ignore his dignity as a person, with all the rights attached to that identity. To speak of forgiveness, without considering a person's right to a just and dignified life, is to deny one a right of God and does not build peace.

Truth and justice, divorced from forgiveness, have the same limitations. Asserting the need for truth and justice is a sacrosanct activity. Yet if these are separated from a desire for forgiveness, for overcoming the evil committed, they put one's adversary in a corner, with no way out. One becomes a defendant, confronting him with his responsibilities, but without overcoming them, without offering any prospect of a solution. Ultimately it becomes recrimination, and that is all. Indeed, all this can provoke an even more aggressive reaction of opposition.

Therefore, it is necessary for church pastoral care to know how to place these three elements in continuous, difficult, painful, complex, lacerating, tiring dialogue with each other. But it is a process that is fruitful and respectful of God's and man's rights and that builds prospects of peace—little by little, since our time is not our own. For what sustains these three ways of being in life and relations between us is not an ideology but love. "God's love has been poured into our hearts through the Holy Spirit who has been given to us" (Rom 5:5). It is that love that drives our desire for peace. Nothing else.

Conclusion

In conclusion, in my opinion, the peace ministry in the Church consists of nothing more than simply being the Church. Remaining ourselves, anchored in what sustains us, living, proclaiming, and bearing witness to this without fear or hypocrisy.

In this regard, allow me to add a small reflection. In the Holy Land, we are painfully witnessing the growing crisis of multilateral organizations, such as the UN, which is increasingly ineffectual and, for many, limited by the great powers (just think of the various powers of veto). The international community is increasingly weak, and so are the various other international organizations.

In sum, those at the international level who are deputed to maintain and promote peace, to defend rights, and to build decent models of society, have shown all their weaknesses. Local leadership is in even more trouble, of all kinds. A reality that is unfortunately well-known to all.

What is lacking, in short, are political and social references capable of making gestures in the territory, building trust, capable of courageous choices for peace, negotiating reconciliations, accepting the necessary compromises, and so on.

In this desolating context, pastoral workers, pastors, and the Church must be careful not to fall into an easy temptation: that of substituting themselves for those organizations and becoming involved in the dynamics of political negotiations that by their very nature are subject to never easy compromises, often indeed painful and controversial ones. The temptation to fill the void left by politics is easy, and the demand by many to fill that void is also always insistent.

But this is not the task of the Church, which—as I said—must remain a Church, a community of faith, which means not being detached from reality, but rather always being willing to engage with anyone to build peace, to facilitate the creation of contexts that help build political perspectives, while nevertheless remaining true to herself, without entering into political dynamics that do not belong to her and that by their very nature are often foreign to the logic of the Gospel.

Peace ministry has only the Gospel as its reference. The characters and criteria for building peace are all to be found there. One must start from there and always return to it. The contribution that we can bring to the social life of our troubled diocese consists of fostering in the community the desire, the disposition, and the sincere, loyal, positive, and concrete commitment to meet with the other; to know how to love despite everything, to help interpret one's pain in the light of faith, to know how to make unity between faith and life. We begin by listening to the Word of God, which is the main source of every criterion for interpreting our reality of life.

Blessed Are You Who Know Him

Meditation for the
Sixth Sunday of Ordinary Time (Year C)

February 16, 2025

The Gospel passage for this Sixth Sunday of Ordinary Time (Lk 6:17, 20–26) recounts Jesus' words on the Beatitudes.

The evangelist sets this discourse in a flat place, or rather, in a place where Jesus is descending (Lk 6:17). He was on the mountain where He prayed and where He chose and called His disciples (Lk 6:12). Now He descends and stops in the plain, where He finds a large crowd waiting for Him.

They are mainly poor people: sick, hungry, possessed. People who have been wounded by life (Lk 6:18–19).

The first thing Jesus does is not to heal them, to help them, but to go among them and stop. Jesus did not come primarily to change people's lives by solving problems, healing everyone and always. He comes down and remains in their midst, making Himself one of them.

Jesus comes down, stops, and then begins to heal them. In short, He does not begin with His thaumaturgical work, through which He frees them from various illnesses, but with a Word that gives them a new perspective on their own lives.

This new view is summarized in four beatitudes and four corresponding "woes": Blessed are you who are poor, blessed are you who hunger, blessed are you who weep, blessed are you who are hated (Lk 6:20–22). And parallel to this: Woe to you who are rich, woe to you who are full, woe to you who laugh, woe to you when everyone will say good things about you (Lk 6:24–26).

There is one great beatitude in the Bible that summarizes all the countless beatitudes with which the Old and New Testaments are teeming—namely, that of knowing the Lord.

This is our calling, our greatest joy: to know Him. That is our bliss.

Jesus sees in these people before Him the first recipients of this promise of joy; He sees people who will be put in a position to know God. They will come to know Him, not because He will change their destiny for the better, but because of the simple fact that He descended to them; because He descended into the depths of humanity and found them waiting for Him, with their desire to listen to Him and be saved. And there He stopped.

So Jesus is not saying that the poor are blessed because they become rich: that is not the justice He wanted to bring. It would still be a purely human justice that would change the lot of all and create new rich but also new poor. There would be nothing really new.

The poor are blessed because the Kingdom of God belongs to them, that is, because they can recognize God.

The blessed are therefore those whom life has enabled to experience God.

It is to experience that God gives life and that only He can do this. Blessed are those whom history has placed in a position to understand that every other place where we seek life sooner or later reveals its deceptive face: wealth, satiety, pleasure, honor, and fame—not that they are negative or sinful realities. They are just incapable of giving eternal life because they keep people trapped in a state where everything is already there, where there is nothing left to look forward to or hope for.

Blessed is the one who knows that life is also other and who expects this other from God with trust.

This awareness often comes at the price of great hardship, great suffering.

And those who suffer are not blessed because they suffer, but because this suffering is a great and valuable school of truth: the truth that we are not enough for ourselves, that we cannot make it in our own strength, that our nets are empty even after a night of work, as we saw last Sunday (Lk 5:5).

And that is the point at which the Lord comes down and stops.

A Call That Heals

Meditation for the Thirtieth Sunday of Ordinary Time (Year B)

October 27, 2024

We are now at the gates of Jerusalem, and what we read today (Mk 10:46–52) is the last of the miracles reported by the Evangelist Mark. It is the last, and it is also an indicative miracle with deep symbolic meaning.

The protagonist is a blind man, and strangely enough, Mark mentions the name of this blind man: Bartimaeus (Mk 10:46).

This is the only case in which we know the name of a person whom Jesus heals, and this is no coincidence.

By mentioning the name, the Evangelist wants to establish a connection between Bartimaeus and the other people in the Gospel whose names are known—namely, the disciples. Bartimaeus is in fact the figure of the disciple, the one who follows Jesus on His way to Jerusalem.

In verse 49, the verb "to call" is heard three times. Bartimaeus is sitting by the roadside, and when he hears that Jesus is passing by, he begins to call out loudly for mercy.

Then Jesus stopped and called out to him, and the same people who had previously been scolding him to be quiet called out to him: "Jesus said, 'Call him here.' And they called the blind man, saying to him, 'Take heart; rise, he is calling you.'" Bartimaeus is a called man, and his call says something about the lives of the disciples, who are not perfect, different, better people, but like all people are in need of salvation, of light. Jesus calls fragile people, and by calling them, He can heal them.

When Bartimaeus heard this, he immediately jumped up, threw off his cloak and came to Jesus ("And throwing off his cloak, he sprang up and came to Jesus," Mk 10:50). This is also another detail that tells us something about discipleship. For the disciple is the one who leaves everything he has behind, just as the first called ones had done. Not out of an effort of will, but because he has found the treasure, something greater and more important than his own security in life.

Finally, the last reference: Bartimaeus, called, healed, no longer sits by the roadside, but follows Jesus, just as the disciples are asked to follow Him ("Immediately he received his sight and followed him on the way," Mk 10:52).

However, Bartimaeus shows us that following the Lord Jesus means more than just following Him on the road. Following Him means learning to look at life and situations in the same way, to call things by the same name, and to give them the same meaning. That is why the last miracle, the miracle that can create a disciple, is the healing of blindness, because the disciple is the one who slowly learns to look at things from God's point of view.

How is it that this man, the beggar, the blind man, becomes the figure of the disciple, the figure of us all?

Bartimaeus is above all a man who will not and cannot remain silent. We see him begging quietly on the street, but when Jesus passes by, his cry explodes, and nothing can stop him. He is not intimidated and is courageous, because that is what faith is all about.

Bartimaeus is a person whom Jesus sees.

He is not the one who sees Jesus, for he is blind. But it is Jesus who hears his cry, as is always the case in the biblical stories: God hears the cry of the poor and does not ignore it. Jesus stands still (Mk 10:49) to hear his cry; he does not pass by without looking him in the face and giving him the opportunity to return this look.

In his encounter with Jesus, Bartimaeus experiences profound existential changes. He goes from weeping to praying, from sitting to walking, from being blind to seeing, from being a beggar to being a free man.

The disciple is the one who emerges transformed from the encounter with Jesus.

It is not possible to remain the same as the man who asked Jesus what he must do to have life (Mk 10:17) and who went away sad because he did not accept to enter a process of transformation.

And finally, the key to this whole process of transformation is found in verse 51: "What do you want me to do for you?"

The turning point in our lives happens when, among the thousands of desires that populate us, we recognize the deep and true desire that unites our existence. This happens to us above all in prayer, in our relationship with the Lord, the One who stops to hear our cry and lets us hear His voice.

The Gift Before the Need

Meditation for the Eighteenth Sunday of Ordinary Time (Year B)

August 4, 2024

Chapter 6 of John's Gospel opens with an unexpected and remarkable gift: Jesus feeds the crowd with an abundance of bread, ensuring that everyone has enough. The evangelist underscores this: everyone ate until they were full, and twelve baskets of leftover bread were collected (Jn 6:12–13).

This principle of starting with a gift recurs throughout John's Gospel in every major scene: from the wedding at Cana to the living water offered to the Samaritan woman, from healing the man born blind to raising Lazarus. In every case, the initial action is a gift, grace given freely to all whom Jesus encounters.

In the first place is the gift of God, which forms the core of our faith.

Yet, this also presents a significant challenge in our relationship with God. This is evident in the interaction between Jesus and Philip in last Sunday's Gospel: Jesus asks Philip where bread can be bought to feed the crowd. Philip's response, rooted in conventional logic, reveals its inadequacy: to feed such a crowd, even a large sum of money would be insufficient (Jn 6:5–7).

This reflects the logic by which we habitually interpret our relationship with God: if we want something, we must acquire it, buy it, or deserve it. If we fail to get it, we assume the fault lies with us. Often our life is caged within this way of thinking. This mindset contrasts sharply with God's logic, which starts with the gift rather than our needs and wants.

Today's Gospel highlights this point: the crowd, having been satisfied, seeks Jesus again, but their search is driven by their own needs: "You seek me, not because you saw signs, but because you ate your fill of the loaves" (Jn 6:26). Animals seek only what they need, while humans also seek something that gives fullness to life, beyond merely satisfying physical hunger.

Thus, before need comes the gift, which in turn shapes our needs. It does not suppress them, but expands them, teaching us not to settle for merely satisfying our appetites but to enter a relationship characterized by gratuitousness and friendship.

However, when faced with this expanded horizon, the old mechanism of merit and gain reappears when Jesus invites the people to seek what offers eternal life; they immediately ask what they must do (Jn 6:27–28). At this juncture, Jesus reveals another way of living, not based on personal effort or merit, but through faith: this is the work of God. Jesus frames it significantly: we are called to fulfill God's work, which is our faith (Jn 6:29).

Believing is God's work because by believing we open our lives to God, and this enables Him to work in us what He desires, which is the fullness of our lives, the beauty of a fully real relationship with Him.

These two logics in today's Gospel are in some way symbolized by the two shores of the lake (Jn 6:25) and by the crossing that the disciples are called to make: faith is not an intellectual act, but a continuous passage between two logics, between two choices: one that begins with God's gift and one that starts from ourselves and our search; one that is based on our works and one that is founded on God's work in us; one that focuses on our small needs and one that opens up to God's desires and the greatness of His heart.

Those who listen to His Word can make this crossing and arrive at the shore where God is waiting to accomplish His work in us.

When the Bridegroom Arrives

Meditation for the Thirteenth Sunday of Ordinary Time (Year B)

June 30, 2024

A key reading that can help us in understanding today's Gospel passage (Mk 5:21–43) is verse 33: the woman afflicted with hemorrhages, after stealthily being healed by Jesus, is invited to come out, to show herself (Mk 5:30). And she does, but she does so "in fear and trembling" (Mk 5:33).

These are not two random nouns.

We find them in the Letter to the Hebrews (Heb 12:21), in the chapter in which the author reflects on the two covenants, the one stipulated on Sinai (Ex 19) and the one renewed with the Passover of Jesus.

The author of the Epistle, speaking to his readers, says that they did not approach a tremendous and dramatic event, such as that recounted in the Theophany on Sinai: in that case, the spectacle was so terrifying that even Moses said, "I am terrified and trembling" (Heb 12:21).

Moses, too, before the Sinai Theophany, is like the hemorrhagic woman before Jesus: both afraid and trembling.

But why was Moses afraid? Certainly, because the theophany was awesome: lightning, thunder, earthquakes, and fire. But not only because of that. There had to be a space, a definite distance between the people and the place of God's presence. There was to be no contamination. Anyone who approached the mount of Theophany, or contaminated the sacred space, was even to be put to death (Ex 19:12)! Even in the Temple, a clear separation would later be made between the sacred place par excellence, accessible to a few and only at certain times, and the rest of the people.

Then we are faced with two different ways of seeing God: that of Moses, where one cannot approach God. That of the hemorrhaging woman, where there is the opposite: she who touches God lives.

If anything, one can die not from touching Him, but from not touching Him. Indeed, the woman's whole plan, once she heard about Jesus, revolved around the possibility of a touch: "If I touch even his garments, I shall be made dwell" (Mk 5:28).

The woman is trembling because she is afraid. After all, the woman has an idea of God that is common to so many, a God from whom to snatch salvation, a God who is frightening.

Jesus urges her to come out, not confirming this face of God to her, but overthrowing it, and He does so with words capable of healing the heart: "Daughter, . . . go in peace" (Mk 5:34).

First of all, this is the only time in Mark's Gospel when Jesus calls someone "daughter". This woman, who dared to touch the God-with-us, has fully found her identity, her truth, that of Daughter of the Father.

This daughter can now go in peace, because the time of fear is over, and the time of trust and love has begun. To touch Jesus, the ultimate presence of God among us, and to be touched by Him, to meet Him, is no longer forbidden. There is no longer a separation between the sacred and the profane.

We can also see that this time of trust and love has begun in the other scene recounted in today's passage, with which the Gospel had begun: a synagogue leader, that is, a man of religion, cannot do anything for his sick daughter and comes to Jesus. As we have seen, Jesus immediately sets out but gets interrupted by the woman afflicted with hemorrhages. And by the time he arrives at Jairus' house, there is nothing to be done: the child is dead (Mk 5:35).

At that very moment, when all hope seems to disappear, the union between God and humanity is celebrated.

The child is twelve years old, which is the traditional age of marriage. And Jesus brings everyone out of the room, except the father, mother, and those who were with Him, and enters the room where the little girl is.

This room of death becomes a wedding room: Jesus takes her by the hand (Mk 5:41), as a bridegroom takes his bride by the hand; and the parents hand the bride over to the bridegroom, in front of the witnesses.

The union is complete.

The Word, today, opens the door to a new time for us: a time in which we let go of all our feelings of unworthiness, all our fears, and all our unconscious mechanisms that lead us to think we have to earn salvation by our own efforts, to believe that, in Jesus, the relationship with God is freely given to us, and it is only a matter of opening our hearts to Him more and more, of bringing our every desire for salvation and life to Him.

When Seeds Take Root

Meditation for the Fifteenth Sunday in Ordinary Time (Year A)

July 16, 2023

The Gospel passage for this Fifteenth Sunday (Mt 13:1–23) is the beginning of Jesus' third discourse reported by the evangelist Matthew. It is the discourse that Jesus delivers by telling a series of parables, of which today we hear the first one, that of the sower.

It is a complex passage, which is structured in three parts, preceded by an introduction (Mt 13:1–3): in the first part (Mt 13:3–9), Jesus tells the parable; in the second part (Mt 13:10–17), the disciples approach Him and question Him as to why He speaks to people in parables; in the third part (Mt 13:18–22), Jesus explains the parable to the disciples.

First and foremost, I would like to pause on an apparent oddity: Jesus tells the parable to everyone; then He seems to say that only the disciples can understand it. Finally, He explains the parable precisely to the disciples, who seemed to be the only ones who understood it.

Now, this seems to me to be an important detail: Jesus tells the parable to everyone, like the sower who sows his seed in all soils: He does not choose only some, He does not make distinctions, He does not spare His gift. He accepts the risk that His gift will be lost, for this is the logic of love. The parables highlight the different types of listening, of accepting Jesus' proclamation.

The parable, then, is like a seed, which does not immediately reveal its mystery, which does not immediately bear its fruit: it depends on who welcomes it, on how one welcomes it. Some understand it, some do not; some harden their hearts, some open them; some listen without understanding, some listen and understand and bear fruit.

We find the difference in these diverse attitudes in verse 10: "Then the disciples came and said to him, 'Why do you speak to them in parables?'"

What allows the Word to go down deep, to bear fruit, is the attitude of the disciples who have the courage, after listening without understanding—like everyone else—to approach Jesus and ask questions. The disciples are not better; they do not have something more than others. They simply remain within a relationship with the simplicity of those who admit they do not understand, who accept that they do not know, but do not run away, do not close their hearts.

Jesus remains a mystery that exceeds the possibility of any man's knowledge, but different are the reactions of those who meet and hear Him, just as different are the soils on which the seed falls.

The disciples "came to" Jesus, an expression that recalls the one we heard last Sunday, when Jesus invited all the weary and fatigued to come to Him (Mt 11:28) to know the Father and find rest: and "coming to" says a movement, a decision of the heart, a search, a willingness not to stop in the face of what eludes us, a desire to know and to be open to the power of the Father's love, which, like a seed, makes life blossom. This is what the disciples do in today's Gospel; they draw near.

In the Gospels, it is often Jesus who draws near, accomplishing the movement of one who does not leave the other in his pain. Today we are told that "approaching" is also *our* verb, our identity: we come close to the One who has made Himself close.

The parable seems to mean that the knowledge of the Father, the knowledge that Jesus had proposed last Sunday to all the weary and oppressed, is not a matter of a moment, but is a process that asks to "come to", that requires a long time of patience: it is, in fact, a matter of letting the seed go down deep. Which is so difficult, especially in our times, and yet so necessary.

The place where life germinates is thus man's interiority: for those who live at the surface of themselves, the danger of dispersion and distraction is very close.

And to the contrary, the parable of the sower tells us that we need depth and that only listening to the Word can bring us to the depth of our lives.

What happens within this depth of heart?

We must understand that in a sense, God always speaks in parables or, to be more clear, that our life revolves around the Word of the Father, which asks to be received, treasured, and meditated.

And for this to happen, we are asked to draw near.

Flipping Our Image of God

Meditation for the Third Sunday of Lent (Year B)

March 3, 2024

Last Sunday, we went up to Mount Tabor, where Jesus revealed His face as the beloved Son (Mk 9:2–10). We saw that the disciples Peter, James, and John were with him, as well as Moses and Elijah, who appeared before them. Those two prophets who, during their lives, also participated in an epiphany, a transfiguration: they went up a mountain, where God made Himself present, but without ever seeing Him face to face, but rather only from behind, after the Lord had passed over.

However, on Mount Tabor, God reveals His face, and He does so in Jesus. In His story, and especially in His Passover, God makes Himself known.

Today this process of the unveiling of this revelation takes a further step.

We are at the beginning of John's Gospel (Jn 2:13–25), where we find an episode that the Synoptics put immediately after Jesus' triumphal entry into Jerusalem instead of at the end of their narrative.

The episode is the so-called cleansing of the temple.

Jesus enters the temple and sees everything that revolves around the temple's wealth: people selling the animals needed for the sacrifices, the animals themselves, and the money changers.

And, in the face of this scene, Jesus makes a prophetic gesture: He sends everyone out, spills the money on the ground, overturns the money changers' stalls, and forcefully tells them not to make His Father's house a marketplace (Jn 2:15–16).

To enter into the understanding of this passage, let us start with one word, which is found in verse 15. Here we read that Jesus throws the money on the ground and overturns the stalls.

Jesus overthrows, reverses, overturns.

He overturns the money changers' counters, but first of all, He overturns an image of God and a way of believing.

Each Gospel tells of this overturning. The four evangelists place at the beginning of their narration a gesture or a word, which displays it.

In Matthew, it is seen in the Sermon on the Mount and the Beatitudes (Mt 5:1–12).

Blessed are the poor, those who mourn, the meek, those who wait for justice, the persecuted . . . : the logic of the world is precisely reversed, because God looks at reality from another perspective. Life is not measured by success and possessions but by the benevolence of God the Father, and His great compassion for anyone who awaits His salvation and relies on Him.

Mark places this turnaround in the first words spoken by Jesus (Mk 1:15), where he announces that the Kingdom of God is at hand and the time for repentance has come for all.

He does not say that one must first be converted for the Lord to draw near, but the opposite: First, the free work of salvation is offered by God, who saves, and from here comes all the possibility of a new life. Not an effort or a toil, but a possibility for all.

In Luke, this is even more explicit, and it is evident in Mary. Not only because of how God makes Himself present in her life: not in a temple, but in a house; not in Jerusalem, but in Nazareth. But also because she herself speaks of it, explicitly, in her Magnificat: "He has put down the mighty from their thrones and exalted those of low degree" (Lk 1:52). Mary is the woman of overthrowing.

By putting the episode of Jesus in the temple at the beginning of his Gospel, John wants to tell us this:

He wants to tell us that the time has come for a new relationship with the Father, which he speaks about with the woman of Samaria a few chapters later (Jn 4): no longer only in Jerusalem, no longer through sacrifices, but with humble readiness to accept God's gift, His Spirit, His mercy.

The relationship with God has been overturned: it is no longer man who needs to make sacrifices to obtain God's benevolence, but it is the contrary. It is God Himself who offers Himself for us, who sheds His blood, who gives His life out of love for every man.

And just like last Sunday, the three disciples have been told not to tell anyone about what they have seen on the mountain (Lk 9:28–36). Today this element returns: the disciples do not understand the words with which Jesus explains his gesture. But they will remember them later, after the Resurrection, when it will be evident that the Body of the Risen One will have become, for all, the place of encounter with the Father and with His salvation.

Make Room at the Inn

Homily for Christmas Midnight Mass

Church of Saint Catherine, Bethlehem

December 24, 2023

Dearest Brothers and Sisters,

May the Lord give you Peace!

Tonight's Gospel echoes the voice of a deep feeling, which I believe we all share: "there was no place for them" (Lk 2:7). As it was for Mary and Joseph, so it seems for us today that there is no room for Christmas. For too many days, we have all been caught up in the sad and painful feeling that there is no room this year for the joy and peace that the angels announced to the shepherds of Bethlehem in this Holy Night, not far from here.

At this moment, our thoughts cannot be far from those who have lost everything in this war, including their closest loved ones, and who are now displaced, alone, and paralyzed by their grief. My thoughts go, without distinction, to all who are affected by this war, in Palestine and Israel and the whole region. I am especially close to those who are in mourning and weeping and waiting for a concrete gesture of closeness and care. Tonight, I remember the hostages kidnapped from their families, as I remember the people who languish in prisons without having had the right to a trial.

My thoughts go to Gaza and its two million inhabitants. Truly the words "there was no place for them" describe their situation, which is now known to all. Their suffering ceaselessly cries out to the whole world. No place or home is safe for anyone. Thousands of people have been deprived of their basic needs; they are hungry, and they are even more exposed to incomprehensible violence. There seems to be no place for them, not only physically, but also in the minds of those who decide the fate of nations. This is the situation in which the Palestinian people has been living for too long. Though living on their own land, they continually hear "there is no place for them". For decades they have been waiting for the international community to find solutions to end the occupation under which they are forced to live and its consequences. However, today it seems to me that each of us is entrapped by his own pain. Hatred, resentment, and the spirit of revenge occupy all the space in our hearts and leave no room for the presence of others. Yet, we need others. Christmas is precisely about this: God making Himself present in a human way and opening our hearts to a new way of looking at the world.

Not that the world has always been hospitable to Christ: it isn't news that the Christian faith and the Christian meaning of Christmas are but a faint memory in today's secularized and materialistic culture. Yet this year, here and elsewhere in the world, the noise of weapons, the children's tears, the suffering of the refugees, the cry of the poor, the grief of so many mourning families, seem to make our songs lose harmony. It seems difficult to rejoice, and our words seem empty and void.

Let it be clear: Christ's coming into our world has opened for us and for all "the way of eternal salvation", which nothing and no one will ever be able to close. The faith, hope, and love of the Church of God are unfailing and solidly rest on the faithful Promise of the Lord. They do not depend on the changing times and the adversity of the circumstances that surround them.

However, it is just as evident that we struggle, especially here, especially today, to find a place for Christmas in our land, in our life, and in our heart. We risk losing that way which Christ opened for us in the labyrinth of war-torn roads, rubble, and abandoned homes. Our heart, so overburdened, may fail to fall in tune with the Christmas message. Too much pain, too much disappointment, too many broken promises, crowd that inner space in which the Gospel of Christmas can resonate and inspire peaceful and life-giving actions and behaviors.

Let us ask ourselves then: Where is Christmas this year? Where can we look for the Savior? Where can the Child be born when there seems to be no place for Him in this world of ours?

As we have heard, Mary and Joseph asked themselves this question as they faced the difficulty of finding lodging that night. The shepherds asked the same question as they looked for the Child, and so did the Magi as they chased the star. It has been the question of the Church every time she lost her way. It is our question tonight: Where is there place for Christmas today?

The angels give us the answer. On that night, and in every night, God always finds room for His Christmas. Even for us, here, today, despite everything, even in these dramatic circumstances, we believe so: God can make room even in the hardest of hearts.

The place of Christmas is first and foremost God. Christmas, the Nativity of Christ, is in the beginning, within the merciful Heart of the Father. His infinite and endless love eternally generates the Son and gives Him to us in Time, even in this time. The salvation of man was decided upon in His good and holy will. "For God so loved the world that he gave his only-begotten Son that whoever believes in him should not perish but have eternal life. For God sent the Son into the world, not to condemn the world, but that the world might be saved through him" (Jn 3:16–17).

In the present circumstances, if we want to find the true joy of Christmas and if we want to meet the Savior, we, the whole Church, must return to God and to His love. We must go beyond the social and political explanations of violence and subjugation of others. These phenomena are ultimately rooted in having forgotten God, having made a false image of His face, and having used a fake and utilitarian religious relationship with Him. This happens all too often in our Holy Land.

If we are unable to call our fellow men brothers, neither will we be able to call God our "Father". It is even more true that we cannot recognize ourselves as brothers unless we return to the true God by recognizing Him as a Father who loves everyone. If we don't find God anew in our lives, we shall inevitably lose the way that leads to Christmas, and we shall find ourselves wandering alone in the night without a destination and fall prey to our violent and selfish instincts.

Mary and Joseph's "yes" is also the place of Christmas. Their obedience and faithfulness were the home in which the Son came to dwell. God's will is not a power that subjugates and bends, but Love that exerts all its strength only if welcomed by a faithful and generous personal freedom. True freedom is not only the capacity to choose but is being able to choose with loving responsibility for our good and the good of others. The Son of God, begotten of the Father, has entered the spectrum of time through the open door of human freedom. Christmas, the Nativity, is found everywhere a man and a woman say "yes" to God! Wherever a person's life is at the service of the Peace that comes from on high, rather than serving his own interests, that is where the Son is born and where He continues to be born.

If we want it to be Christmas, even in times of war, we all need to increase our actions that speak of brotherhood, peace, acceptance, forgiveness, and reconciliation. Allow me to add: we must all commit ourselves, beginning with me and those who, like me, have a responsibility to lead and direct the social, political, and religious spheres, to develop a yes-based mindset rather than no-based strategies. Saying yes to what is good, yes to peace, yes to dialogue, and yes to others, should be not a rhetorical exercise but a responsible commitment. It should make room, not occupy it; find a place for others and not deny them one. Christmas was made possible by the space that Mary and Joseph offered to God and the Child who came from Him. It will not be different for justice and peace. There will not be justice and peace will not come unless we make room for them through our open and generous "yes".

It would not be Christmas without the shepherds. Their staying awake in the night is also a part of the Gospel. They are the first to find the Child. Luke the Evangelist does not dwell on their social condition but focuses rather on their inner disposition. That night, the shepherds found themselves alert and down-to-earth as always, ready to act and open-minded. They did not overthink or make excessive calculations and were thus ready for Christmas. In a time inevitably marked by resignation, hatred, anger, and depression, we need Christians to be like the shepherds so that there may be room for Christmas!

To this my beloved diocese, to its priests, seminarians, religious men and women, committed lay men and women, and all the parish communities with their groups and associations: I feel that I must remind us all that we are heirs of those shepherds. I know well how difficult it is to remain alert, willing to welcome and to forgive. How difficult it is always to be ready to begin again, to set out on the way even if it is still night. This is the only way for us to find the Child. This is the only witness that ensures that Christmas will find room in this time and in this land, so that it may enlighten the whole world. We are here, and we intend to continue being the shepherds of Christmas, that is, those who, in their poor and fragile conditions, have found the Child and have experienced His grace and consolation and desire to announce to all that Christmas is yesterday and today true and real.

Dear brothers and sisters, my heart's wish is my prayer: may our will to do good, which becomes concrete through our responsible and generous "yes" to our commitment to love and serve, may that be the room that Christ finds so that He may always be born anew in us! I ask this for myself, for my Church in the Holy Land, and for every Church. May the Church be a home for all and a space of reconciliation and forgiveness for those who seek joy and peace! I ask all the Churches in the world, who look to us in this time, not only to contemplate the mystery of Bethlehem but also to support us in this tragic war: please convey to your people and their governments your "yes" to God, your desire for the good of our peoples, for the cessation of hostilities, so that all may truly find again a home and peace.

I pray that Christ be reborn in the hearts of those who govern and those who lead the nations and that He may suggest to them His own "yes", which leads Him to become a friend and brother to us and to all. May those who govern commit seriously to stopping this war. Most of all, may they once again begin a dialogue that finally leads to finding just and dignified solutions for our peoples. The tragedy of the present moment tells us that it is no longer time for short-lived tactics or for references to a theoretical future. Rather, it is time to state, here and now, a clear and definitive word of truth that may heal the root of this ongoing conflict by removing its deep causes and unlock new horizons of serenity and justice for all, for the Holy Land, and for our region that is marked by this conflict.

Words like occupation and security and many other similar ones, which have dominated our respective narratives for too long, must be strengthened by trust and respect. This is what we want for the future of this land. Only this shall guarantee a real stability and peace.

May Christ be born anew in this land, His and ours, and may the way of the Gospel of peace for the whole world begin again from here! May He be reborn in the hearts of those who believe in Him, moving them to witness and mission, without the fear of night and death! May He also be reborn as a desire for peace and goodness, truth and justice, in the hearts of those who do not yet believe!

May Christ also be born in our small community of Gaza. My dear brothers and sisters, I used to spend a few days with you, before Christmas. This year it was not possible, but we won't abandon you. You are in our hearts, and the whole Christian community in the Holy Land and around the world gathers around you. May you feel the warmth of our closeness and affection as much as possible.

Finally, may Christ be reborn in everyone's heart, so that for everyone it may still be Christmas!

Merry Christmas! (*Wulida Al Masih—Alleluia*)

The Speed of a Lamb

Homily for Christmas Midnight Mass

Church of the Nativity, Bethlehem

December 24, 2024

Dearest brothers and sisters,

I frankly admit that it is hard for me this year to announce the joy of Christ's birth to you here and to all those who look to Bethlehem from all over the world.

The angels' song of glory, joy, and peace seems to be out of tune after a tiring year full of tears, bloodshed, suffering, in addition to shattered hopes and crushed plans for peace and justice. A sad cry seems to choke the song, and powerless anger seems to paralyze every path of hope.

Over the past few weeks, I have asked myself several times how to live with this burden and even more so how to leave it behind. I have struggled with the unpleasant feeling that words, even faith-based ones, are useless when faced with the harshness of reality and a suffering that plainly seems to have no end in sight.

The figure of the shepherds (of the Christmas story) came to my rescue as the inspiration for me to follow together with the bishops and priests of this land. We are to keep vigil in the night watching over the flock. On that night, which is this very night, they listened to the angels and believed them.

That is why I, too, chose once again to listen to the Christmas story, within the suffering in which we find ourselves, a context not so very different from the one of that time.

As we have just heard, "In those days a decree went out from Caesar Augustus that all the world should be enrolled. This was the first enrollment, when Quirinius was governor of Syria. So all went to be enrolled, each to his own city. And Joseph also went up from Galilee, from the city of Nazareth, to Judea, to the city of David, which is called Bethlehem, because he was of the house and lineage of David, to be enrolled with Mary his betrothed, who was with child" (Lk 2:1–5).

I was struck by this aspect: Joseph and Mary experienced the grace of Christmas, the true birth of Christ, not in a way chosen by them or at a time chosen by them or under circumstances chosen by them, or even particularly favorable to them. At that time, an overpowering empire ruled the world and decided its social and economic destinies. At that time, this Holy Land of ours was equally subject to the game of international interests, no less than today. Poor people had to be registered. Their labor and their toil served other people's quality of life. Yet, without complaint, without refusal, without rebellion, Joseph and Mary went to Bethlehem and *here*, they were open to receiving the birth of Christ in that way. Was their choice driven by resignation? By doubt, powerlessness, or incompetence? Certainly not! It was driven by faith! And faith, when genuine and deeply rooted, brings a fresh and enlightened perspective on history, for "believing is seeing!"

And what did Joseph and Mary see? They saw, through the word of the angel, God in history, the Word made flesh, the Eternal in time, the Son of God made Man! And that is what we also see here, tonight, enlightened by the Word of the Gospel.

This Child shows us the unprecedented and unheard-of gesture, of God who does not flee from history, does not look at it indifferently from afar. He does not reject it with indignation as if it were too painful and evil, but embraces it, loves it, enters it with the delicate and strong pace of a newborn Child. Thus eternal Life finds a place in the harshness of time, through hearts and minds willing to welcome it.

The Nativity of the Lord is all about this: in His Son, the Father personally gets involved in our history and bears its burdens, He shares our sufferings and tears to the point of bloodshed and offers us a way out filled with life and hope.

However, He is not in competition with the powers of this world. The power of divine love is not simply stronger than the world, but it has a different kind of power. This Child, having lived a life like ours to the fullest shall reveal it with luminous clarity: "My kingship is not of this world; if my kingship were of this world, my servants would fight, that I might not be handed over; but my kingship is not from the world" (Jn 18:36). The pace with which God enters history is the pace of the Lamb. Only the Lamb is worthy to receive power and strength; to Him alone belongs salvation (Rev 5:12). The Caesars of this world are entrapped inside the vicious circle of strength, which eliminates enemies only to create new ones in turn. (We must bitterly note this every day.)

The Lamb of God instead, sacrificed and at once victorious, truly wins by healing the violent heart of man at the root through a love that is willing to serve and die and thus generate new life.

Mary and Joseph seem only to obey passively the history

that overshadows them, but in fact they have walked through it and mastered it at the pace of one who looks to God and to His plan. It is thus that they have allowed glory and peace to enter history.

We, too, can and must dwell in this earth and in this our history. We, too, must live our history. We should not be forced or resigned to do so, or be ready to flee as soon as possible. We are called by tonight's angels to live in faith and hope. We, too, like Joseph and Mary, like the shepherds, must choose and decide whether to welcome the angel's announcement with faith or to go our own way: believe or leave. We either decide to side with Christ and make the style of Bethlehem our own. This is the style of people who are willing to serve with love and to write a history of brotherhood. Alternatively, we can choose to adopt the style of Caesar Augustus, Herod, and many others, and thus be akin to those who write history through power and overpowering others.

The Child of Bethlehem takes us by the hand tonight and leads us with Him into history. He accompanies us so that we make history our own to the very end and so that we walk through it at the speed of trust and hope in Him.

He was not afraid to be born into this world or die for it (*non horruisti Virginis uterum*). He asks us not to fear the powers of this world, but to persevere in the path of justice and peace. We can and must, like Joseph and Mary, like the shepherds and the Magi, walk on the alternative ways that the Lord shows us. We must find adequate spaces where new styles of reconciliation and brotherhood may be born and grown. We must make our families and our communities cradles for a future of justice and peace, which has begun already with the coming of the Prince of Peace. It is true: we are few and perhaps even insignificant in relation to the constellations of power and the chessboard where the games of economic and political interests are played out. Yet like the shepherds, we are the people to whom the joy of Christmas is destined. We are sharers in the Paschal victory of the Lamb.

For this very reason, we feel that the Holy Father's invitation, which resounded for the entire Church just a few hours ago, is especially for us. By crossing the Holy Door, he inaugurated the Jubilee of 2025; we are now pilgrims of hope.

We Christians, in fact, do not walk through history as careless and unconcerned tourists or as wanderers without a destination, thrown here and there by the events of the world. We are pilgrims, and though we know and share in the joys and the hopes, the griefs and the anxieties of our fellow wayfarers, we walk toward the goal that is Christ, the true holy door flung wide open to God's future (see Jn 10:9). We dare to believe that since the Word became flesh here, He continues in every flesh and in every time to make history fruitful and to orient it to the fullness of glory.

And so dear friends, it is in this year, it is here that it makes even more sense to hear the song of the angels who announce the joy of Christ's birth! It is precisely now that it makes sense, and it is beautiful to live the Holy Year of the Lord, indeed, the Holy Year that is the Lord! That song, in fact, is not out of tune; quite the opposite—it shows how out of tune the noise of war and the empty rhetoric of the powerful are! That song's voice is not too feeble but resounds with strength through the tears of those who suffer; it encourages us to make vengeance powerless through forgiveness. We can be pilgrims of hope on the roads and between the destroyed homes of our land, because the Lamb walks with us toward the throne of the heavenly Jerusalem.

The Jubilee year, according to biblical tradition, is a special year in which prisoners are set free, debts are forgiven, property is returned, and even the earth rests. It is a year in which we experience reconciliation with our neighbor. It is a year in which we live in peace and promote justice. It is a year of spiritual renewal, of both people and communities. This happens because, with the Jubilee, God is the first who forgives our debts. It is the year of reconciliation between God and man, where everything is renewed. God desires this reconciliation to be fulfilled in the renewal of life and the relationships between human beings. This is my prayer for our Holy Land, which has the utmost need for a true Jubilee. We need a new beginning in all spheres of life, a new vision, the courage to look to the future with hope, without surrendering to the language of violence and hatred, which instead closes off any possibility of a future. May our communities experience a true spiritual renewal. May there also be this new beginning for us in the Holy Land. May debts be forgiven, prisoners be freed, property be returned, and may serious and credible paths of reconciliation and forgiveness, without which there will never be true peace, sincerely begin with courage and determination.

I want to thank our dear brothers and sisters in Gaza, whom I recently visited again. I renew our prayers, our closeness, and our solidarity with you. You are not alone. You are truly a visible sign of hope in the midst of the disaster of total destruction that surrounds you. But you are not broken, you are still united, steadfast in hope. Thank you for your wonderful testimony of strength and peace!

My thoughts also go out to you dear brothers and sisters in Bethlehem. This year, too, has been a sad Christmas for you, marked by insecurity, poverty, and violence. The most important day for you is once again under the banner of weariness and the expectation of better days. To you, too, I say: take courage! We must not lose hope. Let us renew our trust in God. He never leaves us alone. And *here* in Bethlehem, we celebrate the God-with-us and the place where He made Himself known. Take heart! We want the same proclamation of peace that resounded from *here* two thousand years ago to resound again to the whole world!

Together with the shepherds, let us go and behold again and again this unfolding event that the Lord has made known to us.

Let us also celebrate Christmas with outward signs of celebration, for a Child has been born for us and has filled history and the whole world with hope. He has transformed sorrows into labor pains and has given us all the opportunity to anticipate the dawn of a new world.

The Spirituality of the Empty Tomb

Homily for the Easter Vigil

Church of the Holy Sepulcher

April 11, 2020

Dear brothers and sisters,

Strange as it may seem, the experience we are living in these days is nearest to the Easter one and the dearest and ever-powerful sign of the Holy Sepulcher of Christ next to which we celebrate.[1]

The days we are experiencing are marked by a great void: void of rituals, void of faces, void of presences, void of contacts. A widespread and violent pandemic has taken away our certainties, our habits, our feasts, our meetings. A fear, mixed with disorientation and bewilderment, has taken hold of us. We feel lost, confused, blind. We cannot read what is happening very well; we cannot see or glimpse what it will be, how we will be, how and if we will resume our life.

Didn't the women on that first Easter sunrise feel that way? Weren't these the feelings of the disciples after the pain of Good Friday and the silence of Saturday? Wasn't their drama like what we are experiencing? The Master's place at the table was now empty. The center that made them a community was lost. The holy city, strange and empty, had

[1] This homily was delivered at the beginning of the worldwide COVID-19 pandemic. Though the Church of the Holy Sepulcher was closed to the public, the Mass and the homily were livestreamed.

now become an enemy, by weakened friendship from betrayal and infidelity. And even when a new and strange hope pushed them to go out, they found themselves in front of this tomb . . . empty . . .

We should therefore not escape this feeling too quickly. Educated by Good Friday and Holy Saturday, we Christians should know how to stand in the face of death, before the grave, in front of the silence of God and men. The joy of Easter is not a banal *happy end* of the story of Jesus, it is not the happy end of the Gospel for which they all lived, nor is it the cancellation of the pain of the world or the simple removal of the many bleeding wounds of history.

Easter joy, the real one, is born and consists precisely in a new ability to look at emptiness, to dialogue with pain ("Woman, why are you weeping?" Jn 20:15), to see the signs of death and believe.

Here, right here, moreover, the beloved disciple "saw and believed," he who had already seen Jesus' side torn open and turned his gaze to the One who had been pierced.

So here, today, for me, for you, for our Diocese, for the Church, for the world, I want to ask the Lord for an Easter gaze, a new vision to respond better to the One who continues to repeat: "Come and see."

I am convinced that the emptiness we have to live with these days, and who knows how much longer, is not simply the absence of people or things or habits, but it looks very much like the emptiness of the Sepulcher of the Lord. As on that early Easter morning, the disciples were led to understand that it was not a question of absence but of a new mystery of life; the Easter proclamation that was just proclaimed also leads us to believe what a mystery wants to reveal to us, a new word wants to be born from this silence.

I therefore believe that, in the days and months to come,

we will all need a renewed capacity for contemplation, we will need a new vision. It will not be enough, and perhaps courage only will not help to face the inevitable difficulties and the announced human, social, and economic crisis that this tragedy will provoke. Courage thrives on vision and perspective; otherwise, it is only muscular performance, which soon gets tired.

Vision: here is what we ask, here is what we want. Knowing how to comprehend pain and death, new things that God creates and recreates.

With Mary of Magdala, we must go beyond tears and lament for what we believe lost and open ourselves courageously to renewed relationships in which listening to and amazement for the other and his life, especially if weak and fragile, come before self-interest, prejudices, and personal advantage.

With the women we will need to know how to recognize the Risen Jesus and worship Him (Mt 28:9): that is, we will have to return to see God and, in Him, our origin and destiny, acknowledging ourselves as sons and brothers, members of a more humble, more fraternal, more supportive humanity. Our weakness can no longer be camouflaged behind proud and presumptuous political and economic strategies but will have to be accepted and lived within a greater trust in the Father and the brothers.

We will need a new look at the community, both civil and ecclesial, done by mutual welcome, shared responsibility, concrete and renewed affection. A new humanity will be possible if a new community will be its womb and its school. No virtual reality, no social media, however useful to make up for in extraordinary times, can replace the concreteness and depth of the brother's face. "No one saves himself" is not only the refrain of these days but also the very truth of living. And if in certain moments it is right and proper to "stay at home", it is only to be able to emerge more aware of the gift of giving and receiving.

And with Peter and John we will have to know how to say, again and again, to those who will be discouraged and distrustful (and there will be many): "We have seen the Lord!" (Jn 20:25). In the face of the suffering and death that are looming over humanity in these days, we realize that we will have to return to the Easter proclamation of the Resurrection of Christ and ours, which too often we Christians have kept silent. We will only be able to base our hope on the invincible certainty of a Love that has conquered death. Only then will we be able to say—as it echoes today in some parts of the world—"Everything will be all right." Without Easter faith, every consolation, every commitment to justice and peace will be a short-lived recipe for the heart of the man who yearns to rise again.

Brothers and sisters, from this empty sepulcher, and in the emptiness we each experience in our unique way, I announce once again that Christ is living and breathes His Spirit of life upon us and on the Church: that this Easter is still a new creation and the chaos of the world finds order and beauty through it. And God gives us His eyes to see the good things He does for those who believe and hope in His love. Amen!

Sinners, Witnesses, and Mary Magdalene

Homily During the Octave of Easter

Duc in Altum Church, Magdala

April 10, 2021

Dearest brothers and sisters,

May the Lord grant you peace!

We have listened several times to the Gospels of the Resurrection and the stories of the Risen Jesus' first appearances during these days. All accounts have something special of their own. Still, in all of them, two points reappear and are, in a small way, the common thread that unites them: Mary of Magdala as the first person to whom the Risen Lord appears and the sending of the incredulous disciples to Galilee or to all people. They are two essential points of Gospel narration regarding the Resurrection. There may be additions or changes, but these two points are present in all, one way or another.

The Gospel just proclaimed is that of Mark, who is more concise. For some, it is even a later addition. The passage announced summarizes the Resurrection stories of John the Evangelist. We are, however, trying to understand what the Gospel passage communicates.

The first apparition to Magdalene is not an insignificant detail; it is instead an important detail of the evangelical announcement. Why does Jesus appear first to Mary of Magdala? At the beginning of the Gospel, we have a woman, the Virgin Mary. At the end of the Gospel, there is another woman, Mary of Magdala. In the beginning, there is a woman who consents and accepts to become the Mother of the Lord and welcomes Him in her womb, beginning the history of redemption. At the end of the Gospel, we have a woman, Mary of Magdala, who enters first into a relationship with the Risen Lord.

The Fathers of the Church take another approach, through Eve. "A woman first tasted death, but in Mary of Magdala a woman first saw the Resurrection; this is to testify that the woman could not carry the guilt of the transgression among men in perpetuity" (Bede the Venerable).

With the Passion and death of Jesus, the disciples lost faith, except for the Mother of the Lord. Mary of Magdala, therefore, is the one through whom God, through the encounter with the Risen Lord, reconnects with the men. Why Mary of Magdala?

She is the symbol of the unfaithful bride that God calls back to intimacy. In the Old Testament, there are many images through which God calls to himself and forgives the unfaithful bride. (Hosea, Jeremiah, Ezekiel speak of the infidelity of the bride, but also of God's forgiveness). The announcement to Mary of Magdala is the announcement of the forgiveness of the unfaithful man, of the man who once again with the crucifixion of Christ said "no" to God. Mary of Magdala was possessed by seven demons. Seven is a symbolic number and indicates fullness. In other words, Mary of Magdala was truly immersed in sin. We don't know what kind, but sin had become a constitutive part of her life. But her encounter with the Lord freed her, forgave her, saved her. She represents, in short, sinful and forgiven humanity. That is the reason for the appearance to Mary of Magdala. We could not be represented by the Virgin Mary because she has always remained faithful; she is without sin. Mary of Magdala is, therefore, the woman who represents us. On the Cross, the Mother of the Lord becomes our Mother, while after the Resurrection, Mary of Magdala is the one who introduces us to the encounter with the Risen One and gives us access to forgiveness. The alliance of God with man, in conclusion, is restored in the meeting of Jesus with Mary of Magdala.

She is also an image of the Church. The Church that the Fathers of the Church called "Casta Meretrix", saint and sinner, is represented by Mary of Magdala. The Virgin Mary is a mother of the Church and our Mother, as the Council reminds us. On the other hand, Mary of Magdala is a figure of the Church, which is composed of sinners but is at the same time reconciled with the Father through the presence of the risen Christ.

The Risen One, encountering Mary of Magdala, meets the unfaithful but forgiven bride, sinful humanity in need of mercy. She reconnects the bond with the disciples who had broken with the crucifixion and death of Jesus. The apostles' difficulty believing in the Resurrection calls for witnesses in the same league, who are like them, like Mary of Magdala.

Mary Magdalene, however, as we see above all in the Gospel of John, is not only the forgiven sinner. She is also the woman who holds in her heart the desire for Jesus and searches for Him alone. In John's Gospel, after the two disciples found that the tomb was empty, they returned home (20:10), while Mary remained in the garden, still searching for the Lord. She didn't give herself peace; she didn't give up. Her insistence on seeking the Lord was repaid by the encounter with Him, who then called her by name. Jesus is first found by those who have their hearts turned in search of Him. He did not go first to the incredulous disciples but to Mary of Magdala, who was in search of His body, considered lost. In the Gospel, we see first of all with the heart, an open heart, and then with the eyes. The eyes recognize what the heart has already welcomed.

The other point of the Resurrection stories, we said, is the sending to Galilee and the people.

The Resurrection cannot remain a closed act in itself. It is the heart of our faith and the culmination and the sense of the whole life of Jesus. And it is intended for all men.

There is irony in this Gospel passage. Those men whom Jesus scolded for their disbelief are the same ones sent to preach his Resurrection to all the people in the world.

The apostles needed witnesses like them, sinners like them, like Mary of Magdala, who was possessed by seven demons, but who was saved by the encounter with Jesus. So, the men of that time and of today need witnesses like themselves, sinners like the apostles and like us today. Jesus needs normal men, sinners, but who are at the same time happy to have met the treasure that has upended their lives: ordinary people, but who have the full flavor of life, of the resurrection. May they become by themselves witnesses to something greater than they are.

The invitation to become witnesses is addressed to all believers. We, forgiven sinners, are all called to become witnesses to the Resurrection of Christ.

In short, the path is clear, and Mary of Magdala expressly indicates it to us: to recognize ourselves as sinners; meet Christ and allow ourselves to be forgiven by Him; love Him; recognize Him alive in us; testify.

If we do not recognize ourselves as sinners, we do not need Christ and the forgiveness of God to which He alone gives us access. We can't even love Him because we don't feel the need for Him; he's a presence that doesn't communicate anything to us, and so we have nothing to witness to except ourselves.

But if we recognize we are sinners and, with humility, allow Him to forgive us, we will have access to His love, to His life that will break into us and that alone will become an announcement. Rediscovered salvation is the lost-and-found drachma of the Gospel of Luke. Once it is found, the woman calls all her neighbors to rejoice; she can't contain her joy (Lk 15:9). One cannot retain a great joy for oneself; it must be communicated.

Let us ask ourselves how much Mary of Magdala represents us, how much she is our figure. Do we recognize ourselves among the forgiven sinners? Does our life explode with joy for the salvation we have experienced? Do our hearts burn with the desire to meet Christ? Or are we not rather like the disciples of the Gospel, closed in the cenacle in mourning and crying? (Mk 16:10).

We are all here together to ask Mary of Magdala to intercede for us and to introduce ourselves to the joy of the risen Christ. May it become our proclamation here, today, and in daily life.

Between Bitter Realism and Christian Hope

An Interview with *Il Foglio*

April 14, 2025

IL FOGLIO: *Your Eminence, we see what is happening in the Holy Land on our television screens every day. A political interpretation of the events prevails, but we know less about the impact this war is having on people, on society.*

PIERBATTISTA CARDINAL PIZZABALLA: This is not the first time we have had a conflict in the Holy Land. But this conflict has had an impact like no other. There is the time before October 7, 2023, and the time after, even if we struggle to define or understand what this "after" will be like. The emotional, economic, psychological, and human impact has been enormous for both populations, Israeli and Palestinian. For the Israeli population, it has been a tremendous shock. Israel was born as the home where Jews are safe, and suddenly it became clear that this is no longer true. The issue of the hostages is the decisive point for Israel. We see street demonstrations continuing all over the country. Israelis are divided on many things, but on one thing they are in agreement: the hostages. It is an enormous issue. For the Palestinians, too, what happened after October 7, in Gaza but also in the West Bank, has been an incredible shock—for the Arab population in general, I would say. We are dealing

---

Translated by Matthew Sherry. Original: Matteo Matzuzzi, "Alla fine di un mondo. Dialogo con il card. Pizzaballa, tra amaro realismo e speranza Cristiana", *Il Foglio*, April 14, 2025.

with fear and feelings of hatred and resentment on a scale that had never been seen before. Also to be considered is the economic impact that the war has on social life. Part of the Palestinian population has been left without work, but in Israel, too, the situation is not easy; one need only consider that in effect there are no more pilgrimages. Working people have been called back into the military. Life is very hard. There is a deep sense of distrust that permeates social life at all levels. It will be very difficult to rebuild trust after all this, partly because there is no telling what will happen after, when it is all over.

And on the religious level?

It is difficult to distinguish between the social and religious aspects. Religion plays a comprehensive public role for the whole population. There are also different interpretations of the meaning of war. For Palestinians, what happened on October 7 marks the beginning of a new phase, but of a war that began eighty years ago. For Israelis, instead, it is something decidedly new and unexpected. They are completely different perspectives. Before this war, on the religious level, we had interaction between various religious authorities. Today this is not seen. It is very difficult to meet, especially for public events. Everything is at a standstill. Everyone is shut up within his own religious narrative.

It has been 1,700 years since the Council of Nicaea. Among the decisions adopted was the condemnation of Arianism. To us this may seem like pure archaeology. And yet less than twenty years ago the pope condemned "modern Arianism". Benedict XVI said that the denial of the true divinity of Jesus is still a temptation for Christians today, to the point of necessitating a comprehensive catechesis. Indeed, how often do we hear Jesus spoken of as a man in love with

God, and as his emissary who did many good things, yet who can hardly be considered the only-begotten son of God? Is the danger denounced by Pope Benedict still felt?

I studied for a few years at a Jewish university in Jerusalem. My classmates were all Jewish; I was the only Christian. They started asking me about faith, about Jesus, about the Gospel. I replied: "It's pointless for me to explain to you who Jesus was; the Gospel is there, it's all written there. Let's read. You ask me questions, and I'll answer." I was naive and didn't realize what I was proposing to them, because, having been born in lower Bergamo where one was Catholic even before birth, I was used to the classical, traditional catechism. My questions and answers about Jesus were those of the catechism, not mine. So I realized that when they started asking me about Jesus, I didn't know how to respond adequately. The catechism wasn't much use in that circumstance. They wanted to understand the meaning of those pages from me, but I could only babble out readymade phrases. At a certain point a young woman said to me, "I can't come to these meetings anymore because I have to work, I have a young child, and besides, this reading disturbs me a little." Then she added, "I like Jesus—he's not what they told me. And the Gospel is such a beautiful book. There is one thing, however, that you have to explain to me: the Resurrection. Why does he have to rise? Why do you make him rise from the dead? Already without the Resurrection, Jesus is fascinating." In that instance, too, I answered as the catechism answers, and I could tell from her face that she hadn't understood a thing. I couldn't make myself understood. It took me a while to see that the Resurrection isn't a matter for explanation. It is not *explained* in the Gospels. There are only encounters with the Risen One. To answer your question, then, it's true: it is very easy, in every age, to reduce Jesus to a figure that we can encompass within our human understanding. It is the perennial temptation; such a Jesus is easy. He is not a sign of contradiction. The Church's task, however, is to be able to testify that Jesus is the son of God, as the Council of Nicaea said. She must find a way to say this. Catechesis, formation, and the liturgy are indispensable. But without an experience of faith, without an encounter with the Risen One, they become just something more to study, to learn, or to do, which does not give life. The task that we have as the Church is to be able to say that Jesus is Kyrios, he is the Lord—to say it convincingly, to say it because we believe it, having experienced it. This is perhaps what we lack today. We must find a way, in today's language, to say the same thing as 1,700 years ago. The Truth is the same; we must find a way to express it convincingly. It will be understood if the one who says it also believes it, in the sense that he has experienced it, that our witness is not limited to saying things from the catechism and calling it a day, like I did with that young woman.

Speaking of Nicaea, let's go to the question of the date of Easter. Pope Francis expressed the hope on numerous occasions that a single date for the celebration of Easter might be found. You work in a context where divisions among Christians are evident, just considering the liturgies, the calendars, etc. In your judgment, is it possible to arrive at a common date between the Julian and Gregorian calendars?

The very simple answer is probably not. Over 90 percent of Christian families in the Middle East, not just in the Holy Land, are mixed. Catholics and Orthodox marry each other. You will never find a totally Catholic or totally Orthodox family. Children go to Mass depending on the situation. In some areas there is even intercommunion between Catholics and Orthodox. Families continually insist on wanting to celebrate together. For us, therefore, the issue is pastoral, not theological. In much of the Middle East there is already an agreement on Easter. Two-thirds of my Latin diocese (which includes Jordan, Israel, Palestine, Cyprus), for example, follows the Orthodox date for Easter. Only Jerusalem, Nazareth, and Bethlehem follow the Gregorian calendar. Depending on the year, it can happen that when I celebrate Easter at the Holy Sepulcher, two-thirds of the diocese is beginning Lent. This is for pastoral reasons and to meet the needs of families, which are mixed, as I said. Changing the criteria for Easter is complicated; it would take a Council or something similar—not just Catholic, but for all the Churches. I would add that there are also questions of power; Moscow will never agree with Rome on the date of Easter. But even if Moscow and Rome were to reach an agreement, would the Protestants or evangelical churches follow? And even if all the Churches were to agree, would the civil authorities consent? The division between the Churches is a deep wound that has real-life consequences, and we must accept the responsibilities and consequences of what happened in the past. They cannot be erased so easily. There are no ideal solutions. In the Holy Land we have become aware that there are problems that can be solved, others that have no solution.

Let's get back to modern Arianism. "Sometimes, in some sectors of the Catholic world, one even goes so far as to think that divine Revelation must adapt to the prevailing mentality in order to be credible, rather than that the prevailing mentality must be converted in the light given to us from above. Yet one should reflect on the fact that 'conversion,' not 'adaptation,' is an evangelical word." This is a quotation from Giacomo Cardinal Biffi, from his book Pecore e pastori. Riflessioni sul gregge di Cristo. *But today you can't use the word "conversion"; it's out of fashion, as it were. It was already that way when Biffi wrote his book. How can its meaning be rediscovered?*

I think it is obvious that conversion and sin are not talked about today. They presuppose the existence of God. If God is present in your life, you also feel the need to convert. If you are aware of God's presence beside you, you are also aware of sin and therefore of conversion. But if you are not aware of transcendent life, if you are not aware that there is someone who is the source of life and who changes it for you, and you do not think you need Him, neither do you need to convert. Today there is no talk of conversion because we have lost the awareness of God. It is pointless to talk about conversion without first talking about God. That has to be the start. Awareness of God leads you to understand that before him you are always lacking and you need to convert. It is a continuous journey, but the starting point is the awareness of God. Of what use is a Church that does not speak of God?

Hope. This is the theme of the Jubilee year that we are in [in 2025]. One often hears talk about hope; it may even be "the humblest of the theological virtues" (as Pope Francis called it), but it is not clear what hope is. Don't you think that in our societies the concept of hope is understood as the famous "everything will be fine" tagline of pandemic memory?

I remember, from when I was a young seminarian, a homily that Bishop Filippo Franceschi gave at the cathedral of Ferrara. He said something that I didn't understand but that stuck with me: "The Risen Christ is our hope." For you, here in the West, it is easy to confuse hope with optimism. For us, in the Holy Land, it is easy to confuse hope with the end of the conflict or with a political solution. If we identify hope with a purely human horizon, however beautiful and desired, like the end of the conflict, we delude ourselves with the idea that we will be consoled. For you, I was saying, hope seems more synonymous with optimism. Hope, in my view, is not the expectation of something yet to come, but the expression of one's own experience, something within oneself. It is the daughter of faith. Without faith, hope has no foundation to rest on. If you believe in something, you also want to achieve it. You look at the world with the eyes of one who is able to see beyond himself. Faith, in fact, transcends; it makes you capable of looking beyond. The prophets of the Old Testament, for example, sought to get the people to see something that lay beyond. When things were going well, they called the people to conversion; they used words of condemnation for their unjust behavior. They said, "You are living unjustly. You must convert." When things were going badly, theirs were words of consolation. Isaiah, before a Jerusalem desolate and destroyed, described it as a marvelous city. He was not a visionary, but he was capable, through faith, of looking beyond, of seeing something that could be achieved. To return to that phrase of the bishop of Ferrara, this is possible for us Christians if the awareness of Christ's Resurrection is a lived awareness. If Christ is risen and I have met him, there is nothing that can become the end for me. So I would do all I could to build, to live in a different light. In the Book of Revelation, there is a description of Jerusalem coming down from Heaven: in it there is no temple and there is no sun. The Lamb is the source of light. We do not see light, but it is what allows us to see. So that ability to see is needed. Thinking about my experience in the Holy Land, within this sea of hatred, wars, pain, and fear, it means being able to see the beautiful realities, to seek out the people who give their lives for something beautiful: they are the risen ones of today who tell you that there is still light. For me, this is hope.

If we went to a church and asked what the theological virtues are and in what they consist, how many people do you think would answer us correctly? How ignorant have we Catholics become?

My mom knows what the theological virtues are. I don't know if she's able to explain them, but I know that she learned them by heart from the catechism of her time. But she has a solid, simple faith, like that of many of our moms and grandmas, who perhaps didn't know all of theology and the catechism, but had a beautiful, well-founded, simple faith, received in the family. The problem today is that people not only don't know the catechism, but most of the time they didn't even receive the faith in the family. I believe that the catechism has never converted anyone; it is useless if you don't have faith. The catechism serves to help you put the experience of faith in order. But if you haven't received faith, again, it's just one more thing to study and likely forget. I am convinced of this. Today, the problem is not how to teach the faith, but how to communicate it, transmit it, give it. We older people received it from our parents, then we indeed went to catechism, but we already had something inside us that simply needed to be ordered. When I had to guide adults to the sacrament of baptism, an experience that is always powerful if done well and that takes time, I didn't start with the catechism. I started with the Gospel, because you must first get them to meet Jesus, get them to know him directly. You need to know this

Person. Then it is they who must understand how to live this experience, how to translate it into life, and that's where the catechism comes into play. If there is not this encounter with the Lord, catechesis and formation become like a beautifully constructed cornice on a building, but without the framework within. In the past, it was families that transmitted the faith; the Church brought order. Today, families no longer transmit it, and we delude ourselves that with catechesis we are solving the problem. I don't have solutions, but I see the problem. With us [in the Patriarchate of Jerusalem] it is a bit different: Christians are born into a world made up predominantly of Muslims and Jews. But if you asked me if my Christians know the catechism, I would say they know it like they do in the West.

You have spoken of the lack of transmission of faith in families. The Church is unable to fill this void, sometimes seeming disoriented by this "new world".

I would like to make two brief observations, again referring to my experience in the Middle East. Here, catechism was taught in Christian schools. In the early 1970s, Assad's Syria nationalized all the private schools—including Catholic ones, which thus became public. From that moment on, therefore, the catechism could no longer be taught in the schools. So the Church was forced to create afternoon catechism programs in the parishes, which are still in operation. Today, I notice a great difference between Syrian Christians, who do not study catechism in school, and those of other countries. The latter study catechism as they study mathematics and literature, while Christians in Syria do not. For them it is a different experience, in every sense. A model of the Church is coming to an end, and this is no mystery. The Church that Pasolini knew is coming to an end, but it is a drawn-out ending.[1] A biblical passage comes to mind, Jeremiah 27:1. In the Old Testament, there are some significant and evocative expressions. The word *bereshit* is one of these, the first word in the Bible. It means "in the beginning," an expression that indicates the start of something new. There is another time it is uttered, in Jeremiah. We find it in a context of total destruction, and therefore in apparent contradiction with the meaning of that expression: everything is over, Israel is driven into exile. And yet, precisely in that context of failure, we find an expression that speaks of a beginning. Even when everything seems finished, faith is capable of opening to a new beginning, of seeing the inception of something new. What is ending is a model of the Church, not the Church herself. Perhaps the apparent relevance of the Catholic Church is ending, but not the Catholic Church. The challenge is not to recover, but to be the Church. To be what we must be. Without fear over numbers. We must concern ourselves with being able to tell today's world—which is hungry but does not know it—that Jesus is the Lord. At the Wedding of Cana they had run out of wine, but no one noticed. Only Mary saw. We must be able to understand how, where, and with whom to find the wine.

Can the Church of Jerusalem teach something to us in the West?

We are the mother Church, after all! You in the West are also becoming a multireligious and multicultural society. We are a minority Church, as always. This may seem like a tragedy to you, but we are used to it. The problem is not relevance, but having something to say. It is not a given, in such a

[1] Pier Paolo Pasolini (1922–1975) was an Italian filmmaker, best known as the writer and director of *The Gospel According to St. Matthew* (Arco Film, 1964).

polarized situation, to open up perspectives that do not close off, to build trust. In this sense, with all its limitations, the Church of Jerusalem has something to say.

There are a few isolated cases, counter to the trend. I think of Scandinavia, small communities where, however, Catholics are on the rise. One of the bishops of that region, Erik Varden, contradicted me some time ago: I presented a picture of a "post-Christian" society, and he replied: "If we want to talk about 'pre' and 'post,' it seems more appropriate to suggest that we are on the threshold of an era that I would call 'post-secular.' Secularization has run its course. It is exhausted, devoid of positive purpose. The human being, meanwhile, remains alive with profound aspirations. The Church possesses the words and signs with which to transmit the eternal as reality." What do you say?

I am in complete agreement with Bishop Varden. Man who wants to do without God, fails. In the end he comes to experience emptiness. A void of meaning. He is unable to build long-term prospects. In this postsecular society, man is left hungry within. Man does not live by bread alone, but by every word that comes from the mouth of God. The Inquisitor from *The Brothers Karamazov* comes to mind: "Give them bread and they will be fine!" Let us give bread, let us give human justice—all things we have already seen. Then man realizes that he remains hungry, in search of something to fill his life and his heart. This is where the Church must intervene with her proposal. Pope Paul VI, in *Evangelii Nuntiandi*, says that the community of believers must, with its way of life, be able to raise irresistible questions: Why do those people live like that, and how are they so happy? Who? How? The Church must be there, not with a wealth of explanations, but with a way of life. Christianity is not simply a religion, but a way of being in the world. This passes through the community, and this is the problem that we have in the Church today: being a community where life flows. I think the future of the Church will depend on this.

You were speaking of community. Yet we are immersed in the paradox of a society that has never been so hyperconnected and yet never been so full of loneliness—young and old alike. What can the Church say and do?

She must be able to build community, to offer something beautiful and attractive. This is not about following the fashions and the times, or starting to have dances in church. If someone needs to dance, he goes to a nightclub and finds things done better. The Church must be able not only to make a difference but to create difference in societies where everyone has to be the same. When you enter a church, you enter for a liturgy; you enter a different dimension. This must be perceived. It is not just an *agape*, but also an encounter with transcendence. Do we need to change the message? No, the message is always the same. Do we need to be more convincing? This is not a matter of marketing. It is a matter of being able to express the faith seriously, in a solid way. But to be convincing one must be convinced.

Would a conversion like [the French poet] Paul Claudel's be imaginable today? The feeling today is that of a Church who stays a bit too much within the ordinary, very often speaking from the pulpits about issues that have little to do with transcendence and much to do with the things of this world.

The risk is always there, both within the Church and outside the Church, of not wanting to complicate life, of staying within the ordinary, made up of normal horizons that fall within a purely human understanding. Instead, the encounter with God always breaks the mold, and on this, Christianity—I repeat—must make the difference. If it doesn't, you can have many churches and beautiful basilicas, but you become irrelevant because you have nothing important to say. But it's not a question of programs, but rather of witnesses. The testimony becomes effective if the witness is credible. If he isn't credible, the message doesn't get through, even if he says the best things one could possibly hear.

"It is difficult to speak to [young people] today about God and perhaps even more difficult to talk about the Church, because they see in God only the limit of our freedom." These words are from Benedict XVI. He said them in Loreto in 2007, responding to a young woman's question about the burden of "God's silence" and the difficulty of speaking about God to her peers. We can say that almost twenty years later this difficulty has become widespread. How can a priest respond to such a dramatic question?

Within this war, with the hatred, the mistrust, the destruction, the deaths, the injustices, the question of where God is returns. I would respond first by asking where man is. We must not reduce God to the one who solves our problems. God created us free and entrusted us with the life of the world, which is ours. And it is up to our freedom to decide what to do. If you choose good you will live; if you choose evil you will die. We cannot accuse God of what we do. God gives us the criteria; God is the criterion, the light. He is the Lamb who illuminates, to stay with the example of Jerusalem. But I can decide to stay outside of Jerusalem. The question about God becomes a question about man. I think of Mother Teresa, of the darkness that she experienced. Saint Francis experienced God's silence for years. I think of Job, who lived this silence for a long time. I think of John the Baptist, who announced, "Behold the Lamb of God," then finds himself in prison and asks, "But are you really the Lamb of God who was to come?" Well, I think of all these people who were able to continue addressing this question to Him. We can resolve the question about God here, completely and exhaustively, but that doesn't make much sense. Scripture, the Church, and the sacraments are enough for us. What is asked of us by faith is to remain in the question and to address the question to Him. Then we will live our experiences. But we must not ask God for what is man's task. Faith, moreover, the relationship with God, when authentic and lived, is not a limit to human freedom, but is what gives this freedom its shape. The Church today is perhaps perceived by young people more as an imposing institution, with its laws and its "noes", rather than as a community that joyfully lives its "yeses". As we said before, one must start again from the communities within which life flows—and from witness.

In the 1950s a new archbishop, Giovanni Battista Montini, the future Paul VI, arrived in Milan from Rome. Montini looked around and saw, behind the curtain of "religious hegemony", very different evidence: growing "irreligiosity", catechesis almost deserted, low attendance at Sunday Mass, parish priests distant and busy with bureaucratic duties, superficial celebrations. Almost the same problems that we see today.

We must not fear change; we must not live in fear. As I said before, a certain model of the Church is coming to an end. I think Benedict XVI said it well: we know that something is coming to an end, but we don't know what it will be like afterward. It will be defined over time. Also, in the Acts of the Apostles we see that great moments in the history of the Church were the result of great struggles: the question of deacons and the opening of evangelization to the Gentiles, for example. Therefore this crisis, too, will produce something. Our assessments are always very human; there is the temptation of power, numbers, visibility. And hey, these things do help. We must be visible. But we must not worry about all this too much, because there is also God. There is also the Holy Spirit. There is the Church, who, through the testimony of so many realities, still creates something good. Here and there, we have many beautiful experiences of the Church—of life and growth. I wouldn't be too afraid. We must be concerned—I repeat—about being authentic, genuine. The Church must not do marketing: the Church must say that there is nothing better in life than meeting Jesus Christ.

I return to the situation in the Holy Land. Your Eminence. Will things ever go back as before?

Absolutely not. An era has ended for us, too—ended painfully, in the worst possible way. We are still not emotionally free to think about what comes after. It is a distressing situation. I don't know what will happen; it will also depend on the ability of religious and political leaders to help the population to look up, to consider the reality. We are so blinded within our narratives that we cannot see anything else. We will all stay there in the Holy Land, Christians, Jews, and Muslims. We will not disappear; there will be no "rivieras". So we need to be able to rebuild something that will at least make this coexistence bearable. It will take a lot of time; the wounds are very deep. The healing phase will be very long. But there will be no healing if there are no doctors to advise on the cure, who know how to guide. The risk, for you in the West, is to think that you will always have peace. For us, the risk is the opposite: to think that we will always have war. I don't know which of the two is worse off. The Church's task is to be a voice that opens horizons, a different voice. Here in the Middle East, when we talk about "making a difference" it means something else, I think, than what it means in the West. For us, it means to say something that doesn't close off, that isn't born of fear. It's not easy, but I believe it's as necessary as the air we breathe.

As happened before with the withdrawal of the Islamic State, scars will remain between neighbors who denounced and betrayed each other. Can there be no reconciliation?

We are human beings, marked by pain and wounds. There are individuals who have been able to forgive. They are wonderful and powerful examples, which we need. At the community level the dynamics are necessarily different. In a social context, forgiveness takes time. It requires a shared awareness, which cannot be imposed from above. Reconciliation requires healing processes. We must do it, even if it takes a long time. Faith asks it of you; the encounter with the Risen One asks it of you. I think of Jesus asking Peter, "Do you love me?" We must make this experience our own. Eleven years ago, during the war in Syria and Iraq, Christians were told to convert or leave: they all left rather than leave Jesus Christ. We see it today in our little community in Gaza, where they have lost everything. They have nothing left, yet they are there, firm and steadfast in their faith.